'In recording his attempts to grapple with ... realities, he allows the rest of us to step through that looking glass' *Sunday T.*

'Macfarlane masters a wealth of exotic detail into an elegantly arranged narrative that takes in everything from the mythical roots of sumo to the ubiquity of Shinto shrines' *The Times*

'Through conscientious research and lucid prose, he triumphantly decodes this enigmatic country... hides no truths and avoids no complexities' *Japan Times*

'On his journey through Japanese society, he encounters subjects from the most public to the most intimate and uncovers a nation that is even more extraordinary than he first thought' *Herald*

'Alan Macfarlane layers many years of careful contemporary observation, dialogues with important Japanese thinkers, an impressive breadth of reading in scholarship on Japan to reach with informed imagination for the *gestalt* that is Japan ... a disarming, engaging, and provocative book' Andrew Barshay, University of California, Berkeley

'Wise, judicious ... [a] fine book' *TLS*

'Subtle and searching exploration of every aspect of Japanese society ... eschewing myths and clichés and making a serious attempt to investigate and explain manners and mores that can be hard for the casual visitor to understand' *Good Book Guide*

'If you've the remotest interest in Japan, and certainly if you've plans to visit, it should be top of your list' *Bookbag*

ALAN MACFARLANE trained as a historian and is Professor of Anthropology at Cambridge University. He is the author of sixteen books inclu ... *The G ... y: On How the World W ...*

JAPAN THROUGH THE LOOKING GLASS

ALAN MACFARLANE

P

PROFILE BOOKS

This paperback edition published in 2008

First published in Great Britain in 2007 by
Profile Books Ltd
3A Exmouth House
Pine Street
London ECIR OJH
www.profilebooks.com

1 3 5 7 9 10 8 6 4 2

Typeset in Poliphilus by MacGuru Ltd
info@macguru.org.uk

Printed and bound in Great Britain by
CPI Bookmarque, Croydon, Surrey

A CIP catalogue record for this book is available
from the British Library.

ISBN 978 1 86197 967 4

For Rosa

In the hope that one day she will enter the Japanese looking glass

'Long ago the best and dearest Japanese friend I ever had said to me, a little before his death: "When you find, in four or five years more, that you cannot understand the Japanese at all then you will begin to know something about them." After having realised the truth of my friend's prediction, – after having discovered that I cannot understand the Japanese at all, – I feel better qualified to attempt this essay.'

Lafcadio Hearn, *Japan – An Interpretation*, 9–10

'But in truth ... there is nothing behind the veil. The Japanese are difficult to understand, not because they are complicated or strange but because they are so simple. By simplicity I do not mean the absence of a multiplicity of elements ... The religious practice even of the ordinary man is highly complicated ... The cause of what strikes us as alien and impenetrable in Japanese minds is not the presence of a bewildering array of conflicting elements in their psyche, but rather the fact that no conflict is felt to exist between them.'

Kurt Singer, *Mirror, Sword and Jewel*, 47

'I ca'n't believe *that*!' said Alice.

'Ca'n't you?' the Queen said in a pitying tone. 'Try again: draw a long breath, and shut your eyes.'

Alice laughed. 'There's no use trying,' she said: 'one *ca'n't* believe impossible things.'

'I daresay you haven't had much practice,' said the Queen. 'When I was your age, I always did it for half-an-hour a day. Why, sometimes I've believed as many as six impossible things before breakfast.'

Lewis Carroll, *Through the Looking-Glass,*
And What Alice Found There

Contents

Preface: companions on the journey   xi

1   Into the mirror   1
2   Culture shock   19
3   Wealth   51
4   People   75
5   Power   109
6   Ideas   141
7   Beliefs   175
8   Out of the mirror   211

Major eras in Japanese history, conventions   231
Frequently cited early visitors   233
Sources for quoted passages   234
Website, bibliography and recommended reading   240
Index   246

Companions on the journey

When Alice went into Wonderland and through the looking glass, she met numerous creatures who explained their world to her and tried to sort out her confusions. This book is likewise the result of many conversations, much advice and an enormous amount of support. Over the sixteen years since my wife Sarah and I first visited Japan I have been helped by many people, only a few of whom I can acknowledge here.

It is not easy to understand Japan. My attempt to do so would have failed entirely without the help of two Japanese friends, Professors Kenichi and Toshiko Nakamura, hereafter called Kenichi and Toshiko. If I had spent the many years it requires to speak and read Japanese, I would not have been able to make the comparative studies of other civilisations which inform this work. Because I do not speak or read Japanese I am heavily dependent on informants. For example, the key works of several of the most important Japanese historians, anthropologists and political philosophers have not been translated. I thus rely on Kenichi's and Toshiko's summaries of their ideas.

We have discussed the themes in this book many times. I have made six visits to Japan with my wife and on each occasion we have met, and often travelled through Japan with, Kenichi and Toshiko. We have asked them innumerable questions and they have taken it upon themselves to try to teach us as much about Japan as possible, both in Japan and when they have come to England. They have done all this partly because of their fascination with English culture and partly as a result of what they have seen and their consequent desire to learn from us. In Japan, we have become their intellectual children and they have crossed into our world of ignorance and gently led us to a gradual comprehension. They have had the heavier burden of translation, working in English.

In order to meet the most astute and well-informed current Japanese scholars it is necessary to have the right intermediary. Kenichi and Toshiko, drawing on their academic links, have provided the introductions and the contexts for numerous invaluable discussions with others who have thought deeply on Japan.

Nor is it easy for Japanese scholars to be openly critical of senior foreign academics, but the particularly direct and unusually self-confident character of our friends has meant that they have been excellent co-workers and critics, reading and commenting with honesty and originality on many drafts and essays.

The collaboration started with an invitation to talk about Western concepts of romantic love, and the cross-cultural friendship that has developed is another form of love, which Sarah and I deeply appreciate. This love has been shown not only in intellectual and social ways, but in many practical details which made the collaboration possible. In particular, Kenichi has arranged funding for most of our visits to Japan, a place which would otherwise have been prohibitively expensive to visit so often.

Given that the book is, in effect, the narrative of a joint exploration, a long-term conversation in which we have attempted to understand each other's history and culture, it might have seemed only appropriate to indicate joint authorship on the title page. We have agreed not to do this for a simple reason. While quoting or paraphrasing Kenichi's and Toshiko's ideas, in the end it was I who structured and wrote the book. They do not fully agree with everything I write. Thus it is important to stress that I am alone responsible for the ideas in this book, even though it is deeply informed by our mutual work on a joint project.

There are many others who have also contributed greatly in the adventure of trying to understand Japan. Toshiko and Kenichi's family made us feel very welcome and gave us invaluable insights into Japanese life when we stayed with them. I thank Subaru, Yuri and Ai Nakamura; Sumie, Michio and Ayako Kashiwagi; Yoshihiko, Fumiko and Jun Ito.

I have learnt a great deal from the Japanese and Korean postgraduate students whom I have supervised: Sonia Ryang, Mariko Hara, Mikiko Ashikari and Jun Sato. Sato read the book in various drafts and offered a great amount of useful criticism and fresh ideas and I would like to thank him in particular. Ashikari read part of the book and made a number of useful comments. Several of my other doctoral research students, Mireille Kaiser, Srijana Das and Maja Petrovich, read parts of the early draft and offered new insights.

I have discussed Japanese issues with a number of Western experts and learnt a great deal from them: Carmen Blacker, Ian Inkster, Arthur Stockwin, Ronald Dore and Andrew Barshay. Filming in Japan with David Dugan and Carlo Massarella of Windfall Films was a great pleasure, and the support and interest over the years of Patrick O'Brien was invaluable.

A number of friends have read the whole draft through carefully and offered numerous suggestions for improvement. I thank Gabriel Andrade, Andrew Morgan and Mark Turin (who read three drafts). Harvey Whitehouse commented helpfully on the chapter on beliefs. Or Dr Susan Bayly read and commented helpfully on two of the chapters.

It has been my privilege to have had lengthy discussions in Japan with a number of eminent experts on many aspects of Japanese history and society. These include the following professors from various fields: Masachi Ohsawa, Anthony Backhouse, Shing-Jen Chen, Tadashi Karube, Takami Kuwayama, Jin Makabe, Takayoshi Matsuo, Eiji Sakurai, Toshio Yamagishi, Tomoharu Yanagimachi, Toshio Yokoyama, Hiroshi Yoshikawa. In particular, I met Hiroshi Watanabe on three of our visits to Japan and he has commented on early drafts of the book, as well as spending much time explaining Japanese history and political structures to us.

A number of Japanese scholars have become friends and we have had ongoing discussions with them, either in their homes or when travelling through Japan together, or when they have visited us in England. Ken Endo and his wife Hilda Gaspar Pereira and their daughter Anna, Takeo Funabiki, Akira Hayami, Masako Kudo, Kaoru and Nobuko Sugihara, Yoh and Himeko Nakanishi, Emiko Ochiai, Osamu and Nobuko Saito, and Airi Tamura and her husband Susume Yamakage.

As always, it has been a pleasure to work with Profile Books and I would particularly like to thank John Davey and Peter Carson for reading the book in an early stage and for their supportive enthusiasm. Penny Daniel, Nicola Taplin and others at Profile have also, as usual, been greatly supportive and efficient. Claire Peligry read the typescript with immense care and greatly improved the style and grammar. The book owes a great deal to her.

One of my greatest helpers is the late and sadly missed Gerry Martin. We spent time in Japan with Gerry and his wife Hilda and I have discussed the Japanese world many times with them. Gerry was always insightful and added to many kindnesses by providing funds for the project as it progressed. Other funders included the British Council, the Japanese Ministry of Education, the University of Cambridge, the University of Tokyo, the Global Governance project at Hokkaido University, the Research Centre of King's College, Cambridge. The Department of Social Anthropology and King's College at Cambridge provided a wonderful context for creative work and my students have been a constant source of inspiration.

My mother, Iris Macfarlane, has always been a great inspiration and example for me and we have worked together on many themes. Her love of Buddhism and Asian civilisation were among the many influences on my work and I would like to pay tribute here to a remarkable writer, poet, painter, philosopher and linguist whose death occurred in the final months of preparing this book.

As always, my greatest debt is to my wife Sarah. We have explored Japan together. The ways in which she has helped me are too numerous to list. Many of the ideas in this book were shared between us, and without her support, inspiration and several careful readings, the book would not have been written. Not least, she gave me the delight of my younger (step) grand-daughter Rosa, to whom this adventure in ideas is dedicated as a sequel to the letters to her older sister Lily.

1

Into the mirror

Like most good things, my exploration started by accident. In early 1990 the British Council invited me to accept a Visiting Scholarship to go to Japan. The Council wished to send out a British academic to spend a month or two in Japan where he or she would give a few lectures and establish contacts. They asked if I would be interested. I was intrigued, for I had read about the Ainu of northern Japan and wanted to visit them. Furthermore, in my reading I had encountered similarities between England and Japan. I learnt that the official invitation had come from a Professor Kenichi Nakamura in the Law Faculty at Hokkaido University. I later found out he had been urged to invite me because his wife Toshiko had been interested by a book I had written on love and marriage in England. I accepted the invitation.

I knew little about Japan before our first visit. I knew that it was a long thin set of islands east of China. It was, I assumed, more or less a small version of China. I believed that for much of its history Japan had used roughly the same language, had similar art and aesthetics, a similar family system, a similar religion (Buddhist, Confucian), a similar agriculture and diet (rice, tea), a similar architecture, and that both countries had an Emperor system. Only recently had the two diverged, China becoming a communist, Japan a capitalist society.

I knew Japan to be an ultra-modern and efficient country, home to more than a hundred million people. It was the first industrial nation in Asia by more than two generations and the second largest economy in the world. It seemed, from afar, the epitome of a modern, capitalist, scientific society, a country with incredibly large cities, hard workers, efficient transport systems, sophisticated arts and crafts. It was famous for its engineering and electronics.

I knew no Japanese people personally, but I had heard that they were reserved and that many of them wore glasses. In the past, some had been samurai warriors and there were some excellent films on this part of their history. The Japanese, I had been told, ate rather strange foods such as raw fish, and drank a rice wine called *sake*. Traditionally they had enjoyed a free sex life with women called *geisha*.

If I had been asked to set up a balance sheet of my preconceptions, it might have read as follows. The positive side would have included the beautiful arts and crafts; wonderful gadgets; exquisite temples and gardens; a samurai culture of honour; tea ceremony and ethic; intriguing games and arts including *sumo* wrestling and *kabuki* theatre. The negative would have included the behaviour of the Japanese military in the Second World War; violent suicide; organised crime and the *yakuza*; over-conformity; pollution and urban blight; violent pornography. This book will try to explain the background to all these impressions and to dispel some of my own prejudices and ignorant judgements.

I repeat this jumble of preconceptions because it may resonate with you. You may be aware of some of these, but have other images of things of which I was ignorant at the time which have since become part of world culture, for instance the communal singing called *karaoke*, or Japanese comic books (*manga*). You may have seen some recent films of life in Japan, perhaps the hit movie *Lost in Translation*, about the difficulty of inter-cultural understanding. You may carry around in your head as distorted and confused a picture as I did when, at the age of forty-eight, I embarked with my wife Sarah for Japan.

❀

I did not consider myself to be ethnocentric. My moving out of the only culture I had known into something different did not cause the increasing sense of shock that I experienced during my encounter with Japan. It is true that up to then I had worked mainly on European and British history and culture, and I had lived in England for forty years. Yet I had also spent over eighteen months in Nepal and visited my anthropological fieldwork area there five times, travelling through India on the way. I had been teaching anthropology at the University of Cambridge for sixteen years and had read about, taught and supervised many students working on tribal, peasant and modern cultures around the world. Yet it is now clear to me that I did hold a number of largely unexamined assumptions which caused difficulties in understanding what I was about to encounter.

When I went to Japan, putting it rather over-simply, I thought there were only two major forms of society. There were integrated, largely oral, worlds, such as the ones I had read about in Africa, South America and the Pacific, and visited in Nepal. They were 'enchanted' because they did not divide off the supernatural and natural worlds and 'embedded' because their economy and society were not separated. These places were the main focus of most anthropological studies. They were small, often peripheral worlds struggling to retain their otherness on the fringes of civilisation.

Civilisations with money, writing, cities and complex technologies originated about ten thousand years ago. They were initially peasant civilisations, where the economy was still part of kinship, and religion and politics were undivided. Nations where the economy, kinship, politics and religion were, in theory, separated emerged only five hundred years ago, ushering in the modern world.

What I expected to find in Japan was a modern civilisation which was totally removed from the undivided type. Whatever its form, it would be a variant on the great civilisational systems around the world. Thus while France, England, America, India or China were all very different, they were clearly within a similar order of world history. Even if they were not entirely 'modern', they had most of the elements of modernity.

In many ways I was like Alice, that very assured and middle-class English girl, when she walked through the looking glass. I was full of certainty, confidence and unexamined assumptions about my categories. I did not even consider that Japan might challenge them. It was just a matter of seeing where it fitted.

Having temporarily lost our luggage on the way in Colombo, we landed in Japan cheerfully enough at Narita airport, near Tokyo, to await the flight for Sapporo on the northern island of Hokkaido. Our first impressions, as recorded in our joint diary, show a certain disappointment that Japan seemed so familiar and prosaic.

'Met at Sapporo by Professor Nakamura. He drove us to the city, which is some distance from the airport. Again, nothing much to surprise one. The Japanese drive on the left as we do, and the roads, houses and street signs, etc., look similar to any large city in England.' The university flat we were given was 'nice and Western. Nothing much here says we're in Japan. Went shopping for food, etc., with Mrs Nakamura. Again, nothing very startling, except for the range of food, especially fish.'

When we visited the university, set in attractive wooded streets, we found on the surface very little difference from many universities in Britain, except that there was a surprising absence of computers. When we visited Professor Nakamura's flat we were struck by how small and crowded it was, with the family apparently having to sleep on the floor of a room that also doubled as the living room. The furniture was simple and inexpensive, and we noted, 'Odd to see that all the wealth of Japan has not given a particularly impressive standard of living.'

These are just hints of what many Western visitors may experience in Japan. Its huge cities are to a large extent very similar to big

Western cities. The cars, shops, underground were all sufficiently familiar to lull us into feeling that we had travelled across the world only to find a country similar to home. The smells, sights, sounds, shapes were different, but of a similar order to those we knew.

This sense of slight disappointment began to dissolve as we started to talk to our hosts and to visit a number of Japanese institutions. A sense of otherness, of something unfamiliar and strange, began to stir. As Alice found in 'Looking Glass Land', the familiar began to display less familiar, and at times quite odd, aspects, each of which could be explained away, yet increasingly surprising us.

The shrines we visited seemed neither fully religious places, nor secular ones. On 1 July we went to a Shinto shrine to the west of Sapporo. It was very hot and after a quick lunch we walked to our destination which was at the bottom of wooded hills. Here is an extract from our diary:

> Startled by its size and beauty. All built of wood with golden embel-
> lishments. To our surprise we noticed that there was a service on,
> and managed to step inside and sit down. The whole place is like a
> theatre stage which one can see standing outside. Don't know how
> they manage in winter, but very attractive now. The interior equally
> impressive. A priest was kneeling before an altar, chanting. The only
> other 'performers' were three young ladies. One later played a drum
> and the others danced, accompanied by the priest, playing a flute and
> drum. Transpired that the 'audience' were mainly parents who had
> brought their babies to be blessed. Like our christening. Some of the
> mothers and grandmothers wore kimonos ... Moving, as the setting
> so splendid, but the feeling overall was much like an English church.
> Around the courtyard, all sorts of activities, including photographing
> the participants and selling charms. At one point we noticed modern
> offices behind the traditional façade. Many of the participants had

brought bottles of *sake* for gifts, so the Shinto priests do well. Tried to see another building we thought was behind the shrine, but instead found ourselves outside the baseball stadium, and the drums of the Shinto shrine gave way to cheerleaders.

Here we had suddenly stepped into a ritualistic world, familiar yet unfamiliar, mixing Shinto with baseball, practical utility with an apparent survival of religion. This was a constant feeling, rather like walking round Cambridge and stepping out of the roar of the twenty-first century into something timeless and medieval and peaceful.

On 3 July we went with Toshiko to her eldest daughter's school. We spent nearly four hours there, observing her daughter's classes through the day and eating lunch with the children. We noted:

Directly after lunch they had a school photograph taken, and then we asked questions, through Toshiko, of a similar nature to those we asked Nepali children. These 10 year olds were self-confident, deci-sive, and not a bit ashamed to answer questions which ranged from general knowledge to intimate details of their future lives – whether they would marry for love, or have arranged marriages ... Perhaps the only real oddness was in relation to our questions on religion. We asked, 'How many religions are there in Japan?' Only one person guessed at four or five; the rest did not know what 'religion' meant. We were told that the concept could not be translated into Japanese. We had been under the impression that Japan was a mixture of Shinto, Buddhist and Confucian, with a little Christianity, which is what we were asking about. But when we asked the children if they could name the founder of any of those religions, only one or two had any idea. One answered the Buddha, but did not know what religion he had founded. No one had heard of Shinto and no one had heard of Confucius. Toshiko suggested that this might be explained by the fact that Shinto was not a 'religion' at all. All very strange and needing further exploration.

The entry for 10 July records:

Spent much of the day in court. First the High Court – Sapporo
has one of the eight High Courts in Japan. Saw three cases in all.
One of tax avoidance, one of threatening behaviour, and the third of
burglary. All three defendants had links with organised crime, with
gangsters. Lunched with the Judges in a large banqueting hall where
weddings are also carried out, near the Court…. Later we went to the
Family Court and saw a juvenile case … There is the strange intersection with organised crime, and the high emphasis on apology, and the
involvement of the family who are weeping in court and part of the
proceedings. Something different is happening here. Another oddness occurred at the meal with the judges. When we asked why it often
took many years for quite simple cases to be decided, they said that it
was because as judges they found it so difficult to come to a decision.
Life was complicated, things were not black and white. Binary decisions of 'guilty' or 'not-guilty' were not easy in a Japanese context. So
there are a number of intriguing hints to follow up here.

The court cases are just three examples of another world behind the
apparently urbane and westernised exterior. Such examples accumu-
lated over the years. For as I experienced Japan in a variety of contexts,
learnt about its history, absorbed its culture and later compared it to
China, I felt as if I were walking through an unfamiliar forest, whose
trees were no longer those I knew, and whose animals and birds were
foreign species. The familiar became unfamiliar and the recognisable
became increasingly incomprehensible.

When I started to read seriously about Japan after my first visit, I
discovered that my sense of strangeness at what I had experienced was
part of a very old tradition. Wondrous tales of the strange, upside-
down world of Japan can be found through the centuries, from early

accounts by Portuguese visitors in the sixteenth century onwards. Western writers from the seventeenth to the early nineteenth century, when a succession of Dutch and German observers frequently relayed the oddness of Japan to their European readers, commented on the strange world they were encountering, though generally from the confines of the island of Deshima lying off Nagasaki.

The impressions of Western travellers, visiting Japan around the time of the Meiji Restoration in the second half of the nineteenth century, are particularly interesting because travel through Japan was now possible. Experienced Victorian travellers did not merely say that Japan was different from other places they had visited. Isabella Bird, who was already widely travelled, commented in 1880, 'Japan offers as much novelty perhaps as an excursion to another planet'. Edwin Arnold, with long experience of India, wrote that he was 'in a new world, life in which is almost as strange and different as would be existence in the moon'. A particularly elegant account was given by W. E. Griffis who spent several years in Japan:

> A double pleasure rewards the pioneer who is the first to penetrate into the midst of a new people. Besides the rare exhilaration felt in treading soil virgin to alien feet, it acts like mental oxygen to look upon and breathe in a unique civilisation like that of Japan. To feel that for ages millions of one's own race have lived and loved, enjoyed and suffered and died, living the fullness of life, yet without the religion, laws, customs, food, dress, and culture which seem to us to be the vitals of our social existence, is like walking through a living Pompeii.

Lafcadio Hearn, who also spent many years in Japan, marrying a Japanese woman and taking Japanese citizenship, gives one of the most forceful accounts of the surprise he felt. He was able to observe a world as yet not totally overlaid by a veneer of modern industrial and urban development. He comments on both the strangeness and the sense that there is something enchanted about the country, a mysterious world of magical otherness which lay behind the surface of life.

As first perceived, the outward strangeness of things in Japan produces (in certain minds, at least) a queer thrill impossible to describe, – a feeling of weirdness which comes to us only with the perception of the totally unfamiliar ... Further acquaintance with this fantastic world will in nowise diminish the sense of strangeness evoked by the first vision of it. You will soon observe that even the physical actions of the people are unfamiliar – that their work is done in ways the opposite of Western ways ... These and other forms of unfamiliar action are strange enough to suggest the notion of a humanity even physically as little related to us as might be the population of another planet.

What most observers found particularly puzzling were the paradoxes, contradictions and topsy-turvy inversions which they could not understand. Percival Lowell wrote:

What we regard intuitively in one way from our standpoint, they as intuitively observe in a diametrically opposite manner from theirs. To speak backwards, write backwards, read backwards, is but the *a b c* of their contrariety. The inversion extends deeper than mere modes of expression, down into the very matter of thought. Ideas of ours which we deemed innate find in them no home, while methods which strike us as preposterously unnatural appear to be their birthright. From the standing of a wet umbrella on its handle instead of its head to dry to the striking of a match away in place of toward one, there seems to be no action of our daily lives, however trivial, but finds with them its appropriate reaction – equal but opposite ... Humour holds the glass, and we become the sport of our own reflections.

It might be thought that with the supposed Westernisation of Japan in the later nineteenth century, as it turned into an industrial society, these difficulties of comprehension, this feeling of indefinable otherness, which cut across our ways of classifying our experiences would have ended. Yet the sense of surprise has not diminished. Japan continues to be an anomalous case within comparative anthropology, challenging our cultural logic.

The economist Kurt Singer commented in the 1930s:

A stranger landing on the islands of Japan will soon perceive that he has entered a world that follows a law of its own in every province of action and contemplation ... the sense of orientation and the scales of preference are subtly disturbed by a general 'topsy-turvydom' expressing itself in almost systematic exchanges of left and right, before and after, speech and silence. Every gesture, shape of vessels, the cadence of a sentence, the etiquette of a household or of a school-class, and arrangement of flowers in a vase – each bears an unmistakable mark peculiar to just this country.

Ruth Benedict noted some of this peculiarity in her book *The Chrysanthemum and the Sword*, written at the end of the Second World War:

During the past seventy-five years since Japan's closed doors were opened, the Japanese have been described in the most fantastic series of 'but also's' ever used for any nation of the world ... Japanese are, to the highest degree, both aggressive and unaggressive, both militaristic and aesthetic, insolent and polite, rigid and adaptable, submissive and resentful of being pushed around, loyal and treacherous, brave and timid, conservative and hospitable to new ways.

Most westerners still find that they cannot understand Japan. When they do attempt to write books about it, these works are dismissed as shallow and incorrect by Japanese scholars. Many Japanese would agree with the teacher who remarked, 'You have to be born a Japanese to appreciate the subtlety of Japanese thinking', and all the educators and businessmen interviewed by Kosaku Yoshino 'considered it impossible for foreigners to learn to "behave and think like the Japanese"'. Yet when outsiders ask in what ways they are wrong, and what would be a more accurate representation, their informants are silent. As Kenichi put it to me, Japan is a one-way mirror out of which the Japanese can look, but which outsiders cannot look into. It also seems to be a world that even those inside the mirror find difficult to understand.

We went to Japan for our second visit in July 1993 and it was then that we had our most intense conversations. Evening after evening, and on long journeys around Japan to see the wonders of Kyoto, Ise, Nikko and elsewhere, our friends patiently tried to answer our many questions and explain Japan to us. It was then, I think, that we began to see how some of the jigsaw fitted together and to get a little sense of order and understanding.

Building on earlier drafts, I set about writing on many different aspects of Japanese history and culture, on property, law, kinship, politics, and economics and to compare Japan with China and Europe. Through a deeper study of the institutional history of Japan, when compared to the West, I began to see why the Japanese had become so different and how some of the inner forces worked. I was still in 'Looking Glass Land', but I felt that what I perceived to be the culture was beginning to make a little more sense.

This is the second phase of the normal experience of an anthropologist, following the initial 'culture shock'. After some months, you can partially predict behaviour, understand why a person says a particular thing, and begin to see the underlying grammar of a society. You not only see the surface confusion, but the more patterned currents that run through the society. Usually this process takes some months, in the case of Japan it took me about four years.

The third phase consisted of further attempts to probe beneath the surface of Japan. I wrote a book comparing ecology, population and material life in Japan and England over a thousand years. I wrote another book comparing the ideas of two great theorists of how the modern world came about, F.W. Maitland in England and Yukichi Fukuzawa in Japan. I helped make a television series which, among other things, involved filming in Japan and discussion of central features of Japanese society and history. Through long conversations, seminars and exchanged writing, I worked with the late Gerry Martin to develop a model of the similarities and differences between Japan and the West.

The final phase occurred when, with Kenichi and Toshiko, we jointly tried to put the pieces of the puzzle together into this book; a summer of discussion and writing, intense meetings with a dozen of the most distinguished Japanese scholars in the spring of 2006, and the final synthesis later that year.

The path into and through the Japanese mirror is made more complicated by three sets of ideas which have been developed particularly strongly in the last forty years: Japanese cultural nationalism *nihonjinron*, and its opposite, anti-*nihonjinron*, orientalism and occidentalism, relativism and postmodernism. Readers need to be aware of the distortions which these are likely to cause to any writing or reading on Japan.

Like every other people, the Japanese have always been interested in their own identity and for many centuries those who attempted to explore this area compared themselves with China and Korea. Then, from the 1850s, as Japan began to measure itself against an aggressive and powerful West, they went through various stages of self-perception, at times thinking of themselves as just like westerners, then as very different, depending on political and economic relations.

After the Second World War the Japanese self-image was largely shattered. However, as they rebuilt their economy the Japanese started to see themselves as not only modernising but westernising. Then in the 1960s and 1970s, a number of writers, picking up ideas from earlier authors who had stressed Japanese uniqueness, contributed to a theory of the essence of Japaneseness or *nihonjinron*.

Nihonjinron is partly a cultural reaction by these writers to the 'ethnocentric universalism' of some Anglo-American thought. As in many other areas of the world, some people in Japan feel assaulted by the modern trend to conform to the institutions and values of the West. They feel under pressure to abandon their own culture, to accept that they are no different except in aspects which are considered 'backward'. In opposition to this, *nihonjinron* thinkers have made a counter-claim that the Japanese are indeed different and unique, and that they should be proud of their 'traditional' culture.

This debate, and the pre-war ultra-nationalist and anti-Western proclamations of Japanese uniqueness, have added to the difficulty of writing about Japan. Although few of the *nihonjinron* writers have actually claimed that the country was superior, they have sometimes stressed that it was unique in a special way, at times even suggesting this was due to its genetic and racial heritage.

This in turn has led to a powerful counter-attack on the idea of Japanese uniqueness, exemplified by Peter Dale's *The Myth of Japanese Uniqueness*, which documents a number of the problems of the 'Japan as unique' literature. In a more measured way Kosaku Yoshino's *Cultural Nationalism in Contemporary Japan* analyses the phenomenon and its roots.

Peter Dale summarises the *nihonjinron* assumptions as follows: 'Firstly, they implicitly assume that the Japanese constitute a culturally and socially homogeneous racial entity, whose essence is virtually unchanged from pre-historical times down to the present day.' My own view is that, as Dale and others argue, this assumption is unacceptable. As we shall see, the Japanese are not homogenous in space or in time and their roots are to be found all over Asia.

'Secondly, they presuppose that the Japanese differ radically from all other known peoples.' That the Japanese are different from other neighbouring as well as more distant countries will emerge in this book. Yet they also share many features with other societies.

'Thirdly, they are consciously nationalistic, displaying a conceptual and procedural hostility to any mode of analysis which might be seen to derive from external, non-Japanese sources'. Clearly, such an attitude towards outside analysis is unacceptable to a comparative anthropologist and indeed the whole of this book is a denial of this view.

Let me state straightaway that my initial premises do not accord with those of *nihonjinron*. Japan is not superior, it is not constructed by racial or cultural uniqueness but rather by historical forces and accidents. Yet while rejecting the extreme assertions, if we rule out all discussion of Japanese distinctiveness put forward either by the Japanese or by others, we make it impossible to understand Japan.

When criticising the excesses of *nihonjinron*, we have to be very careful not to overdo the attempt to go in the opposite direction, for this only inflames the reaction. It also distorts reality. There are indeed real and important differences between cultures. We should be prepared to accept that they exist rather than trying to pretend that they are illusions, or to be so arrogant about our superiority that we do not even notice them.

Assimilating Japan to our categories of thought, for example assuming that it is just another 'postmodern' society, would deny its specificity. We have to allow the possibility that Japan may be a genuine alternative to the Western civilisations with which most readers are familiar.

At this point I want to keep my options open, to suspend judgement. I hope to sail a middle course. On one side is extreme *nihonjinron* and on the other extreme anti-*nihonjinron*. Each has its dangers. I do not have any particular predisposition. I am not Japanese, but nor do I fear Japan. I would like to evaluate what I have found in Japan without fear of political correctness or the reverse. I want to explore the central questions of how far Japan is unique, comprehensible; how it fits with outside (Western) theories. If there is uniqueness, what is it? How have the Japanese preserved such uniqueness against waves of invasion? How continuous is Japanese culture? What have been the effects of massive transformations since the 1960s? What implications does this have for our understanding of our own world and humanity in general?

Another difficulty in seeing Japan relatively clearly arises from 'orientalism' and 'anti-orientalism'. From their first encounters with Japan in the sixteenth century onwards, Western thinkers and travellers have had a long tradition of perpetuating national stereotypes of the Japanese. These largely unexamined projections now impinge on us by way of numerous advertisements and other representations: cherry blossom, chrysanthemums, tea houses, samurai warriors, sumo wrestlers, *geishas* and a host of other cultural stereotypes infest our imagination, and it is extremely difficult to dislodge or avoid them. This distorted gaze from outside is reinforced by tendencies within Japan itself to project images of Japan as unique, ancient and exotic for marketing or nationalistic reasons.

To use the 'mirror' metaphor when writing about Japan could be seen as contributing to an 'orientalist' tendency. In fact, my intention is to remind us that while we may indeed be dazzled by the surface reflections of our own hopes and fears, and may tend to create the 'other' to suit ourselves, it is also possible to abandon some of our own preconceptions and narcissistic concerns and go beneath the surfaces inside the mirror.

However, this task is also made difficult by another tendency which I was not fully aware of when I went to Japan, and even when, after fifteen years, I started to write this book. It is a bias which many westerners are guilty of. It could be called reverse orientalism or 'occidentalism'. In these pages I set out to show that while much of Japanese life seems to be upside down or reversed when considered from a Western perspective, subverting many of our deepest assumptions, as a whole it works pretty well. Yet attempting to argue this may be seen to be orientalism in reverse. As I shall explain in more detail when we leave the Japanese mirror, the encounter with Japan is partly written in that tradition of 'Utopian' thinking which has been a feature of Western thought since at least Thomas More's *Utopia* in the early sixteenth century. In other words, I have constructed the book so that, among other things, it calls into question some of the assumed, 'natural', beyond-question features of a Euro-American world view.

When I tell my friends that I have written a book in order to 'understand Japan better', they often react with surprise. Surely I know that many people today are highly sceptical of such an endeavour? Some argue that we cannot understand 'the other' because we cannot escape from our own categories. Others say that to construct an entity such as 'Japan', flattening time, space, social class, gender and other variations, is ridiculous. Both are important objections. Understanding is indeed limited, there is only less or more of it, and I cannot claim fully to 'understand' myself, let alone others. It is also true that there is a danger of reifying something we call 'Japan' and then giving it enduring characteristics.

I draw encouragement from the studies by Alexis de Tocqueville. *Democracy in America*, *L'Ancien Régime* (on pre-revolutionary France), and the scattered writings throughout his life which, in effect, created another book on England, succeeded in deepening our understanding of three civilisations. Tocqueville achieved this while recognising well enough that understanding another civilisation is, to a certain extent, an impossible task. 'You are right when you say that a foreigner cannot understand the peculiarities of the English character. It is the case with almost all countries', he noted. Elsewhere he wrote, 'Every foreign nation has a peculiar physiognomy, seen at the first glance and easily described. When afterwards you try to penetrate deeper, you are met by real and unexpected difficulties; you advance with a slowness that drives you to despair, and the farther you go the more you doubt'.

Nevertheless, Tocqueville persisted and believed that he had found the basic principles upon which the America of his time was based:

> In America all laws originate more or less from the same idea. The whole of society, so to say, is based on just one fact: everything follows from one underlying principle. One could compare America to a great forest cut through by a large number of roads which all end in the same place. Once you have found the central point, you can see the whole plan in one glance.

Subsequent generations have found that his accounts, like those of Hippolyte Taine in *Notes upon England* or George Orwell in *The Lion and the Unicorn*, do give us a deeper understanding. Indeed, all comparison and communication between civilisations become impossible if we take the extreme relativist and postmodern position that there is no possibility, and therefore no point, in trying to understand 'the other'. If we do take this position, we fly in the face of our own daily experience of interacting with people from different backgrounds.

When I talk about 'understanding' Japan, I am not claiming either that I fully understand the country, or that I have explained it away. What I have tried to do is what many anthropologists proclaim to be their aim, that is to make other cultures comprehensible to us and to do this by describing them as far as possible from inside, thinking through their categories and symbols. If we achieve this, at least partially, it makes it possible for people from very different vantage points to appreciate and make sense of what is going on. I believe that this is only possible if we set Japan in a wide comparative framework, that is if we consider it as a civilisation alongside other civilisations and societies. We need to look at 'Japan' broadly, both over a long time period of thousands of years, and as a whole, integrated civilisation where, however much there may be variations, there are some central organising principles, of the kind to which Tocqueville alluded.

If we examine the Japanese both from close up and also from afar, we can use our imagination and experience of life to help us penetrate sympathetically the material and mental worlds of another civilisation. We can emotionally and intellectually grasp unfamiliar things by relating them at least partially to what we already know. True understanding comes when we are able to re-live in our own hearts and minds the experiences of others, so that we put ourselves in their place and come to understand their actions and decisions. This imaginative leap, which all of us perform daily, when we watch television, play a computer game, interact with children, read a novel or talk to our friends, is part of our amazing but real ability as human animals to comprehend things outside ourselves, temporarily suspending disbelief. When we do this we broaden our understanding.

2

Culture shock

Most outsiders first encounter Japan through its material culture. Yet this entry into the Japanese mirror is particularly confusing. As I tried to approach Japan by this path, I felt a preliminary sense of familiarity, and then shock and surprise at something different. There is a surface recognition, yet inside the mirror there is a growing feeling that the relations between things and the assumptions upon which the actions and symbols are based are different to those with which I am familiar.

Before we try to understand the deeper roots of Japanese civilisation, it is worth elaborating on the culture shock which many foreigners experience when they encounter this aspect of Japan. It is worth outlining impressionistically something of the confusing mixture of the beautiful and the ugly, the sublime and the grotesque, the innocent and the depraved, the spiritual and the material which will follow us through our exploration.

I live in a world which has, since the Renaissance and scientific revolutions, adopted a number of binary oppositions or divisions. Art is distinct from life, craft from art, popular taste from high culture, realism from symbolic art, the Baroque from the Gothic style, the urban from the rural, sports and games from ceremonial and religion, the material body from spiritual purity, nature from culture. I initially found the Japanese experience very puzzling because it challenges all of these separations.

The confusion is only increased by the overwhelming delight many outsiders feel when they first encounter the arts and crafts of Japan. Anyone who reads about or visits Japan will be struck by the Japanese love of the aesthetically beautiful. One of the earliest and most percep-tive visitors was the biologist Edward Morse in the later nineteenth century. After he had gone to an exhibition of Japanese ceramics, Morse commented:

> What amazes one in this work is the originality in all designs, their truthfulness to nature, and their grace and charm. We admire the life-like etchings of grasses by Dürer, the wild bits over which we become enthusiastic; in the Exhibition one sees the work of a hundred Dürers whose names are but little known ... There were beautiful wreaths, cherry blossoms, thorns and little flowers in colours, all made out of porcelain; old Dresden and Chelsea products of a similar nature look weak and putty-like in comparison.

Morse also noted that even young children were visually acute:

> I ought to record the interesting experience I had with the children and other people of the inn when drawing, with a Japanese brush on Japanese paper, a number of objects such as toads, grasshoppers, dragonflies, snails and the like. The little children would recognise the animal intended when I had made no more than a stroke or two.

> Even the most trivial thing was turned into art: 'If a child acci-dentally punches a hole through the paper screen, instead of mending it with a square piece of paper, the paper is cut in the form of a cherry blossom.'

As I came to learn a little more about Japan, I began to have the sense that if the economy dominates America, law dominates England, religion India, culture China, then one of the central threads of Japan is aesthetics. For the Japanese, in Keats's words, truth is beauty, beauty truth.

From the exquisite *netsuke* wood and bone carvings for ornamental clasps, through the *ikebana* art of flower-arranging, to the delicate *origami* paper cutting, the *bonsai* shaping of miniature trees, the delicate art of calligraphy, the wonderful traditional temple architecture, the superb gardens, the amazing lacquer and bamboo work, the ravishing pots and paintings, Japan is arguably the most artistic civilisation on earth.

The Japanese play with form and function in a delicate and entrancing way. This partly explains their great commercial success in recent years. The design of the cars, computers and other electronic gadgets, whose parts are now often manufactured outside Japan but assembled into a Japanese shell, still enchant the world. Now *manga* cartoons and computer games are among their greatest exports.

In its attachment to beauty Japan is unsurpassed. Knowing this makes a walk through many parts of Japanese cities an even greater shock. An unsightly tangle of wires and electric connectors can often be seen there, which, even allowing for the fact that earthquakes necessitate carrying wires above ground, has not been disciplined. The streets are also frequently clogged with ugly signs and incongruous buildings; the neighbourhoods often appear to be unplanned.

In certain cities, particularly Kyoto and Nara, elegant oases can be found, of course. Yet compared to Italy, for instance, much of Japan seems a mass of modern hideousness. It is both the most beautiful, in terms of its arts and temples, and one of the messiest of civilisations. This is but one of the many puzzles which begin to emerge as we try to make sense of the confusing features of this world within the cultural mirror.

❖

An American scholar, Ernest Fenollosa, joined Morse as a professor at Tokyo University in 1878. Fenollosa became an influential teacher and a great documenter and promoter of Japanese art in the West. He worked with his former student Kakuzo Okakura, an art critic and philosopher who later became a high official in charge of arts at the Ministry of Education, to systematise and institutionalise Japanese art. Together they set up the first official art academy, later to become Tokyo University of Fine Arts and Music, in 1889 and published Japan's first art magazine. They organised international exhibitions and wrote extensively on the nature and history of Japanese art, introducing the notion of a Western distinction between 'art' and 'craft', and the technical vocabulary of art appreciation which had largely been absent in Japan. Japanese art, hitherto little known abroad, became famous in the West. It made a deep impact on the French Impressionists, who in turn, through their interpretations, influenced Japanese artists.

For the first time, Japan became part of a world art market. The insatiable Western demand for Japanese art works, from the finest porcelain down to what had previously been considered by many as rather vulgar, if lifelike, woodblock prints of popular life or *ukiyoe*, was welcomed and promoted by the Meiji government.

Many of the distinctions and features of Japanese art were invented in the later nineteenth century to mirror Western desires, in particular through tilting the balance towards the more popular and colourful forms and away from the more austere courtly and Chinese-inspired classical art. In turn, Western desires were themselves shaped by the Japanese inspiration. The international movement known as *mingei*, promoted by Okakura and then taken up by Muneyoshi Yanagi, spread in the early twentieth century, making its mark on the folk arts movements elsewhere in the world, for example those associated with William Morris and John Ruskin.

❖

Before the institutionalisation of its art in the later nineteenth century, there had been no hard divisions between different forms of communication through visual media in Japan. In common with many tribal societies, where the very humblest of objects, whether small pots, gourds, shawls or spears, are made with exquisite and concentrated effort in an attempt to make them superbly beautiful, the Japanese did not make a distinction between utilitarian and aesthetic purpose.

Traditionally the Japanese have always lived in a materially circumscribed world with the majority of the population wearing simple clothes, living in small houses and with few possessions. Yet what they do have has received immense attention, from the buckles of swords, to the fasteners for bags, to the surfaces of anything that would receive lacquer.

At the other extreme, many in the West had an extremely generous material environment which they rigidly divided between the utilitarian and the aesthetic. The utilitarian things were made by technicians and craftsmen. High art, such as painting, beautiful but useless, was produced by artists. This is a division which many attribute to the Renaissance, where the artist and the craftsman became separated, and 'art for art's sake', and not as a vehicle for religious education, became a central organisational principle of Western aesthetics.

Yet although the division began to be instituted in art galleries, exhibitions and art books, and in the vocabulary introduced by Fenollosa and Okakura, the border line between craft and art is still rather indistinct in Japan. The Japanese elevate their artist craftsmen to the highest prestige rank in Japan by designating them 'National Living Treasures'. These include potters, swordsmiths, paper makers, lacquer workers and calligraphers. This tendency to reassert the value of traditional art-crafts has been particularly pronounced since the rise of the nationalist movement after the Second World War.

Within what we roughly lump together as 'Japanese art', there are in fact a number of striking and contradictory traditions and aesthetics.

One opposition is between the Chinese and the native ways of repre-
senting and establishing beauty. From the seventh century, China
and Korea were the predominant influences. Their golds and reds,
their classical forms and symbols, their Buddhist-inspired conceptions of beauty, all shaped Japanese sensibility over a thousand years.
However, their effect was altered in the medieval period, when new,
reformed and puritanical forms of Buddhism, especially Zen, swept
through Japan and a more subdued, minimalist, asymmetrical and
austere taste was established. These two layers can be seen in the still
opposed traditions of Japanese aesthetics represented by the art of
Tokyo, the centre of government from the seventeenth century, and
that of the ceremonial centre through much of that time, Kyoto.

Some Japanese friends stress how they love the 'show-off, *ukiyoe*,
very colourful, very flat, very surprising' art of the *kabuki* drama, of
Hokusai and Hiroshige. Others describe it as 'short, clear, express
yourself, simplify, decisive, keep your distance' art. The bright colours,
the exaggerated and even grotesque figures, the theatrical beauty, the
playfulness and exuberance, all these are central to Japanese art. It is
not the same as Chinese art, but it is direct, deals with everyday life
and turns the world into a huge colourful cartoon.

This tradition of flamboyant, humorous and energetic art is being
rediscovered by the world's young people today through Japanese *anime*
films, *manga* or cartoon books and computer games. Many people
think of this when they call to mind Japanese art.

But there is a shadow side, the reverse of this coin, often associated with Kyoto, which one friend described as 'ephemeral, soon
gone' art. Since the thirteenth century, one strand of Japanese art
has become very pure, ascetic, understated and minimalist – black,
white and grey rather than filled with bright colours. It attempts to
transcend colour. It represents the sadness and unreality of life, the
impossibility of holding on to the present. The falling blossom, the
waning moon, the death of love. Exquisite beauty is depicted as transitory, bound to perish, its moment is short, like life. This strand is

part of a Buddhist tradition which emphasises life's mutability and illusory nature. Describing the effect of this philosophical realism on aesthetics, Basil Hall Chamberlain commented, 'Japanese taste in painting, in house decoration, in all matters depending on line and form, may be summed up in one word – sobriety.'

The difference between the two aesthetic strands is immediately visible by moving between a Korean gallery in a museum, filled with extraordinarily bright reds, blues, greens and golds, and a Japanese gallery, with its subdued greys, browns, gold and silver. The Chinese, while not quite as exuberant as the Koreans, are still relatively far from the largely pastel shades of Japan. The Puritans in seventeenth century England gave English and American visitors some sense of this shadow side, but even they never established something so purified or extreme.

While the bright and the shadow sides are starkly contrasted, at a deeper level they both exhibit certain features which are essential to the Japanese. One of these is that in all forms of art, including calligraphy and poetry, the outward expressions employ well known and powerful symbols which can be deeply appreciated by a well-educated audience.

A great deal of Japanese art is allusive and symbolic, referring to something else. Expanding in the mind, it works indirectly. There is a desire to avoid the obvious and realistic in favour of the suggestive and the more profound. It is, as in Roland Barthes's title, *An Empire of Signs*. This is because artists are trying to convey not the surface of things, as in realist art, but the inner essence, which can only be transmitted to the observer indirectly by symbols. This is illustrated by the story of a Japanese painter who was commissioned at great expense to paint a picture of a garden with trees. After some time he came back with a largely empty canvas. Only in one corner was a sprig of cherry with a small bird perching on it. His patron asked why he had not filled up the rest of the frame. The painter replied, 'If I had filled it up with things, where would the bird be able to fly?'

When I first showed Kenichi the Fellows' Garden at King's College with its wide lawns and huge trees, he was delighted. He commented, however, that I would not find anything like it in Japan. In Japan, he said, everything was miniaturised. A garden is like a written text. One 'read' a miniature garden or a famous rock and stone Zen landscape. Then, as with any language, one interpreted the symbols in one's mind. English art, he realised, is much more literal and realistic.

Indirectness and allusion are found in the Japanese love of subtlety. In his *In Praise of Shadows*, Junichiro Tanizaki explains:

> When we gaze into the darkness that gathers behind the crossbeam, around the flower vase, beneath the shelves, though we know perfectly well it is mere shadow, we are overcome with the feeling that in this small corner of the atmosphere there reigns complete and utter silence; that here in the darkness immutable tranquillity holds sway ... This was the genius of our ancestors, that by cutting off the light from this empty space they imparted to the world of shadows that formed there a quality of mystery and depth superior to that of any wall painting or ornament.

Lacquer-work is one expression of this. Tanizaki explains how 'the lacquerware of the past was finished in black, brown, or red, colours built up of countless layers of darkness, the inevitable product of the darkness in which life was lived'. Morse saw this very clearly: 'It is the reserve, simplicity, and yet audacity these artists show that is so wonderful. Who would think of details in black on a black background! A jet-black crow on a jet-black *inro*! It is unthinkable, and yet it is only one of hundreds of things the Japanese delight to do. The tablet represented night, and night it was.'

Miniaturisation — the obliqueness, single word, brush stroke or curve of an object that signifies a whole world of meaning to the highly educated Japanese public — is well illustrated, of course, in the minute poems of a few syllables known as *haiku*. English poems are often wordy, spelling out the feelings, sights and emotions in an explicit way. What the English do in dozens of lines can be synthe/sised with breathtaking economy in a few words which strike hidden chords for many Japanese. Again, it is impossible to place this partic/ular aesthetic firmly within any other art tradition of the world. Its central features, as the critic Donald Keene has written, are the ideals of suggestion, irregularity, simplicity and perishability. It is a true wonder, both vaguely familiar in parts, yet also strange.

Any visitor, or reader of books on Japan, will soon feel a sense of otherness about traditional Japanese homes and gardens. Yet it is difficult to pin down exactly what is strange about them. When I visited Japan I carried from my background a strong assumption about houses. I thought of them as large, solid, permanent, complex places which endured through time. A house should be as full of objects as possible, as well as being physically comfortable and cosy. It took me a long time to understand that a house is very different for the Japanese.

Nowadays most Japanese live in what look like modern buildings, yet even the most modern apartment surprises by its unfamiliar aspects. Certainly, if I visit the small houses of Japanese friends, or stay in an old/style inn or *ryo/kan*, I feel a sense of shock. The thick rice/straw *tatami* matting, the *hibachi* or heated pit, the ancestor shrine in the corner, the slippers by the toilet, the paper shutters and the bed/roll or *futon,* stored in a cupboard by day and spread out on the floor at night — all remind me that while on the surface the Japanese live alongside us in time, they also preserve features of an otherness, even if, as I have become aware, many of these features are quite modern inventions or reinventions.

A hundred and fifty years ago, the difference would have been much more visible, and the otherness even more striking. Edward Morse, in his classic work *Japanese Homes and Their Surroundings,* wrote that the normal Japanese home has 'no doors or windows, such as he had been familiar with, 'no attic or cellar; no chimneys, and within no fire-place, and of course no customary mantle; no permanently enclosed rooms; and as for furniture, no beds or tables, chairs or similar articles.' He found that it was 'so unlike anything to which we are accustomed in the arrangement of details of interiors in this country, that it is difficult to find terms of comparison in attempting to describe it.'

Kurt Singer captures the essence of the Japanese house in a telling contrast:

> Chinese dwellings are cut into the soil, moulded from it, or joined to it in such a way that they appear to be parts of the earth's crust ... Japanese houses attach themselves only lightly to the soil; they survive earthquakes and hurricanes by not relying too much on their slender foundations; their virtue is in their swinging elasticity ... Relentlessly this archipelago is rocked by seismic shocks, invaded by storms, showered and pelted with rain, encircled by clouds and mists ... they are built like a ship, or a big piece of furniture, held together internally by interlocking beams, and only the most exceptional shock is capable of wrecking them.

Even today houses are made with flexible wooden frames, though the outer cladding makes them look like houses anywhere in the world.

Along with some castles, the temples and shrines were until recently the only large constructions in Japan. Lafcadio Hearn wrote, at the start of the twentieth century, 'A Japanese city is still, as it was ten centuries ago, little more than a wilderness of wooden sheds – picturesque, indeed, as paper lanterns are, but scarcely less frail.' And, like paper lanterns, the houses were as much things of beauty as of utility. Enright wrote that 'The Japanese have never, traditionally, thought of the house as a machine for living – they have thought of it as a work of art.'

For those who have never had a chance to experience the sensation of wandering round a Japanese temple or shrine on a hot summer's day, I can do no better than quote Isabella Bird on one such visit in the 1870s:

> The shrines are the most wonderful work of their kind in Japan. In their stately setting of cryptomeria, few of which are less than 20 feet in girth at 3 feet from the ground, they take one prisoner by their beauty, in defiance of all rules of Western art, and compel one to acknowledge the beauty of forms and combinations of colour hitherto unknown, and that lacquered wood is capable of lending itself to the expression of a very high idea in art.

Coming from a civilisation steeped in monotheistic religions and ideas originating in Ancient Greece, I inevitably assumed there was a strong opposition between the natural and the cultural. Human beings make their cultures, that is to say the intellectual and material objects, which make up their world. In this entirely man-made environment, there is a ring of domesticated objects, farm animals, cultivated fields and gardens. In a second ring are totally wild things animals, forests, climate, mountains – over which we have little control and which are basically hostile. The task of humans is to try either to domesticate, or to eliminate that wild world over which Christianity suggested humankind has been given dominion.

I was shocked when I realised that in Japan there is no opposition of the kind described above. Nature is not separated off; the world is not 'disenchanted'. Everything is simultaneously cultural and natural, domesticated and wild, constructed and free. It is very difficult to articulate this, or to sense what it means to live in such a world.

Clearly the landscape within which most Japanese have lived is, even more than for the English, one created by human effort. Every leaf on every tree is 'man-made' to a certain extent. Every object, and every sentiment about every object, is constructed. Not a bud stirs or blossom falls without permission within the centrally inhabited areas, though large areas of forested mountains remain wild.

On the other hand, nothing in nature is really subject to human will alone. Not only could nature erupt in fire or earthquake, lashing rains or tidal waves, but it is only marginally controllable by human will. Humans are not radically differentiated from other living things. Although few Japanese hold very strong beliefs in rebirth, their outlook on the world is informed by Buddhism: everyone and everything is interfused; all of the things on earth are on a continuum. There is no great opposition between the human and non-human world. It is all a matter of more or less, both natural and human.

It is not just the deep emotional attachments and careful tending of flowers, even in the humblest of gardens, that is special, but the arrangement of the pots and the blooms. 'The foreigner visiting Japan is impressed at the very outset by the Japanese love of flowers,' Morse wrote, 'for everywhere, in gardens, or in little tanks, flowerpots and hanging or standing flower-holders are seen, and he begins to realise that the simplicity and beauty of their arrangement is everywhere manifest'. The elaborate art of *ikebana* or flower arranging is immensely important and widespread with its own schools and teachers. Ruth Benedict noted, 'Chrysanthemums are grown in pots and arranged for the annual flower shows all over Japan with each perfect petal separately disposed by the grower's hand and often held in place by a tiny invisible wire rack inserted in the living flower'.

Flowers seem to have an intense significance for many Japanese. Percival Lowell wrote:

Indeed, they may be said to live in a chronic state of flower-fever
… The intense appreciation shown the subject by the Far Oriental
is something whose very character seems strange to us, and when in
addition we consider that it permeates the entire people from the com-
monest coolie to the most aesthetic courtier, it becomes to our comprehension a state of things little short of inexplicable … Their care
for tree flowers is not confined to cultivation, it is a cult. It approaches
to a sort of natural nature-worship, an adoration in which nothing is
personified.

If we move from flowers to gardens, again there is an intensity of
careful application, the purpose of which is to make perfect works of
art from moss, stones, trees, water and flowers. When Lord Elgin's
mission toured Japan in the middle of the nineteenth century, one
of his entourage noted, 'We are filled with astonishment and delight
at the exquisite taste displayed in the gardens and cottages upon the
roadside. No model estate in England', he thought, could produce
cottage gardens 'comparable to those which adorn the suburbs of
Yedo [Tokyo]'. 'Their very farming is artistic gardening, and their
gardening half necromancy,' commented the American visitor Eliza
Scidmore.

The art is to trick the eye. 'At first sight you might be in the
clearing of a wood', wrote Fosco Maraini, 'Then you realise that
you are surrounded by the work of man, but that the artist's aim was
the unobtrusive recreation of nature. There is no geometry here; or
rather there is a secret, infinitely non-Euclidean and subtle geometry,
a secret harmony that the mind seizes before the intelligence.' Every
object is both natural and cultural, both itself and standing for
something other. The garden is an enchanted place, existing on
several dimensions simultaneously. 'His garden is more human, even,
than his house', noted Lowell, 'To walk into a Japanese garden is
like wandering of a sudden into one of those strange worlds we see

reflected in the polished surface of a concave mirror, where all but the observer himself is transformed into a fantastic miniature of the reality.'

It is indisputable that the Japanese, while living in one of the most crowded and artificial landscapes on earth, adore what they perceive to be natural. As Morse observed:

> No civilised nation on the face of the earth exceeds the Japanese in the love for nature in every aspect. Storm or calm, mist, rain, snow, flowers, the varying tints of the seasons, placid rivers, raging water' falls, the flight of birds, the dash of fishes, towering peaks, deep ravines – every phase of nature is not only admired, but depicted in unnumbered sketches and *kakemono* [illustrated scroll].

The ways in which a society organises its leisure time is a good mirror of its essential character. The divisions between work and play, game and sport, secular and sacred, are all revealed. Let's start with something apparently quite humdrum for which Japan is famous, *sumo*. At first sight this looks like just another competitive sport – somewhat like heavy-weight wrestling anywhere in the world. Two flesh mountains get into a ring and struggle and one is thrown out by the other. End of story. Yet as I watch *sumo* contests broadcast live for hours on Japanese television, or visit a *sumo* 'stable' where the wrestlers are trained, or read about its history and traditions, it becomes clear that it is not just a sport.

Sumo feels, at times, like some kind of ritual. There is sometimes a replica of a Shinto shrine suspended above the ring, as in Tokyo's *Kokugikan* or Hall of National Skill. A referee dressed in Shinto costume and trained by Shinto officials opens the proceedings with a little ritual. The ring has to be purified with salt to make it safe and each wrestler must throw a handful of purifying salt each time he enters the ring. A grand champion becomes automatically an acolyte of the Shinto faith. The *sumo* wrestlers live in monastic-like institutions and have to abstain from sex before fights. They have to wear special ritualistic costumes and dress their hair in an archaic style. No woman is allowed into the ring.

Sumo looks much more like some kind of formalised communion between humans and spirits than a sporting contest. Yet it is also a contest of skill and training. It is on the exact border line between religion and sport. Originating at least two thousand years ago, one theory is that it began as a sacred contest through which shamans were able to make predictions about the rice harvest – divination by wrestling. It became a professional sport about three hundred years ago and a number of the religious ceremonies attached to it are of recent invention or reinvention.

When we attended a *Noh* drama, we were much perplexed by what we experienced. The strange formal gestures, the screeching and wailing, the masks, the darkness, the unfamiliar music, all of these elements felt religious, yet it was not quite clear in what way. Although there were similarities with medieval Christian morality plays, religion and drama were being mixed in an unfamiliar way.

We asked our Japanese friends to enlighten us. They told us that most of the audience would not understand the words or singing in a *Noh* drama. There were about one thousand popular sequences of *Noh* in the late eighteenth and early nineteenth centuries, performed by seven or eight families of players, each of which has its own repertory. The stories of the plays were taken from classics and from folklore. *Noh*, they thought, was pre-thirteenth century; the main textbook was written in the fourteenth century.

Originally wandering players performed *Noh* – outsiders to polite society. It was then taken up by the rich samurai and merchants. It was often played in front of a temple or shrine, a place where people gathered, and was frequently sponsored by ecclesiastical authorities to attract people to the shrines. Dancing in front of the temple was included in the *Noh* repertory.

When a powerful noble or *daimyo* invited another *daimyo*, he would arrange a *Noh* play for the guest. The dancing sequences in *Noh* were then much more coquettish and flirtatious but they were later simplified and made more spiritual. Yet while the stories are often prosaic, there is something mystical or magical about a performance. For the samurai, we were told, it was a spiritual experience to watch a *Noh* play.

Noh may not be explicitly religious, but a number of the main protagonists are Shinto deities (*kami*) and the stories are often based on Shinto mythology. On the other hand, the supporting protagonists are usually Buddhist priests. Singer discerned far-flung origins: 'The dances of North-east Siberian shamans ... seem to survive exquisitely sublimated in the *Noh*-play dances of Japan.' While Carmen Blacker perceived similar spiritual purposes, 'Many of these plays I believe ... are in themselves concealed shamanic rituals'. For the Japanese *Noh* is the sublime expression of a great art, comparable to the stained glass of Chartres, or an exquisite Mozart or Handel aria.

We have twice enjoyed public hot baths in Japan. It was clear that our friends felt there was something special about this experience, something beyond the mere sensual pleasure of hot water. Unlike westerners, Japanese wash themselves before getting into the very hot water where they then lie and soak.

'We think it very famous,' explained our friends, 'We are bath-sensitive people. We were very disappointed with the English bath. Not a bath at all. A bath is one of the most wonderful things in Japan. The most comfortable thing in the world. Once a year, usually in May, people tend to go to hot springs, but they are not relaxing if one has lots of things to do. One needs to prepare oneself and forget everything, forget all human relations. People should behave modestly, talk about the landscape. They are completely naked.'

We were told that it is important to place the bath, if possible, near to nature, in other words outside, near a forest or glade, or (as in a hotel we stayed in which had a bath filled with scented apples) with a window looking out on snowy mountains. This brings together the natural and artificial. This is very important. 'One is borrowing from nature. It's very artistic for us to create artificial nature within a human space'.

So important are these things that Trades Union Congresses are held at hot spring resorts. Kenichi explained, 'No notice is taken of a foreigner in the bath; it is a place where one can be in a public place with strangers. One trusts them. One makes friends in the bath as it is a place to communicate frankly. *Hadaka no tsukiai* – "companions in nudity" or friends who bathe together – are the closest friends of all.'

I speculated at the time that in a curious way a bath seemed to me to be like an English pub, where strangers come in and can become, for a while, close friends. In rural mountain villages there are public baths and hot springs where strangers can come and bathe. 'Even a monkey or bird can share', we were told.

The most elaborate of all the Japanese leisure occupations is the tea ceremony. The British have a tea ceremony of sorts, the tea party being a central institution in their recent civilisation. At its most ornate, the formalised behaviour of host and guests and the array of tea utensils look rather special. As a result, I thought when I heard about the Japanese tea ceremony that I could bracket it with other formal meals and drinks I have experienced in India, China and elsewhere.

Yet as we read the classic accounts of tea ceremonies, experienced them in Japan, and later constructed a version of a tea house in our English garden, we began to feel that there was something else involved. The ceremony is held in a small tea house on a *tatami* matting floor. You crawl in through a low entrance, after having walked along the 'dewy path'. You take off your watch. It feels like the almost universal stage of separation from the mundane world and entry into a sacred space which is found in rituals of many kinds.

There is a *tokonoma* in the background, a sort of shrine that has a calligraphic scroll hanging in it, a flower or other precious object, a reminder of otherness. But there are no gods or spirits present anywhere in the ceremony. It is purely of this world, yet feels at the same time sacred, halfway between the mundane drinking of tea and taking Holy Communion. It might be described as human religion.

The tea ceremony is an anti-ritualistic ceremony, a curious contradiction. There is a ceremony, but no communion with God or gods, etiquette but no morality. To a certain extent, it acts as a functional equivalent to religion, but without the theological system.

The tea house is the outside world (as opposed to the inside), but it is nevertheless safe and neutral, and allows the kind of deep intimacy of communication which normally could only occur in the home. It is thus a place where all class and caste barriers are temporarily suspended. It is a neutral space, an arena where you communicate by the language of movement and gesture.

The essence of the tea ceremony is the saying of the tea master Rikyu, *ichi-go ichi-e*, 'One time in your life you can meet a stranger, and thus you put all your truthfulness into it'. The tea ceremony is simple but spiritual. You can inject everything or nothing into it. The tea, with its mystical and medical properties, is the centre of veneration, where time stops and space is absent. The nearest I can approach it from a Western perspective is encapsulated in the lines of Andrew Marvell on the magic of a garden, where all of time and space is annihilated to 'a green thought in a green shade'.

All of this just scratches the surface. The unfamiliar world of imported and adapted activities like *pachinko* or pin-ball parlours, the extraordinary craze for sing-along clubs (*karaoke*), which is believed to have originated in a snack bar in Kobe in the 1970s, and many other pastimes, each reveal further in-between categories.

Baseball is now the most popular game in Japan. It looks like a straight import. Not being a baseball fan I do not know exactly what the differences are, but the fact that some mutation has happened is suggested by a conversation with our friends. They talked about the importance of baseball and mentioned that the high school baseball tournament is enormously significant, with over four thousand schools participating. Yet the hero of each match is the pitcher of the *losing* team. You should not win. There is great sympathy with the losers, who arouse feelings of loss and beauty. It is not like this in the professional league, I am told. Yet I cannot imagine that even at the high school level this is the same in America.

I am told that field dimensions, ball size, slight changes in rules, playing style, strategy, team management and general ethos are very different from their American counterparts. The victory of the Japanese team in the world championship in 2006 was explained in the newspapers as the victory of more integrated team playing by the Japanese, which defeated their more individualistic, if physically larger, opponents.

The relaxed attitude to nudity in public mixed bathing caused some severe criticism by foreigners when they began to visit Japan. Japanese women breast-fed openly in the streets and fields and often until their child was four or five years old. The skimpy clothing of both men and women, which often revealed all of the body, especially when people were working or in a high wind, is well documented. 'In Japan', commented Lowell, 'the exposure of the female form is without a parallel in latitude. Never nude, it is frequently naked.'

In the middle of the nineteenth century a member of the Elgin mission noted, 'The women seldom wear anything above their waists; the men only a scanty loin-cloth.' And Griffis wrote, 'Even the young girls and maidens just rounding into perfection of form often sit half nude; thinking it no desecration to expose the body from waist up' – while Alice Bacon in the early twentieth century spoke of 'the open bath-houses, the naked labourers, the exposure of the lower limbs in wet weather by the turning up of the kimono, the entirely nude condition of the country children in summer, and the very slight clothing that even adults regard as necessary about the house or in the country during the hot season'.

As Lowell explained, the Japanese did not see the uncovered body as innately sexual. 'In their eyes a state of nature is not a state of indecency. Whatever exposure is required for convenience is right; whatever unnecessary, wrong.' This was an 'Eden-like condition of society' where their unwritten code of propriety on the subject seems to be, 'You must see, but you may not observe ... it is a fatal mistake to suppose the Japanese an immodest people. According to their own standards, they are exceedingly modest. No respectable Japanese woman would, for instance, ever for a moment turn out her toes in walking. It is considered immodest to do so.'

While westerners were shocked, the Japanese were in turn shocked by the way in which westerners used their bodies as sexually provoking objects. Bacon noted: 'A careful study of the Japanese ideas of decency ... has led me to the following conclusion. According to the Japanese standard, any exposure of the person that is merely incidental to health, cleanliness, or convenience in doing necessary work, is perfectly modest and allowable; but an exposure, no matter how slight, that is simply for show, is in the highest degree indelicate.'

Edward Morse made a similar observation: 'The sight of our people in low-necked dresses dancing together in the waltz, a dance they do not have; kissing in public places, even a man greeting his wife with a kiss in public, and many other acts cause the Japanese to regard us as barbarians.' Kissing in public is still shocking for many

Japanese, as it was in the 1930s when Rodin's sculpture 'The Kiss' was exhibited in Tokyo with a sack over its head, and the moment of kissing was cut out of imported films.

There was nothing particularly private or shocking about the bodily functions of excreting. I remember being embarrassed when going into a Japanese men's toilet with very open and communal urinals to find a Japanese lady cleaning round me. Then I read that for centuries some people living on the main highways had placed urinals in the front of their houses so that people, both men and women, could urinate into them and provide valuable fertiliser for the fields.

What is striking, when one is travelling through a big Japanese city, looking at the advertisements in the shops, the trains or on the many television channels, is the absence of sex. Advertising still hardly uses the power of sexual desire to sell things. A moment's comparison of British or American advertisements with their equivalents in Japan shows a vast difference. When women are shown in Japanese adverts, they are usually demure and innocent.

Certainly, until very recently, most Japanese women dressed simply and with no attempt to accentuate the breasts or legs. There is innocence in clothing, make-up, advertising and much of life. This fits with the innocence noted in many tribal societies, where men and women, to the delight or horror of their observers, did not seem to have learnt the message of man's downfall in the garden of Eden. 'In short, the erotic aspect of nudity is something new in Japan,' comments Maraini, 'one of the many gifts to it of the West.' Or, as the editor of the *Japan Mail* in the early part of the twentieth century put it, 'The nude is seen in Japan, but is not looked at'.

On the other hand, there is a prosaic and, to many westerners, quite shocking matter-of-fact attitude towards the exposure of the human body and the extremes of sexuality in the pornographic industry. Historically there has always been a very tolerant attitude to prostitution and the use of *geishas* to provide entertainment is widespread.

Early visitors were amazed at the open prostitution of boys. In the eighteenth century, Engelbert Kaempfer described streets where there were:

> nine or ten neat houses, or booths, before each of which sat one, two, or three young boys, of ten to twelve years of age, well dress'd, with their faces painted, and feminine gestures, kept by their lew'd and cruel masters for the secret pleasure and entertainment of rich travel-lers, the Japanese being very much addicted to this vice.

In the early nineteenth century, Pompe van Meerdevort observed that, 'The Japanese does not regard a free sex life as bad, much less as sin; the word "vice" is therefore not the right term for it. Neither the religion nor the society prohibits intercourse with women outside of marriage, and this is the cause for all the remarkable acts which arouse our amazement.'

A few years later Sir Rutherford Alcock noted that not only did parents sell their children into prostitution but also after a number of years in the trade, these children returned home to marry. Van Meer-devort commented, 'The prostitutes are as keen on going to church [temples] as anyone else, and the law guarantees this as a special right. The Japanese society does not look with contempt on these public brothels, precisely because they are *public*.' When the Europeans arrived, the Japanese were ready for them. 'Before they opened any port to foreign trade', Griffis wrote, 'the Japanese built two places for the foreigners – a custom-house and a brothel'.

The long tradition of erotic art, illustrated by the explicit 'pillow books' (of Chinese origin), has now evolved into a film and video industry where images of extremely violent sexuality are widespread and a world away from the innocence suggested by the clothing and advertising.

When I first went into a local corner shop to buy some food I noticed rows of pornographic magazines and videos available on the bottom shelves. Young people were leafing through the most explicitly sexual materials. Similarly, in most Japanese hotels there is a huge variety of pornographic pay channels on offer, and the Japanese equivalents of the *News of the World* or the *Sun* frequently carry cartoons which show men and women copulating.

When I expressed my shock and puzzlement to my friends, they explained that for the Japanese sex is a neutral subject. If you want sex, that is natural. It is quite normal to have sex with the opposite sex, or the same sex. Pornography, extensive since the eighth century, is thought of as an art like any other – cooking, calligraphy or sword fighting. Sexual behaviour is learnt, just as the playing of musical instruments is learnt, or the proper way to perform the tea ceremony. Sex has long been a very important part of human life. As specialists in this area, the sex workers of the middle ages were able to form a guild, though their status gradually declined and by the nineteenth century they were corralled into particular districts on the edges of cities such as the *yoshiwara* in Tokyo. We can see that there is an ancient technique of showing the body to men, and very detailed sex techniques at a really professional level.

In Japan, women consider their bodies to be their own, to do with as they like, so being a sex worker is not considered shameful and certainly not sinful. There is no moral opprobrium associated with it.

When Isabella Bird visited the great Shinto shrine at Ise, she noted that the brothel house and shrine were side by side. Sex and religion were not seen as contradictory. The Western ambivalence towards the body, considered on the one hand a symbol of Divinity, a copy of the Divine body, and on the other hand as full of sin and temptation, is utterly incomprehensible to most Japanese. For them it is ridiculous to think of the body as subject to ideas of good or bad in the religious sense, just as morality is irrelevant to the activities of eating or defecating, although both are subject to codes of decency and manners.

The segregated sex area or *yoshiwara* in Tokyo continued to exist through the Meiji period right up to the end of the Second World War. During the American occupation, the Japanese authorities set up a similar environment for the troops and persuaded not only prostitutes but ordinary women to work there.

We discussed with our friends the highly contentious use of 'comfort women' during the Second World War, women who supplied sex to the army, an issue which has caused much bitterness in Korea, China and elsewhere. This practice was clearly modelled on the sex industry in Japan and reflected attitudes about the body and sex totally at odds with those of the countries where it was exported. At first the comfort women were paid for their work, but this gradually ceased in many places as war spread throughout East Asia. The Japanese comfort women, taken to China, were not only prostitutes but ordinary women who had been encouraged to go to provide support for the troops. They were usually located in the cities. However, in the countryside, where the Japanese occupiers tried to replicate the system, native women were forced into sexual slavery. Some of them are now seeking compensation from the Japanese government, an action no Japanese 'comfort woman' has taken to date.

As for the violent, sado-masochistic sexual acts depicted in so many films and comics, our friends were as puzzled by them as we were. There are two kinds of pornography, we were told: the kind issued by established mainstream publishers, with art photographs; and the kind produced by many small underground publishers selling their materials on stands and in convenience stores. Pornographic films started being made in the 1960s at the time when television was introduced, plunging the film industry as a whole into crisis, and at first they were not violent. They were made in

increasing numbers in the 1970s, and several of them won international prizes.

Japan appears to be the most desexualised of large civilisations. Under
Western pressures clothing and public bathing were 'reformed' to
meet 'international standards' in the later nineteenth century. I still
have a feeling of being in an innocent society where the body is hardly
noticed. It is neither shunned, emphasised, nor regarded with fear,
loathing, or even delight. The body is just a body; it eats, defecates,
has sex, and dies. What more is there to say?

On the other hand, the Japanese erotic tradition is along with its
Indian counterpart one of the most explicit and graphic on earth.
Just as it startles us by its innocence, Japan also shocks by its explicit-
ness and freedom to enjoy the sexualised body. Sex seems to be treated
calmly as a pleasure to be enjoyed and dissected in exactly the same
way as food, drink, art and company.

Sexual relations have no spiritual dimension; there is no danger
(except possibly to health) associated with them. Sex is sex, not a
symbol of our union with God or each other, as it is in the Christian
tradition. Indeed there are considered to be two kinds of sex: sex
for pleasure and sex for reproduction. Sex as communication is less
common. Such a matter-of-fact attitude makes paying for sex a pretty
mundane event; it is not uncommon for a Japanese wife to settle the
bills for her husband's visits to sex parlours as she makes the monthly
household payments. However, such an unusually prosaic and utilitarian attitude to sex has had widespread repercussions outside Japan,
during the Second World War, and aroused much bitterness about
the treatment of non-Japanese 'comfort women'. When it comes to
sex, I know of no other large civilisation so poised, from a Western
perspective, between innocence and depravity. Conversely, many
Japanese have long found Western attitudes to sex deeply hypocritical,
guilt-ridden, lascivious and puzzlingly mystical.

❀

What we choose to eat and how we eat are reflections of deeply held cultural values. From a Western perspective, the Japanese diet differs most strikingly from our own in two ways. The first is that the strong distinction between culture and nature, or the cooked and the raw, is not observed. If we make a distinction between societies which tend towards leaving foods as raw as possible, and others that cook very fully, the Japanese are the most extreme example of a modern civilisation which tends towards rawness. The still-living fish off which bits are sliced and eaten are just one element of the whole wide range of raw dishes for which Japan is famous. Apart from a number of tribal societies where raw grubs or meat are consumed, I know of no parallel.

Nearly all world civilisations have devoted enormous energies to transmuting the raw into the cooked. Compared to the notoriously over-boiled and baked traditional foods of the English, or the pan-frying of the Chinese, Japanese food is cooked minimally. Perhaps the shortage of fuel, which we see reflected in the tiny traditional stoves heated by charcoal and straw, has something to do with it. The minimalism the Japanese apply to every part of life is also active here. Apart from soy sauce and a little salt, not much is added in the way of herbs or spices.

A second feature is that the strong aesthetic sensibility the Japanese express in all aspects of life is extended to food, and the presentation of a meal is almost more important than the meal itself. 'It has been said of Japanese food that it is a cuisine to be looked at rather than eaten,' commented Junichiro Tanizaki. 'I would go further and say that it is to be meditated upon, a kind of silent music evoked by the combination of lacquerware and the light of a candle flickering in the dark.'

The Japanese delight in the way in which food is delicately arranged. A good meal is a miniature painting. But turn off the light, we were told by our friends, and there is hardly any flavour. On the other hand, Indian or Sechuan curries may not look very elegant, but they taste even better with their rich spices when eaten in the dark.

By the seventeenth century, the Japanese had the most urbanised society in the world. The court was based in the great city of Kyoto; the merchants in the equally vast city of Osaka; the rulers were building up their power in what was shortly to become the largest city on earth, Edo, or as it was later called, Tokyo. However, there were many other large cities in existence outside of these three famous places, and the Japanese then, and to a far greater extent now, seem to be city people. A train ride through central Japan, or visits to the extreme tips, Nagasaki or Sapporo, reveal few remote villages or even small towns. People tend to crowd into the cities, and show little interest in exploring the neighbouring countryside, which is often thought to be inhabited by rather backward agriculturalists.

Yet if we look at the content of Japanese paintings over the centuries, or study the literature, a strong rural bias emerges celebrating a romanticised countryside. Similarly the love of the townspeople for spring blossom, or the popularity of pilgrimages to rural shrines at Nikko, Ise or to Mount Fuji, tell us a different story.

Living in Tokyo we were struck by the many small gardens and parks dotted between the tightly packed houses, and the many walks along clean canals filled with golden carp. Even in the massive and densely populated modern cities, one has the feeling of living in a cluster of villages, each with its own identity and air of rurality. It is clear that nature is relished.

In the nineteenth century, Morse was struck by this desire to bring nature into the cities:

> In the city houses of the better class much care is often taken to make
> the surroundings appear as rural as possible, by putting here and there
> quaint old wells, primitive and rustic arbours, fences, and gateways

... In the crowded city, among the poorest houses, one often sees, in the corner of a little earth-area that comes between the sill and raised floor, a miniature garden made in some shallow box, or even on the ground itself.

This paradox could be explained by the influence of the quasi-religious traditions in Japan. The nature worship of the animistic Shinto beliefs, the anti-consumerism and rural flavour of ascetic Buddhism, even the austere rural values of neo-Confucianism have worked to inject something different from the usual urban values.

For many centuries, middle-sized towns, surrounded by satellite villages, were very important in Japan. While the northern, southern and western domains might be at a great distance from Kyoto or Edo, they were sophisticated places. The Japanese practice of an alternating residence during the seventeenth to mid-nineteenth centuries, whereby the powerful lords had to spend half of their life at court in the city, but then went back for the other half to their remote domains, had an enormous effect. With the constant processing of their huge entourages back and forth along the main highways every couple of years, they linked all of Japan and they were never for long away from the latest gossip and developments at the centre.

If I stand back and reflect on the relation between humans and the world around them, I can see certain patterns. I can understand the creation of an artificial nature, a symbolic raft on which each Japanese can bob through the tempestuous ecology, politics and emotional turmoil of their environment. The decorations of each individual's personal space are important as a self-contained protection against chaos. Yet they simultaneously help each Japanese to open the shutters, the delicate paper *shoji*, with little effort, and then to move out through symbols into 'other lands and other seas', a world of enchantment and eternity.

The Japanese are able to do this by living in an almost entirely symbolic environment, in which each element of nature and culture, when carefully re-shaped, stands for something else much grander, an emotion, a thought, a whole philosophy. This symbolism is at its most extreme in the Zen gardens. Where an object is placed, its exact colour, its texture, everything is significant. Zen masters consider the garden to be a mixture of poetry, philosophy, landscaping and symbolic art. Almost everything around the Japanese is highly artificial, crafted, yet the final effect is to make it seem natural and unforced. As in true art, there seems to be no other way things could be. All possibilities are encompassed, even if only one is chosen.

Thus in contrast with many societies, the Japanese have bridged the perceived gap between nature and culture and nullified it. Everything is both natural and cultural. The moon, the falling water, the rocks and sand, are fully natural. Yet they are framed into a composition which is highly manufactured. It is artificial nature. Likewise the buildings, the tea houses and temples and many ordinary houses are cultural artefacts. Yet their roughness, unevenness and shadows, make them simultaneously natural objects.

We find this also in the calligraphy, which is highly artificial, elaborately inscribed and carrying human meanings, yet in its spontaneity and beauty a work of natural freedom. All these meanings of the constructed Japanese environment glimmer on the edge of my comprehension. I absorb the experience, but cannot put them into words.

This refusal to make a distinction between nature and culture fits with the argument that the Japanese have never separated out their worlds. Religion does not exist separately, as another dimension. The world is both constructed and outside human control, filled with some kind of spirit or essence beyond human knowledge. All things – wood, stone, flowers, water – are expressions and signs of other powers. They constitute a magical landscape of the kind which I had only previously encountered in fairy stories and the poetry of

Wordsworth, Keats and Yeats. This is the last great fairy-land on earth, but it did not take Disney to create it.

The first cultural shocks within the magic mirror that is Japan, however impressionistic and preliminary, give us some hints of what to look out for in the further parts of the journey. The mirror itself reflects many things: ancient features of Japan, the huge Chinese influence, especially through Confucianism and Buddhism, the Korean inspiration, as well as the influence of Western nations, especially since the opening up of Japan from the 1870s. There is no 'Japan', but many reflections of reflections, and the way Japanese art affected Western artistic sensibilities, and simultaneously boomeranged back into Japan is one complex part of this.

The mirror constantly changes as the Japanese re-invent themselves. Sometimes the civilisation and the art which expresses it seem very 'Chinese', then 'Japanese', then 'Western'. It is a moving surface which, chameleon-like, reflects the powerful faces that gaze into it. Yet it is unlike an ordinary mirror in that it has memory. Earlier traces are not lost. It is extraordinarily retentive, as is demonstrated by its ability to keep side by side the most ancient forms of drama such as *Noh* and relatively modern forms such as *kabuki*, or ancient pottery from the Jomon period in its celebrated tea bowls alongside the most exquisite later porcelain. It is a cumulative mirror: each new image which enters it finds itself amidst many thousand earlier symbols.

The artistic patterns suggest a set of unreconciled and contradictory forms. Japanese art is not one thing but many. There is both the brash, direct, grotesque, brightly coloured, and the oblique, indirect, subdued. They are all aspects of one aesthetic. The art is both flat and full of perspective, both practical and art for art's sake. All are forms of Japanese art.

Indeed, it is in the relations between art forms and between man and man, man and nature and different forms of nature, that much of the pleasure resides. The interaction between sand and stone, between the wooden temple and the mountains and forest behind, between foreground and background, is a very important part of Japanese aesthetics. Everything is related and brought together through the choice of colour, space and form so that the divisions and separations which cause such unrest to the mind are resolved and harmony prevails.

The great classical art of China with its divisions of space and design, its symmetry, its baroque and centralised tendency was absorbed and then stripped of much of its essence and its separations. In the same way, although the Japanese temporarily institutionalised their art and allowed it to fit into Western categories – art or craft, high or low, traditional or modern art – all these now are mingled again and anyone visiting Japan will find strange juxtapositions which show the coalescence of temporarily contradictory and opposed categories. We shall see this effect of the transforming mirror in much of what we examine in Japan.

If we begin to go deeper, to explore what lies beneath the cultural surface, move beyond the first phase of surprise and only partial comprehension, we need to look within the economic, social, political, ideological and religious worlds which the Japanese have created over the last two thousand years.

3

Wealth

Japan is a very rocky island, with thin soils and steep slopes. Most of its landmass cannot be used effectively for agriculture because it is too high, cold or steep. Among ridge after ridge of mountains there are only a few flat plains or broad river valleys. The soil tends to be poor, deposited black volcanic ash with little nutrient value. Even grass suitable for animals does not grow in much of Japan.

The huge Japanese population, fluctuating through the fifteenth and nineteenth centuries at between ten and twenty million persons, something like four times that of Britain during the same period, tried to live off a cultivatable area about the size, but with less of the productivity, of an English county. A current population of over 120 million people, nearly half that of the United States, lives in an area which is similar to a small American state.

The immensely labour-intensive and skilled agriculture, until recently very dependent on the use of human excrement as fertiliser, makes sense in this context. In the same way, the virtual elimination of domesticated animals by the nineteenth century is quite logical. Animals such as sheep or cattle would have competed for the tiny areas of potential crop land.

Some recompense for this extreme scarcity of reasonable soil comes from the sea. Japan is above all a water empire. A sharply indented coastline means that the sea is seldom far away. The Japanese have always harvested the sea and their many lakes and rivers. Their food-obsession with fish, whales and other sea products reflects a long history where much of their protein came from the water.

In the past, the presence of the sea also lessened communication problems. Across the land, travel, and particularly the carrying of heavy goods, was very difficult. Paths had to pass over steep rocky mountains and even packhorses found it challenging. However, most parts of Japan could be reached by water. Heavy monsoon rainfall only adds to the impression of a misty, water-logged civilisation, so beautifully captured in Japanese paintings and literature.

The length of Japan and the Ryukyu archipelago as a whole – whose southern tip is almost on the equator and northern tip almost adjacent to Siberia – is also important. Imagine a very thin civilisation stretching from Morocco to Finland, or from Mexico to Newfoundland, and you will have a sense of the changing ecologies involved in Japan.

There are micro-ecologies, with the eastern and western, the northern and southern parts of Japan, each very different in its flora and fauna. These helped to encourage local trade, for instance, between areas that provided tropical fruits in the south, and those producing furs and salmon, in the north. They also helped to buffer the civilisation from the terrible forces of an unusually savage physical world.

Nature has inflicted much of its most destabilising power on the Japanese. It is no coincidence that the word we use for a tidal wave caused by an earthquake is Japanese, *tsunami*. The minor earthquakes which occur every few days in Japan, from time to time with huge and disastrous effects, give life a transitory instability which those living in much of the rest of the world have never known.

Anyone who visits Japan for any length of time will experience sizeable earthquakes and will know that they are not only physically but psychologically destabilising. Watching the ground sink and swim from the tenth floor of a building in Tokyo, I felt that Japan seemed like a civilisation camped on a living creature. Much of Japanese spirituality, philosophy and art are linked to this awareness.

Then there are the volcanoes, always active and periodically pouring their lava down into the surrounding valleys. In the past, active volcanoes periodically caused localised famines, and again they remind the Japanese, particularly in the hot springs and thermal baths, of the seething, unstable and thin mantle on which human civilisation temporarily crouches.

Like the earthquakes, the volcanoes have shaped not only the psychology but also the built world of the Japanese. The traditional insubstantial houses in which most Japanese lived until recently were really the only response possible in this volatile environment. Glass windows or heavy buildings would have been useless. Thin bamboos, strong mulberry paper and wood were supple and flexible and could bend with the forces of nature.

Finally there are the monsoons, when lashing winds and rains hit the high mountains and pour huge volumes of water down the steep slopes, ripping up the thin soil in devastating landslides. The control of too much water, both along the dangerous sea fronts and coming down the mountains, has been a central concern of the Japanese. I have often wondered why they have left most of their mountains covered in forests. With so little land, why did they not build terraces, as do the Nepalese or southern Chinese, and inhabit the high mountains in the kind of mountain villages we find in those other rice-growing areas?

Part of the answer may well be the realisation that to strip the hillsides of forest cover, which holds the thin soil on to the rock, would risk triggering disastrous flooding and erosion. Better by far, if one has the money, as the Japanese now have, to preserve one's own forest and import the timber from elsewhere. Certainly a monsoon world brings constraints which people from the non-monsoon West can easily overlook.

❊

Rice is central to understanding Japan, and historically one could almost say that Japan is rice, and rice is Japan. Eliza Scidmore noted, 'Twenty-five synonyms for rice are given in Hepburn's smaller dictionary, all as different as possible. Rice in every stage of growing, and in every condition after harvesting, has a distinct name, with no root common to all.' When we first went to Japan in 1990 much of the conversation was about the forced dumping of, as the Japanese saw it, less tasty American rice on their country.

The sacred drink of Japan, *sake,* is made from rice, and some of the central rituals in Shinto revolve around it; the courtyards of shrines often have frames piled high with empty *sake* barrels. Every year the Emperor prepares a diminutive rice field for cultivation in his imperial gardens in Tokyo. As one Japanese informant commented, 'Rice follows us everywhere as a nation ... and as individuals. When we get married, it is the nine sips of *sake* that sanctify the union of man and woman. And rice is offered to the dead, and to Buddha, and to *kami,* the Shinto gods.'

At first glance we might be tempted just to bracket Japan with other south Asian rice areas. Yet things are not that simple, for Japanese rice agriculture has for long had distinctive characteristics which make it different even from that of its neighbours.

A feature of most wet rice cultivating societies is that rice is grown alongside domesticated animals. In much of south-east Asia pigs, chickens, ducks and buffaloes (and sometimes cows and oxen) coexist with the rice. These animals give traction for the ploughing of the rice fields and manure for the vegetable plots, as well as meat and in some cases milk.

What is most striking about Japan in the last five hundred years is how far it has departed from this almost universal pattern. Up to the seventeenth century, there were some domesticated animals, particularly horses and cattle. But there was no heavy emphasis on the pig-duck-chicken-buffalo pattern of places like Vietnam. And from the seventeenth century onwards even the existing animals had almost disappeared. By the time that the traveller Isabella Bird visited Japanese villages in the second half of the nineteenth century she noticed that there were hardly any animals. All that visitors saw was rice, with some subsidiary crops in the fields, hedges and forests. Hence there was no meat, manure, milk or eggs. The Japanese were lactose intolerant, that is to say they were sick if they ate dairy products such as milk, butter or cheese, well into the twentieth century. There were hardly any animals to help with ploughing or carrying.

Roughly between 1600 and 1850, as labour and land-intensive rice agriculture increased, the Japanese systematically eliminated two of the fundamental technologies which had revolutionised agriculture about 10,000 years ago, ushering in the first peasant civilisation: the use of the wheel and of domesticated animals. They knew of the Chinese wheelbarrow, but saw no point in importing or improving on it. They also knew of carts and of grinding wheels. Yet they scarcely used them. Nearly everything was carried on the human back.

Although many of the new crafts such as spinning, weaving, pottery and metal work were developed to perfection, in terms of agriculture, by the time the West struck against them with great force in the second half of the nineteenth century, the Japanese were feeding a huge population from a tiny cultivated area largely on the basis of rice and foraging from the sea.

The Japanese have traditionally worked very hard in gruelling conditions to sustain a reasonable standard of living. Comparative studies on hours worked suggest that while peasants in Spain, Italy or India worked extremely long hours, those in Japan characteristically often worked even harder.

This background of disciplined and almost non-stop hard work stood the Japanese in good stead when they industrialised. It partly explains how in one generation they moved from a very low-technology society to surpass the far more populous and previously advanced civilisations of China and Russia both industrially and militarily. The tradition of unremitting labour also helps to explain how, out of the ashes of Hiroshima, Nagasaki and Tokyo, they were able to create one of the foremost economic powers in the world within a generation.

Those who wish to understand the Japanese need to be aware of this long experience of minimalism, hard work and tough endurance. Only then will they begin to see the Japan which still lies just beneath the surface. Japan, if anywhere, has been a hard nurse of men, and even more so of women, who worked as hard in the fields, but also bore and raised the children, and kept the homes.

The Japanese were intensely curious about the technologies of other cultures and very skilled in adapting those they felt were useful. Charles Peter Thunberg, in the eighteenth century, commented:

> This nation ... carry their Curiosity to a great length. They examine narrowly every thing that is carried thither by the Europeans, and every thing that belongs to them. They are continually asking for information upon every subject, and frequently tire the Dutch out with their questions ... During the audience we had of the emperor, the privy counsellors and others of the highest officers of state, we were surveyed from head to foot, and also our hats, swords, clothes, buttons, laces, watches, canes, rings etc.; nay, we were even obliged to write in their presence, in order to show them our manner of writing and our characters.

The Japanese were also remarkable for their ingenuity. 'Perhaps in nothing are the Japanese to be more admired', wrote Basil Hall Chamberlain, 'than for the wonderful genius they display in arriving at the greatest possible results with the simplest means, and the smallest possible expenditure of time and labour or material.' Almost immediately after their country came into forced contact with Western powers in the middle of the nineteenth century, Alcock noted, 'In the expositions held in Europe, America, Australia, and India, the artistic ability, manual dexterity, and inventive genius of the Japanese have won abundant recognition.'

This playful inventiveness was particularly apparent in Japanese toys. Griffis marvelled at these:

> We do not know of any country in the world in which there are so many toy-shops, or so many fairs for the sale of the things which delight children. Not only are the streets of every city abundantly supplied with shops, filled as full as a Christmas stocking with gaudy toys, but in small towns and villages one or more children's bazaars may be found.

The toys, Hearn wrote, showed 'that astounding ingenuity by which Japanese inventors are able to reach, at a cost too small to name, precisely the same results as those exhibited in our expensive mechanical toys'. A member of the Elgin mission gives a lovely account of what was to be found:

> We examined the toy-shops on our way back, and bought wonderful jacks-in-the-box; representations of animals, beautifully executed in straw; models of ... Japanese houses, as neatly finished as Swiss models; figures, some of them more humorous than decent, carved in wood; little porcelain figures, whose heads wagged and tongues shot out unexpectedly; tortoises, whose head, legs, and tail were in perpetual motion; ludicrous picture books, grotesque masks and sham head-dresses of both sexes. Enough absurd contrivances were here exhibited to create a revolution in the nurseries of England.

A century later, that inventiveness was indeed to do so, not only in the nurseries and schools, but also in many aspects of Western civilisation. For instance, my granddaughter Rosa has introduced me to the mysteries of the computerised pet, a *tamagotchi*. She is scathing about the inferior look-alike competition made outside Japan.

On the other hand, what has always struck me on my visits to Japan is how uninterested a lot of Japanese are in most technologies. They make state-of-the-art computers and cameras, and have some dazzling cheap stores where these can be bought. Yet computers, for instance, were generally absent from schools and universities in the first part of the 1990s; and when we tried to persuade our friends to get a computer or register for email, we found them considerably resistant to the idea.

This lack of interest has long been a feature of Japanese life. The Japanese largely gave up many foreign technologies. We have seen that animal rearing for agricultural purposes was abandoned, but so was glass, for instance, and, for a time, so were gunpowder weapons. As late as the 1920s, there was a marked reluctance to import new mechanical devices for military purposes. In the case of gunpowder weapons, these were barely used from the seventeenth century until the Japanese were under threat in the middle of the nineteenth century.

It appears that although the Japanese can and do manufacture entrancing gadgets, they do so rather absent-mindedly. In contrast with many in Western, Chinese or Indian societies, they do not seem to have a passion for machines. Rather, the making of machines is considered simply as a way to earn money, and to create novelty in the amazing toys they design, and in their art.

This may be changing among the young, however, as many are retreating from the stress of intense human relations in real life into a controllable cyberspace alternative. Yet I get the impression that even they are not interested in the technology as such, but rather in what they can do with it to move into virtual worlds.

We might partly explain this contradiction by looking at the way in which technologies have evolved in Japan. There have been waves of imports, first from China and Korea, and later from the West. When a benefit was perceived, they were adapted with great skill. The gunpowder weapons of the Portuguese in the sixteenth century or the consumer electronics and car manufacturing techniques of the Americans in the second half of the twentieth century were thoroughly studied, and the Japanese began to make better guns than the Portuguese and better cars than the Americans. Yet there have been few home-grown, world-changing inventions until the crop of electronic products which have flooded the world in the last quarter of the twentieth century.

In many cases, technologies that were successful in Japan reached perfection several centuries ago. For instance, the sword of the thirteenth century was never really improved on, and likewise body armour a little later. The exquisite minimalist furniture and housing Japan is famous for was perfected around the same time, as were its pottery and lacquer work. This first wave was almost entirely based on macro inventions imported from China and Korea.

Beauty, stability, reciprocity, elegance, and mutual respect: for the Japanese, all of these are the goals of life, not the making and consuming of gadgets. Just as Napoleon dismissed the British as a nation of shopkeepers, I suspect that some Japanese would regard the Western obsession with technology as rather vulgar. The Japanese heart and soul are elsewhere.

It could well be argued that the Japanese economy, despite its veneer of modern efficiency and high technical ability, is still an embedded system. In their company and factory ethos, the Japanese encourage lifetime security of employment and mutual trust, even at the expense of short-term economic gains. The *zaibatsu* system whereby a company sticks to the same subcontractors, even if they cannot for the moment match the prices of competitors, is another example. Again and again, people put family-like loyalties above short-term economic returns. As Arthur Koestler wrote, 'the Japanese managed to create a competitive society *sans* competition, and they have stuck to this principle ever since'.

It is indeed a unique feature of Japanese employment that long-term contracts and internal promotion can be traced back several hundred years. However, competition does exist within the huge conglomerates, where there is a highly mobile labour market. Nowadays, many people do not stay in one firm for life – it is only from the 1960s to the 1980s, a period of full employment, that being employed by a large firm became tantamount to lifetime employment.

For a time in the 1990s, it looked as if the Japanese system was collapsing in the face of the competitive Western model and shortages of jobs. But recently, it has begun to emerge from the crisis and many of the largest companies have returned to the assured system, particularly since the economy has started to grow again and the oversupply of labour from the 'baby-boom' years after the war is gradually disappearing.

It is often pointed out that large companies account for less than half of the employment in Japan; small family firms are the predominant form. Yet even here there is a disguised form of more secure employment. In small businesses there is often no room for longer-term employees to rise to the top, since a chosen son will succeed, yet those workers who have a long record of loyalty may well be offered stock, contacts and other support to set up their own businesses. The new ventures thus retain a strong connection with the former employer.

Companies often collude rather than compete with each other, and the stock market does not behave in the way in which it operates in London or New York. The Japanese complain about the Chinese and the Westerners as money-grabbing individualists who seem to be obsessed with profit. In Japanese business there is a huge amount of corporate power, and bureaucracies run the economy on semi-socialist and quite centralised principles.

This curious ambivalence towards money and competition is illustrated in the life of Yukichi Fukuzawa, the great moderniser of Japan in the later nineteenth century. As a young man, when he moved to Osaka, Fukuzawa admitted that he was still wary of money. Later he tried to introduce the concept of Western market capitalism to Japan, using a book on Western economics.

> I began translating it ... when I came upon the word 'competition' for which there was no equivalent in Japanese, and I was obliged to use an invention of my own, kyoso, literally, 'race-fight'. When the official saw my translation, he appeared much impressed. Then he said suddenly, 'Here is the word "fight". What does it mean? It is such an unpeaceful word.'

Fukuzawa tried to explain, but the official refused to take the translation to his superior because the word fight was too aggressive. Fukuzawa then commented acidly:

> I suppose he would rather have seen some such phrase as 'men being kind to each other' in a book on economics, or a man's loyalty to his lord, open generosity from a merchant in times of national stress, etc. But I said to him, 'if you do not agree to the word "fight," I am afraid I shall have to erase it entirely. There is no other term that is faithful to the original.'

The Western concept of a separate institutional realm of an 'economy' free of morality and social bonds, has never been fully implemented in Japan. Apparently the Japanese language has no authentic word denoting 'economy'. *Keizai* refers to 'the politico-spiritual guidance of social life in general'.

When an individual takes a decision about activities which we would classify as economic, he or she considers many factors, including longer-term social relations, what the other thinks, face and status, harmony and goodwill, which are far less important in a possessive individualistic society where extreme competition is the norm. In this we could easily be led to believe that there is a pre-transition, embedded, situation.

On the other hand, what is equally remarkable about the Japanese economy is that it has shown signs of a precocious 'capitalism' since medieval times when the huge markets in grain encouraged speculation and the first 'futures' markets in the world appeared. There were vast merchant cities like Osaka where buying and selling occupied hundreds of thousands of traders. The use of money and an understanding of monetary value were widespread, reaching even the remotest regions. By the later Middle Ages, Japan had a huge trading empire based on silver. It had a manufacturing industry making high-quality goods which were traded all over the country and abroad.

Both Japanese literature and the visual arts depict a bustling, hedonistic merchant nation, and the *kabuki* plays have celebrated it from the seventeenth century. For several centuries, Japan was the most urban, commercially literate, market-oriented society in the world. As Ihara Saikaku wrote in the early eighteenth century, 'A man may be descended from the noblest of the Fujiwara, but if he dwells among shopkeepers and lives in poverty he is lower than a vagabond monkey-trainer. There is no alternative for a townsman: he must pray for wealth and aim to be a millionaire.' This was particularly the ethos of the townspeople and merchants (*chonin*), yet this practical and economistic attitude spread throughout Japan.

So we have a socially embedded yet capitalist, cautious yet revolutionary society, a people who are economically successful, yet
suspicious of (and a little disgusted by) the vulgarity of mere profit
maximisation, which many regard as an uncouth trait of the Chinese
or Westerners. The Japanese remind me somewhat of the Protestants
of the West who made large fortunes by being careful, hard-working
and honest, but eschewed show and followed their vocations as if the
activity were religious rather than economic.

To a considerable extent my puzzlement at the apparently contradictory nature of the Japanese economic system – both highly rational
and competitive, yet embedded and 'sticky' – was resolved when the
medieval economic historian Professor Eiji Sakurai explained the
historical background. Money started to be widely used in Japan in
1270, as the result of the growing influx of small Chinese coins. Tax
payments were made in coins rather than rice, and goods began to be
made to raise money to pay taxes. Supply and demand determined
prices and an efficient market economy in terms of production of
goods was established.

Curiously, however, instead of extending to most social relations,
as it usually does, the use of money was restricted to the sphere of
things, and did not impinge on relations between people. The labour
market was not influenced by commodity prices. For example, the
cost of lodging on the main Japanese highway, the Tokaido, remained
the same from the fourteenth to the sixteenth century, even while rice
prices fluctuated rapidly in terms of supply and demand. Or again,
carpenters worked from sunrise to sunset throughout the year, but
were paid the same amount per day, winter and summer, though the
hours worked were very different.

Working for an employer is seen as a gift of one's labour and the
wages are the return of the gift. The Japanese word for salary is *roku*,
which means 'gift'. Kenichi explained that in the past coins were

believed to have a particular magical power because they cut off social relations, and hence money was often buried, or kept in special places – in shrines or temples, for instance, where money-lender monks were found.

Toshiko enlightened us further. Payments for goods and those for services are considered to be totally different things in Japan, she said. Up to the nineteenth century school fees were not an obligatory but a voluntary payment, usually made in goods rather than money. Schoolmasters could not ask to be paid and would never send a bill, neither was there a legal right to payment as such. Fees were not set but parents would talk among themselves to get an idea of the general rate. Schoolmasters would often accept varying amounts depending on the parents' wealth or poverty. It would have been considered very impolite for a parent to ask how much to pay.

When the library was set up at Keio University in the later nineteenth century, the borrowing fee was very small and it remains so. There are still a lot of 'voluntary' fees in Japan. Toshiko's sister-in-law teaches piano but finds it nearly impossible to ask for payment and relies on the parents of her students to do the honourable thing. Often when fees are paid, presents are also given at certain times of year which underlines the idea of payment as a 'gift'. Thus fee payment is part of a social relationship, not a cold economic transaction. Labour contracts in Japan are formulated in terms of gifts and the exchange is disguised – money should not be paid directly and explicitly. Money for labour should be 'wrapped' as a gift.

This applied in the past to most relationships. For example, the samurai were given a sort of 'retainer' or *on*, and had to show their loyalty to their lords to the same degree whether the gift was large or small. It was the same with employees in the great merchant houses. This feeling that there is a deeper relationship between employer and employee than just monetary wages can do justice to, permeates Japanese employment to this day. Employees feel that they are part of the company and that shareholders have no real ownership of it. Even taxes today are treated as gifts. People 'give' the government money, and then the government, supposedly out of a sense of reciprocity and benevolence, provides services. The belief is that people are not being taxed, but asked to contribute of their own volition to the greater good.

This dual system, a fully market system in terms of things, yet a personalised system where people are concerned, is unusual, but it is reflected in the present state of the Japanese economy. The economist Professor Hiroshi Yoshikawa explained the dual economy: the manufacturing sector is very efficient, and the non-manufacturing sector is only a little over half as efficient as that in the United States. The manufacturing sector makes many products, but does not absorb labour. The labour absorbing sector is in non-manufacturing. The shift from production to services, towards construction, banking, retail and so on at the world level is one that, he thought, does not favour Japan. Anyone who travels through Japan can see that many institutions – hotels, banks and shops – are overstaffed. While one can be ruthless with material objects, humans have to be treated delicately.

In many non-monetised societies, both things and people are treated with respect, in a set of complex and embedded relations. In advanced capitalist economies in the West, people and things are both treated as commodities, often in a competitive and quite brutal, market-oriented way. The Japanese combine elements of both; things are part of the competitive market, people are in multiple and embedded relationships.

It could be argued that the Japanese concept of property has long been similar to that adopted in the idiosyncratic English legal system, and this mostly remains the case today. In both Japan and England, from the twelfth century at least, an individual who held an estate could alienate it as he or she liked. This is illustrated by the medieval

English statement, 'no one is the heir of a living person'. No one person can automatically assume that they will inherit from anyone else, since until the last moment they can be disinherited through the property owner selling the estate, or by making a will which leaves it to someone else. Likewise in Japan, all the children could be asked to leave the farm or business and the estate passed on to an unrelated, adopted heir at any time until the death of the holder.

Japan and England were the only two large agricultural civilisations in the world which had a system whereby just one heir could inherit. The main properties of the larger landowners, and almost all estates in Japan, were normally passed on to only one child from at least the fifteenth century. This in effect disinherited the others, though they might be given smaller portions of money or goods. The usual system of inheritance, whereby all sons automatically received an equal share of their parents' property, and daughters received their share as a dowry, was not followed on these two islands.

The contractual relations of a similar feudal property system in England and Japan set them apart from all other civilisations, and this property system tended towards very individualised ownership. Many have seen this peculiarity, with its security of tenure for those actually in possession and its protection of economic gains running against the almost universal tendency towards constant divisions and subdivisions of estates, as one key to the respective economic success of England and Japan.

In this way, Japan is very different from China with its concept of clan property, India with its peasant holdings and caste groupings, and indeed from everywhere except England. Japan's surprisingly individualistic, calculative and contractual property system, which has held for hundreds of years, has provided a good basis for modern capitalism and the kind of individualistic property with which most of us are now familiar.

❧

Yet if we look a little closer, we shall find that there is something which fundamentally differentiates the Japanese system from the English one, and which places it in another, hybrid, category. For while the head of a Japanese household could treat his property superficially like his counterpart in England, he operated in a very different context. He did not fully own it, or in fact own it at all. He was, in effect, a trustee, part of a long line of people stretching through time, and had a deep obligation to continue the *ie* or 'lineage'. He was in a very similar position to that I find myself in as a Fellow of King's College, Cambridge. I can choose my successor (with the agreement of the other Fellows) through competitive Fellowship Elections. Yet I cannot sell off bits of the College, the Chapel or Library. Consequently my freedom is strictly limited.

Except where the estate was tied to the family through the legal device of the entail, which only covered the very largest holdings, an English property holder could sell off what he (and his wife) liked. They could break up the estate, sell it to the highest bidder, and no one could stop them. There was no institution similar to what the French called 'the restraint of the line', in other words the right of family members to maintain their interests in a 'family' estate.

In Japan there was definitely a kind of 'restraint of the line', the obligation to pass on the property, if possible in an improved state, to preserve the lineage. Yet this system also had the peculiar feature of an Oxford or Cambridge college in that the person to whom the property was passed did not have to be a family member. The successor was selected by the current manager or 'trustee' of the estate. If he (or she) decided that the business or farm would be better managed by a distant relative, or even a complete stranger, such a person could be adopted in, and all the natural children disinherited.

This makes it difficult to decide whether we are talking of absolute private property, or no private property. Both are equally true. There is freedom, but with tremendous constraint. While only a few of the largest estates in England were successfully entailed in this way, in effect every Japanese property holder suffered a restraint which directed them to pass on their property as intact as possible.

This difference may partly explain a feeling of both familiarity and unfamiliarity as I explore Japan. Japan feels more communal and corporatist than England, as if individuals have only a little wealth in their small houses and simple furniture. On the other hand, the national income of the Japanese when notionally divided among the population is immense. They should live like Americans, or even more opulently. Yet they have fewer possessions if we look at their houses, gardens and consumer durables, though their bank accounts are in a much healthier state.

Education, health provision, transport and many other things strike me as much closer to their equivalents in a socialist, centrally planned economy. It is a country of corporations and group assets, not striving for extreme private property. If anything, it appears to have reversed J. K. Galbraith's remark about the capitalist West, 'private affluence, public squalor', and in doing so has eliminated squalor almost entirely. It would seem that paradoxically, while in theory the Japanese were among the earliest societies to institute privatised property, they are still in many ways living in a world of communal assets.

Japan has suffered relatively lightly from famine during the last millennium. Although many thousands died in three great eighteenth- and nineteenth-century famines, the victims were proportionately fewer than the millions who died in the great famines of China, India or Russia. It has largely avoided the devastations of war because of its position as an island, which meant that it was not successfully invaded for a thousand years before 1945.

Likewise, it has been a relatively disease-free country. After a period of serious epidemic diseases up to about the tenth century, many of the great killer diseases either disappeared or did not spread. Bubonic

plague never entered Japan. Malaria seems to have been largely eliminated by the sixteenth century. Typhoid and cholera only struck in
the later nineteenth century and with less than the normal mortality.
Of the epidemic diseases, only measles and smallpox affected the
country severely. Smallpox later became a childhood disease, as it did
in England. The perennial killers, particularly dysentery, were limited
in their lethal effects. In its death patterns, Japan is historically not
dissimilar to England, but different from all other major continental
civilisations.

The century following the reunification of Japan, around 1580, saw
great improvements in agriculture and an upsurge in fertility, and
the population doubled. But then for about 150 years the population hardly grew, despite the fact that people's incomes were steadily
improving. During the nineteenth century the population again
increased greatly until the middle of the twentieth century. More
recently, in the later twentieth century, the Japanese have also had
small numbers of children per family.

The Japanese have tended to use a particular strategy to achieve
exactly the numbers of males and females which, in their highly
constricted and inhospitable terrain, they felt they could afford. Not
only did Japanese women not tend to marry in their middle teens, in
the manner of much of India or China, but a number did not marry
at all. Yet, as women married around twenty, without some positive
check there would still have been rapid population growth, for each
woman could have had an average of eight or more children as the
infant mortality rate was relatively low. Generally they did not have
access to contraception. Even today contraception, particularly the
Pill, is not used to the same extent and with the same freedom as in
the West. The Japanese health authorities officially banned it in 1972
because of health scares about its side-effects and it was only legalised
again in 1999.

Instead the Japanese opted for a solution which is found in remote Pacific communities with a similarly grave population problem. What they did in a number of farming communities, in areas of Japan where land was limited, was to use a combination of abortion and infanticide to fine tune both the number and the sex of surviving offspring. It was a painful, emotionally damaging, and in many ways wasteful system, putting a huge strain on women. Yet it was efficient in that, like the culling of any livestock, it enabled precise calculations to be made and carried into effect.

The high rate of abortion, which continues today, has led to certain parts of selected temples being filled with figures of children which are placed there (at considerable expense) to commemorate the dead. The destroyed infants are called 'water children', and are thought by some to be returned to the lake from where they came, to wait there for a more propitious time to be born.

The pressure to use abortion and infanticide, as well as the poignant regret of generations of Japanese women is illustrated in the words of an old woman in the early twentieth century who had to kill several of her infants: 'In order to survive I had no choice. To keep the children we already had, the others had to be sent back. Even now, rocks mark the spots where the babies were buried under the floor of the house. Every night I sleep right above where they're buried. Of course, I feel love and compassion for the babies I sent back.'

Thus in Japan, economic growth occurred for several centuries just before industrialisation without resulting in rapid population growth: a very different pattern to that observed in the majority of civilisations.

Even today the majority of the Japanese live, with their small flats and often simple furnishings, in a relatively spartan way. In the past they lived on the floor, sitting, eating and sleeping without tables, chairs or beds. They had few clothes. In their often bitterly cold and draught-filled houses they heated themselves with nothing beyond small stoves filled with charcoal. The houses themselves were tiny and flimsy. The food was largely rice and vegetables, with no meat or milk products. Their drink was tea. With no leather readily available, outside the house they wore straw sandals which soon disintegrated, or wooden clogs.

Yet while the material world was simple and minimal, it seems quite different from that of many other poor countries; there seems to have been less destitution. Those visitors who, like Isabella Bird, travelled across Japan, and her antecedents when they were allowed out of their quarantine base in Nagasaki Bay, reported a bustling world of sufficient food, many inns and eating places, serviceable clothing, adequate furnishings.

The Japanese had far less, consumed far less, and recycled much more than their British or American counterparts. Their intake of proteins and other forms of energy was a lot lower than others in much of the affluent West. Yet they had contrived to elaborate a style of living which gave them an expectation of life, a health regime and a general level of 'affluence' in a wider sense which was similar to the well-off middle classes in the richest Western countries.

Professor Osamu Saito explained to me a little of the background to this recycling and resource-conserving attitude. Japan's system of production is resource efficient but labour and skill intensive, reflecting a very heavily populated island with relatively scarce natural resources. This is in contrast with the American system of manufacture, which is skill saving and resource gobbling, as one might expect of a country which started with huge land, mineral and other resources and a thin population. Britain comes in between, as both capital intensive but with traditional skill efficiency through training and apprenticeship.

The Japanese took a different path to that followed in the West. They went for functional efficiency, conservation, working out exactly what was needed and no more. Unlike three quarters of the planet until the twentieth century they have never lived, in the graphic image,

with their noses just above the water, likely to drown when any unexpected disaster or expense occurred. However, they were not always
warm; they worked extraordinarily hard; they ate and dressed and
housed themselves in the simplest of ways.

Problems such as how to get enough food, keep oneself warm, get
rid of excrement, keep oneself clean, arrange space and time in the
home, were often met with solutions that were very different to those
adopted in the West. Much of the topsy-turvy nature (to a Western
visitor's eye) that I refer to is a reflection of these alternative paths.

The Japanese were faced with a particularly difficult set of
constraints in terms of soil, climate and population density. Within
these constraints, by sharing their wealth, through ingenuity, by
recycling, separating the essential from the inessential, they forged a
material civilisation like no other.

When the West, with its profligacy and super-abundance, came
along, the Japanese adopted some of its wasteful ways. Yet to the
despair of many economists, who want the Japanese to be the super-
consumers of Western dreams in order to generate a market for the
wonderful goods made in Japan, there is still a reserve, a ceiling on
desire – caution.

When I visited Japanese homes I was struck by a mixture of
consumerism and a conservative minimalism, by a sense of the transitoriness of life, the need to save. I was reminded of the persistent
thriftiness of some who have experienced war and go on saving bits
of string or old bottles or clothes without really knowing why, except
that there was once a shortage of them. Brought up in austerity,
they cannot bring themselves to consume and waste with complete
freedom.

Following the shattering experience of the Second World War,
the Japanese, too, went through a period of austerity. But they had
lived in a resource-scarce, rationed environment for many centuries,

although there was usually just enough. Everything that moved in water and most plants were eaten or turned into useful things. Houses made of bamboo, wood and paper grew temporarily out of the unstable landscape. Clothing – always basic – was fashioned from the natural, non-animal world around them – of silk, hemp, cotton or straw or even mulberry paper.

The West forged (note the metaphor) its world out of a battle with the earth, extracting the iron, coal, stone and harvesting the animals. The Japanese skimmed what they needed off the surface of their environment like hunter-gatherers. In many ways Japanese nature was more generous than that in the West. Rice, bamboo, mulberry and tea flourished and could be grown without the machinery necessary to produce goods in the West. The richness of natural resources, particularly rice, helps to account for the much higher population densities early on in Japan, as in China. As we have seen, once a ceiling was reached, however, the population was controlled in ways that were different to those in both China and the West.

The Japan we encounter today emerged out of a different material world to our own in the West. This world is one which recent industrial and technical development has made largely invisible. Before the 1960s, it was still a relatively poor country both in terms of income and stock of assets. Since then, it has become an affluent society in terms of salaries and then of goods. Now it is awash with material affluence, so that on the surface a tourist wandering through Tokyo or Osaka and looking in the shop windows or restaurants may feel that he or she is in a modern consumerist society. Yet a great deal of difference remains.

Living for three months in one of the few traditional houses in Tokyo or eating with chopsticks, sitting and sleeping on the floor, taking deep baths and feeling the tremor of an earthquake, was a great privilege and helped me to understand to some extent the sense of shock experienced by the first Europeans on encountering those most visible areas of material culture, namely what people eat, wear, sleep on and live in.

❀

Japan poses a challenge to conventional economies. It is not merely non-capitalist, but also not communist. It is a third way. It has not traversed any of the stages of economic development. It cannot be slotted into the usual sequence of Hunter-Gatherer to Tribal to Peasant to Industrial, as it was until recently all of these simultaneously.

My belief is that it would never have developed science or industrialisation without the West – there was no sign of this. But once these developments were apparent, it was able to appropriate them and run a highly industrialised economy as well as or better than the countries from which they had originated. This is precisely because the inner, undivided system is so efficient, co-ordinated, trusting, hard working, co-operative, once the industrial pattern has been established elsewhere.

The surface of the Japanese mirror reflects Western technology, science and economy. When we enter we find everything to be different. Western economic rationality, based on the assumption of individual profit maximisation, does not really apply in large parts of Japanese society. Indeed, it could be argued, somewhat paradoxically, that in the most efficient and second largest economy on earth, there is no 'Economy' at all.

4

People

From one perspective it appears that there are no individuals in Japan. Western-style individualism has never penetrated below the surface. I remember being struck by the force of this strange idea when I started to read about Japanese concepts of the self before I met my first real Japanese person.

Although there are many words equivalent to personal pronouns in Japanese, they are seldom used. By the age of six, a Japanese boy must have mastered at least six terms of self-reference, a Japanese girl at least five. Usually no self-referent equivalent of 'I' is used at all. The individual stands outside the 'I' and refers to themself as if looking through the eyes of the person they are talking to. Such is the complexity that in a conversation the question of who the self is, and who the other, is not unambiguously settled. The 'I' and the 'You' are relational, intermixed.

Another example of the lack of any fixed concept of the individual is the way in which personal names are used. In the West we have one given name. Though a woman may change her surname at marriage, the very personal first name is usually retained throughout life. 'I' am 'Alan' all through my life. In Japan in the past (as in Vietnam and Thailand) people had names appropriate to their stages of life, and they were even changed when they died. 'As soon as a child is born,' wrote Charles Thunberg in the eighteenth century, 'it receives from the parents a certain name, which, if a son, he keeps till he arrives at years of maturity. At that period it is changed. If afterwards he obtains an office, he again changes his name; and if, in process of time, he is advanced to other offices, the same change always takes place ...'

Morse gives an example of the wide set of names a single individual may have, each of which can be changed: *sei* (clan name), *uji* (family name), *tsucho* (equivalent to Christian name), *go* (scholastic name), *azana* (additional scholastic name), *imina* (legal name for contracts, etc.), and a name after death. When addressing a letter in the West, the individual given (Christian) name comes first, moving outwards to the widest geographical location. In Japan until recently it was exactly the opposite, with the personal name tucked away unobtrusively at the end.

An overview of the four categories of given names in Japan in the past was provided by the historian Yoshihiko Amino. There is the childhood name, affectionate and often a diminutive, names like *maru*, meaning a round, pretty thing. The name used by others, a term of address, such as *ichiro*, meaning first son. The real name, carefully given by the father, usually includes two Chinese characters, one of which echoes the grandfather's name. Finally, there is the name which a person has when they become an adult and can choose their own name, which usually aims to be humble and traditional.

The situation is different today, with fewer changes of names over the life cycle. Furthermore, this absence of fixity is less troubling because people tend not to address each other by their personal names, but rather by their positions. They call each other *sensei* (teacher), president, section chief, or whatever is appropriate. When the status relationship changes, so does the way people address each other. Hence the importance of name cards in Japan, not for the 'name' but for the status and position.

Many have noted that the 'meaning' of an individual in Japan is not intrinsic, implanted in a single person, as in the West. There is no unique soul or substance. The meaning is in relation to another. We can see this in the very word for 'human being'. It is composed of two Chinese characters, one meaning 'human' (*nin*) and the other meaning 'between' (*gen*). One way of interpreting this is that a human being is by definition a relationship, not a self-sufficient atom. Thus the very idea of the separate, autonomous 'person', the basic premise of Western thought and Western individualism, is missing in Japan.

There are a mass of observations to support this essential difference. The Catholic novelist Shusaku Endo tried to explain through the words of Father Valente, a Jesuit missionary, why an individualistic religion like Christianity, based on the concept of the unique human with his or her divinely implanted soul, cannot succeed in Japan:

> The Japanese never live their lives as individuals. We European missionaries were not aware of that fact. Suppose we have a single Japanese here. We try to convert him. But there was never a single individual we could call 'him' in Japan. He has a village behind him. A family. And more. There are also his dead parents and ancestors.

The group tends to claim priority over the individual, society is imagined as an organic whole of which the individual is a part, a finger or toe, of no great significance if chopped off. Japanese life is based on a series of groups – familial, social, political, scholastic, trade union, business. The Japanese, by common assent, have the least individualistic civilisation in the world.

There are many possible reasons for this relational, anti-individual world. The absence of a dominant monotheistic religion and of a belief in an individual soul related to one God is clearly a factor. The Japanese forms of Buddhism tend to deny the existence of the individual soul. Some have suggested that the flimsy, communal, traditional Japanese house where everyone lived and slept in one room and where it was impossible to obtain privacy is another.

Whatever the reasons, the effects are well known. It is very difficult for the single person to stand out against group pressure. The word for individual in Japan has the connotation of selfishness. The Japanese proverb that the protruding nail is hammered down (*deru kugi wa utareru*) is often quoted. In schools, families, business organisations, the army and elsewhere the pressure to conform, which is felt in most societies, is extreme.

Even children's stories emphasise the collaborative model for life. Joy Hendry describes how, 'A Japanese version of the Three Little Pigs, for example, usually has the first two little pigs escaping the attacks of the Big Bad Wolf so that they can join the third pig and co-operate in their efforts to entice him down the chimney into the cooking pot.' In the English version the first two little pigs are 'eaten up for their lack of foresight, whereas the third pig uses his individual cunning and cleverness to defeat the wolf'.

Yet the opposite, namely that each Japanese is alone, could be argued equally well. The mid twentieth-century philosopher Masao Maruyama used the metaphor of the 'octopus pot society' to describe Japan. Each Japanese is alone in his or her pot, cut off from others, only linked by a piece of rope that holds all the pots together. An earlier metaphor was suggested by the nineteenth-century philosopher Fukuzawa: 'The millions of Japanese at that time were closed up inside millions of individual boxes. They were separated from one another by walls with little room to move around.'

The loneliness and separateness are compounded by the fact that inside the innermost box or octopus pot is a being without a centre. When we were in Japan we were told by a friend that the Japanese feel empty; there is nothing, a space, at the centre of each person. All of life is in what surrounds this empty space. Our friend seemed to be saying that he imagined that westerners feel filled at the centre with an individual soul and personality, while a single Japanese is like an empty room.

If ever there was a 'lonely crowd', filled with single, discrete individuals who find it very difficult to communicate with others, it is Japan. It is not surprising that there is an undercurrent of deep loneliness in much of Japanese art and literature, associated with concepts such as *wabi*, derived from a word which originally meant 'to decline into a sad and helpless state', or *hie-sabi*, 'the sphere of the cold and the lonely'.

From a traditional Chinese or Indian point of view, Japan appears individualistic, flexible and competitive. We are far from the Chinese clan system, with its all-dominating village community, or from the Indian caste system. Japan is sometimes described as a 'small group' society.

Yet what is odd is how very small and temporary these groups may be. They can consist of just two persons meeting; they can be full of significance for a moment, then over, as momentary as the falling blossom or the full moon in the sky — which Japanese love for their sense of transitoriness.

The most obvious such tiny group occurs in the tea ceremony. A ceremony where there is only one person is meaningless. Yet with two people, tea master and guest, a full ceremony can take place. The 'group' may only meet once, and for an hour, yet in a sense it then lasts for ever in the memory. The individual has become complete in the eyes of the other.

In metaphors which are often alluded to by modern Japanese, people are both part of the sticky, root-entwined bean curd (*natto*) and lonely octupuses. Each person is an empty mirror, searching for themselves as reflected in others. The Emperor was in the past the ultimate empty mirror, reflecting everything. The mirror is the absorption of every particle of light. This is *kyo*, the capacity of a person to absorb the expectations of others, as the Emperor and superiors are meant to do. Japan is the ultimate 'other-directed' society, to use David

Riesman's term, where each person is constantly picking up and then relaying back signals.

Socio-psychological studies have shown that Americans are, on average, more co-operative and trusting than the Japanese. Yet when they are embedded in a social structure in which they are monitored and sanctioned, then the Japanese appear to co-operate very well. In Japan collectivism seems to be based on personal networks of known people. Americans tend to identify themselves with the group category, for example in the context of patriotism to the country, or school, or the football team. We can see that there are two kinds of collectivism, one is face to face, and the other, as in America, is more abstract.

I asked several leading intellectuals in Japan what they considered to be the worst aspect of Japanese society and they all agreed that it was the overwhelming pressure to conform. This makes it hard to live in your own way. Japan is a tightly knit society where being an individual is not easy. It is often suffocating. 'We act in groups and we have a colourless life as opposed to the colourful and individualistic foreigners. Thoughts here are equal and tending towards the average. I can always anticipate what people will say before they say it, which makes things boring.'

The Japanese tend to be influenced by the majority mood and move as a group. Society consists of collections of relationships, because relations are more important than the individual. Small groups can stand out against the majority, for instance a new religious sect or trades union, but within each of them it is difficult for the individual to resist group pressure.

At first sight it looks as if the Japanese are a strongly family-based society, not too dissimilar to the Chinese or Indian systems. Japan is thought by many observers to be based on the principle of a group of related people called an *ie*, which was a male-linked lineage from grandparents down through sons to grandsons.

These kinship-like groups have influenced much of Japanese life. The ancestor tablets are handed down the line. The farms, business enterprises and craft activities of Japan are based upon such groupings and demand extreme loyalty and political allegiance. Much of Japanese social life and sentiment is based on an extension of family ties. Visitors to factories, shrines and schools feel a strong sense of family-like sentiment.

Yet as we delve deeper and watch more carefully, we begin to notice an oddness. In the normal clan-based systems around the world, all children have birthrights and certainly all males have equal rights. Yet in Japan, as we have seen, any child can be disinherited, including the oldest son. Only one heir is chosen, and the chosen one may be an adopted stranger. The borders between kin and non-kin are artificial and a household that looks as if it is blood-based may, in fact, be filled with unrelated strangers who have put on the mantle of kinship. Anyone may be recruited, or sacked, from the *ie*. What at first looks like a family group may in fact be an artificial creation, a co-operative enterprise group.

When we look at the way in which people trace their family links, we find that for over a thousand years the Japanese have used exactly the same method as the British or North Americans do now. Equal weight is given to the male and female line; a person's mother's mother is as close as their father's father. Such a system cannot create any kind of strong, bounded, kinship group since each individual has a widening set of circles of relatives spreading out from himself or herself which is not identical with any other person.

Likewise, the way in which the Japanese term their relatives is identical to that in America or England. It isolates out the close family of parents and children, who are given special terms. Then the system groups relatives into categories which are not distinguished by which side of the family they are on: aunts and uncles, nephews and nieces, and a wide range of cousins.

Thus we have a civilisation which has two levels. There are fictional groupings of a kin-like nature which influence much of life, based on the sentiments and loyalties of kinship, but not necessarily based on blood or marriage. Beneath this there are families that are identical to the modern Western family system in their ways of conceiving of how people are related and should address each other.

The kinship system is a contradiction in terms, for it is an 'artificial family'. Family sentiment feels much more powerful and pervasive in its reach than in the West and seems to a considerable extent to underpin economic, religious and political life. Yet it is founded on entirely different principles. It is based on human choice rather than birth and blood. It is a hybrid.

One could equally well argue that all of Japan is based on the family, or that the family hardly exists. To support the latter view there is plenty of evidence of the fragmentary and weak nature of practical kinship in Japan. Many have noted that neighbours are more important than kin; the Japanese place less weight on their kin outside the nuclear family than do any other societies, including the English.

Even the link between brothers and sisters is often weak. As the anthropologist Chie Nakane notes:

> The wealthy brother normally does not help the poor brother or sister, who has set up a separate household, as long as the latter can somehow support his or her existence … A married sibling who lives in another household is considered a kind of outsider. Towards such kin, duties and obligations are limited to the level of the seasonal exchange of greetings and presents, attendance at wedding and funeral ceremonies and the minimum help in case of accident or poverty.

Even daughters become strangers.

The Japanese have created a flexible, family-based yet non-family system. Any particular family is weak and fragmentary, but everybody is 'family'. A family is constructed, artificial, and people can be brought into its heart through adoption. Even strangers are 'honorary' family, including neighbours, workmates and friends. Life is filled with the emotion and commitment of a giant family, with high levels of trust and warm feeling, alongside the flexibility and openness that the efficient business organisation of modern Japan requires.

Traditionally it would be parents who put pressure on their children to marry. They often asked an intermediary to find a suitable partner and to arrange the introductions. In the seventeenth century, Saikaku wrote, people complained, 'Nowadays a marriage-broker is no longer a friendly mediator, but a business-woman who makes a profit.' He also cautioned, 'Marrying off your daughter is a piece of business you may expect to do only once in a lifetime, and, bearing in mind that none of the losses are recoverable later, you should approach the matter with extreme caution.'

Even today, the marriage sponsor or negotiator is an important figure at many Japanese weddings. About half of married couples in Japan have been united using a go-between, though the situation is changing and 90 per cent of couples married at the end of the twentieth century took the initiative themselves.

Until very recently, most marriages did not follow a long courtship, or the initial impulses of the young people themselves. The parties were brought together by others and told that they were suitable marriage partners and that they should therefore seriously consider getting married to each other. On the other hand the institution of marriage in Japan has a flavour which does not fit smoothly with the kind of arranged marriages which I have encountered elsewhere.

The couple were not chosen on the basis of their respective family positions, and cousin marriages were neither particularly preferred nor avoided. In contrast to the Chinese system, for example, it was possible for parties with the same surname to marry. The people who made the decisions were close relatives – the mother, father, perhaps uncles and aunts, not a wide kinship group. There was little significant economic exchange of wealth at the wedding.

Furthermore, the psychological compatibility of the young people was considered important. They were left together alone a few times before the marriage was finalised in order to see if they liked each other. If they were unhappy about the arrangement it would probably be called off. As the marriage was mediated by a broker neither family lost face.

What place has love in all this? Japanese literature and folklore is filled with romantic love stories, often ending in the joint suicide of the young couple who refused to be parted despite their parents' decisions. Love is widespread. What has long been shocking to the Japanese, though, is the Western desire to base marriages on romantic love and thereby to elevate the relationship between husband and wife above the duty to parents.

As Hearn, who taught literature in Japan at the end of the nineteenth century, noted:

> Our society novels do not strike them as indecent because the theme is love. The Japanese have a great deal of literature about love. No; our novels seem to them indecent for somewhat the same reason that the Scripture text, 'For this cause shall a man leave his father and mother and shall cleave unto his wife' appears to them one of the most immoral sentences ever written.

Even today, it is doubtful whether most marriages in Japan are based on that overwhelming passion which lies at the heart of romantic love in parts of the West. The account given by a close Japanese friend of his marriage sums it up from the male standpoint. Having decided he was at the age when he should marry, my friend cast his mind over his closest female acquaintances to find a suitable partner. Three of them made his shortlist in terms of intelligence and character. It was quite a methodical approach, which he might have adopted when making an appointment to a job, which is exactly what he had done. For the Japanese wife is seen as the 'headmistress' of the school in which the children, as they are born, are nurtured and taught. The husband is the 'headmaster'.

From what I have heard in conversations with my married Japanese friends, there is little talk, in relation to marriage, of the overcoming of loneliness, the joining of hearts, the passionate uniting of blood with blood, the finding of a soul mate, or any of the stuff of so much romantic literature and television in the West. Marriage is a practical, utilitarian arrangement, often gone into with great fondness, but somehow less emotionally than in the West. Above all, the couple are joined by their shared investment in and love for their children.

This half-arranged system is often acted out in the theatre of the extraordinary marriage hotels of Japan. Having been brought together by a broker, the future spouses go to a wedding hotel. There they inspect the selection of wedding costumes and for a moment the woman is transformed in her *kimono* into a traditional Japanese bride. The couple then move along the conveyor belt of slick consumerism to the large hall where hundreds of tables are filled with their workmates, friends and some family. After presents, dances and speeches, they retire upstairs to the bridal suite. Next day they leave for a short honeymoon in Guam or Australia. A week of romance, and then they return home. The husband drops all pretence of being a romantic lover and reverts to the salary-man or businessman that he has never stopped being.

This is a caricature, but it roughly captures the humdrum nature of many Japanese marriages. The bond between man and woman in marriage remains relatively weak. They are fused neither by love and intense desire, nor by an ideology which suggests that they have become one flesh and one blood. They remain strangers who, as our friends openly admitted, feel closer to their children than to each other.

The system is changing rapidly, and it is difficult to tell where it is heading. We were told on a recent visit that there has been a huge increase in dating agencies in the previous three years as young people are getting busier and do not have a chance to meet potential partners. Marriage arranging in the past was termed *omiai*, but there is no specific name for the new model. Since 2005 the government has been keen to encourage these agencies, so it is introducing quality-assurance guides to promote the best. There is a sliding scale for their services, from nothing to about three thousand pounds – which will more or less guarantee a good match. Much of this dating trend is related to the development of the Internet.

Traditionally the relationship between a son and his mother took precedence over that with his wife. If his mother ordered him to divorce his wife, he had to do so. In the Civil Code of 1898, the wife's right to maintenance from her husband came third after the rights of parents and children.

I asked my friends the following question: If you had to choose to save the life of one of your daughters or that of your marriage partner, whom would you choose? They unhesitatingly said, 'Our daughter of course, for she is our blood while my husband [or my wife] is a stranger.'

The Japanese are described as having an intense son–mother dependency complex, *amae* as it is called. There is strong affection, loyalty and protectiveness here which colours all of a son's life. There is also historically a lack of symmetry in the husband—wife relation-ship, with the wife closer to the husband, than the husband to the wife. This was commented on by Alice Bacon in the early twentieth century: 'If the wife dies, her husband does not mourn for her, though her children do; but if the husband dies, the wife must mourn the rest of her life, cutting off her hair and placing it in the coffin as a sign of her perpetual faithfulness.'

My friends were surprised to hear how difficult it had been until about 1970 for a husband or wife to get a divorce in England. In contrast, for five hundred years divorce has been relatively easy to obtain in Japan. This difference in attitude towards divorce is likely to be reflected in the respective status of marriage: in Britain, marriage is central to society, whereas in Japan its bonds are weaker and it is less emotionally important.

Yet having spent time with Japanese couples and read Japanese histor-ical and literary works, I can see that there is also a closeness between husband and wife. The children leave home and may end up living a long way away from their parents. The husband and wife share their wealth, with the wife in charge of their communal money. They often treat each other as friends.

I have noticed that many younger Japanese, particularly women, are insisting that they be put first in a marriage, thereby placing the husband with strong loyalties to his parents in an almost impossibly difficult position. However, there is still some way to go before the revolutionary biblical injunction, to prefer one's wife or husband to one's parents, is accepted.

The Japanese have fashioned a mixed marriage system. To the Western observer, the inner dynamics of family life in Japan can be rather puzzling. Partners often treat each other with an arm's-length caution which seems a long way from the Western ideal of a cosy, companionate marriage. They are, in essence, strangers who have come together. Some spouses practise what is called 'divorce within marriage' after the children are born. They no longer sleep side by side or engage in sex. Japanese visitors to Europe are often shocked to find middle-aged couples sharing double beds.

Yet in many respects, Japanese couples seem companionate and overlapping in their lives. The women are not strictly segregated or placed into purdah or harems. They share their husbands' lives and make many of the decisions in the family. They seem self-confident and in many ways equal to their husbands. They even treat their husbands with some derision, referring to them, when they return exhausted from their work, as 'the big rubbish' (like the black bin bags that obstruct small Japanese kitchens), or when they retire as 'the wet leaves', clinging, unwanted, to wives who are used to leading a rich social and aesthetic life without them.

When Westerners travelled to Japan in the second half of the nine-teenth century they recorded with admiration and astonishment the apparently high regard and kind treatment of young children. Isabella Bird in her travels commented:

> I never saw people take so much delight in their offspring, carrying them about, or holding their hands in walking, watching and enter-ing into their games, supplying them constantly with new toys, taking them to picnics and festivals, never being content to be without them, and treating other people's children also with a suitable measure of affection and attention.

The result was extremely well-behaved children: 'They are so perfectly docile and obedient, so ready to help their parents, so good to the little ones, and, in the many hours which I have spent in watching them at play, I have never heard an angry word or seen a sour look or act.' For his part, Morse noted, 'Japan is the paradise for children. Not only are they kindly treated, but they have more liberty, take less liberty with their liberties, and have a greater variety of delightful experiences than the children of any other people.'

As our friends explained, the Japanese socialisation process is one of the keys to understanding many puzzles. The very strong, tactile bond between mother and child, almost swamping in its intensity, creates a deep sense of warmth and trust. The child is supported, encouraged, played with, physically pampered and cosseted, and made the centre of the mother's world. A long period of breast-feeding and carrying, parent and child sleeping together – all create dependency and a sense of a meaningful, encouraging, hopeful and loving world.

There is no attempt to set the child free or to foster independence. The infants are cocooned in love and support. This continues for a surprisingly lengthy time until the child is about six or seven. There is almost no thwarting or disciplining. There is just the occasional withdrawal of total affection if the child misbehaves.

Here is an enchanted world. Wishes and desires turn into reality. Play and fantasy, spirits and reality, are all intertwined. The world is portrayed and seems, within the home, to be dependable, friendly, optimistic, and safe – whatever the savage physical reality of Japan may present. There is little sense of sin, of failure, of instilled and increasing separateness.

Much of the personality of the adult Japanese is formed during this time, and by the age of seven there is a considerable gap between such children and their counterparts in many other societies. They are taught to be relaxed about their bodily functions, trusting in others, appreciative of intense interactions. They are seldom alone, anxious or rejected.

When infants and young children go to school, the transition out of the highly controlled and supportive environment is gradual and careful. In the past in Europe or America, the child was often sent away, or went to a school where he or she was disciplined, taught to be an individual and prepared for adulthood. In contrast, little changes for the Japanese child over the next few years except that the teachers supplement the parents. The child goes to a school where the teachers try to be like older brothers and sisters. They do not beat or otherwise punish the children. Mothers continue to lavish attention on them.

In the first half of their schooling, up to the age of twelve, the child is taught the intricate rules of how to extend and expand the delicate dance of social relations to others. He or she learns that they will be surrounded for life by a thick layer of inter-personal and multi-level relationships. Their language, etiquette and senses are tuned to an infinitely complex set of expectations and responsibilities. They are carefully shaped as if they were delicate trees.

In some ways the period between fourteen and twenty-one is the most interesting. For while in the West this is when the enchanted world of childhood is abandoned and black-and-white certainties turn to shades of grey, this does not seem to happen in Japan. Somehow the social and intellectual world remains largely undivided. Adults in Japan also live in an integrated world. There is no need to take teenagers out of some childhood world and to introduce them to another, colder but more rational, adult existence.

Toshiko and Kenichi said that China and Japan were very different in relation to child-rearing. The Japanese were not patriarchal in the Chinese sense. They told us that when discussing the disciplining of children Hiroko Hara wrote that in the West adults stand in front of the children and formally instruct them, telling them what to do and punishing them if they do wrong. In Japan parents stand behind and watch their children, guiding and protecting them like shepherds.

Shing-Jen Chen, a child development specialist, explained that if we conceive of moving from childhood to adulthood as similar to crossing a river, then there is a basic difference in how this is done in the West and in Japan. In the West parents have already crossed and shout back instructions to their children as to how to get through the rushing stream, leaving it to them to do so. Japanese parents, on the other hand, go back over the river and bring their children across. Quite literally they go down to the child's level in gestures and speech and share the experience of growing up alongside the child. During feeding, while a Western mother will tend to remain in front with her head about three feet above that of the baby, a Japanese mother will sit side by side with the baby, with her eyes at exactly the same level as the child. When women are with their children, we were told, they adapt their personality; they construct the world through language mostly from the child's point of view.

If a six-month-old baby is being fed solids and wants to touch the eating utensils, a Western parent will suppress the waving hand as if to say 'It is too early. I know best, let me help you – the purpose of eating is to feed.' The Japanese mother will give the spoon to the child, hold the hand and help the child feed themself, as if to say 'All that you want to do has value. The very childish wish I do not question; it is what you want and I understand, and let us do it together'. We were told that parents quite frequently see their children as their own shadows, and re-live their early lives through them.

The division between the adult's and child's mental world in the West is often very great; the child's world is enchanted, full of fairies and magic. The adult world is supposed to be rational, sensible, based on logic. Growing up is conceived of as moving from enchantment to disenchantment. This is all rather less pronounced in Japan.

Since children are an extension or shadow of their parents, there is no corporal punishment in Japan (except occasionally with a slap). Our friends were shocked when they read English novels which described the harsh physical punishments inflicted in the past. They explained that in Japan there is a saying that children are treasures or gifts from heaven. In the past young children were regarded as fragile, likely to die, and hence still belonging to the world of spirits rather than humans. They were not just small adults, they were half-wild, driven by imperatives and with a morality that were very different from those of the human world into which they would gradually be domesticated.

Now as then, the goal of the parents is to make their children healthy, happy and socially aware, honest and law-abiding. If children do not achieve this, the parents are failures. If you are a proper human being, you will take on the mixed burden and blessing of bringing up children.

Children start their lives in great freedom and then, gradually, the path along which they are guided gets narrower. They are conceived of as becoming adult very late. Although the age of criminal responsibility is nowadays eighteen, Toshiko believes that a child is only half an adult at fifteen; 80 per cent adult at twenty, and becomes fully responsible at about twenty-eight.

During the process of growing up, the cocooning or protection is made easier by the age-grade system. In many tribal societies, where people either stay in one place throughout their lives or move on together as a group, individuals remain particularly close to their age mates. The children they played with as they became aware of the world grow up with them, a group of easy, no-pretence, friends for life with whom they are always innocent and young. Childhood playmates become members of an age group whose relationships are cemented through the training and initiation they have undergone and later through their experiences as householders and parents, and through old age.

The modern Japanese are not quite like this: they tend to move several times during their lives. But it has been noticed that school and university friends retain an extremely strong bond. Once the effort has been made to fuse with other persons, to reveal oneself and

learn to appreciate the other, to build up a repertoire of shared experiences and memories, this closeness is not abandoned. A warm circle
is developed and surrounds a person through life.

The period of full adulthood, attained very late according to Japanese
ideas, is short. Starting in the mid-twenties, thirty years or so later
it is over, and the retreat back into a warm, child-like existence of
irresponsibility and grandparenthood occurs. Having gone through
five of the twelve-year cycles of life, at sixty, you retire and become a
child again, with all the freedom that implies. You may even choose
to celebrate your re-birth dressed in a red coat and hat, since you are
starting again at the age of zero. It is as though the period in between
childhood and old age had only been a partial suspense, or make-
believe, adulthood.

As they retire people pass their power on to the younger generations. Traditionally the wife of the house used to hand over money
matters to her daughter-in-law. Parents were marginalised, although
their successors had a duty to consult them. However, older people,
both within the family and within organisations, are nowadays still
respected for their experience, wisdom and maturity, though the
huge number of the elderly in Japan, and the changing structure of
families, is posing severe problems.

Accounts of the current situation bear some interesting resem-
blances to earlier descriptions. For example, in the later seventeenth
century Saikaku divided the ages:

A man, it is decreed, is lacking in all discrimination till the age of
thirteen; from then until the age of twenty-four or twenty-five he must
abide by the guidance of his parents; thereafter he must earn his living by his own efforts, on his own responsibility, and if, by the age of
forty-five, he has laid firm the foundations of his household's prosperity in his own life-time, he may then take time for pleasure.

Kenichi summarised the present in these words: 'Childhood is wild, loose; the middle part is contained and restrained and selfless. In old age and retirement you are free and unconstrained again.'

The difference between the Japanese and the Western treatment of the life cycle reflects their different conceptions of human nature. The Japanese child is born into the world wild, without sin, to be gradually domesticated and gently trained. In much of the West, however, the legacy of the Christian vision is still strong, although many are not formally Christian. The child is both a responsible person with a soul, but also full of sin and evil tendencies which need to be restrained. From this different foundation, the life cycle works in an opposite way to that of the Japanese. The West starts with moderate severity (the child is quite soon distanced from its parents, disciplined early in various ways) and this, traditionally becomes harsher through adolescence, until the child is independent and then released into adulthood.

I was told that the aim of my schooling was to 'toughen me up', to make me independent and able to stand alone, to teach me how to control the temptations and weaknesses of my sinful mind and flesh. Then, gradually, I would attain freedom and independence from everyone for the rest of my life. For the Japanese, as we have seen, children are delightful, innocent, yet hardly human. They must be taught to bond very strongly with their parents and other adults, and then gradually to spread this dependence to others. When they become adults, in middle life, they may have to stand partly alone, but then in retirement they can return to childhood.

There is a vast literature on the effects of the Japanese style of child-rearing and the close bonds between parents and children on the Japanese personality. Without going too far into the various theories, it does seem that one clue to this basically benevolent optimistic society lies in its shared experience of a warm and loving childhood. Children sense that there will always be someone who will understand them.

When Europeans visited Japan in the nineteenth century they were surprised to find how equal men and women seemed to be. Siebold wrote, 'The Japanese women are subjected to no jealous seclusion, hold a fair station in society, and share in all the innocent recreations of their fathers and husbands. Their fidelity and purity are thus committed to their own sense of honour ...' He added, 'The minds of the women are cultivated with as much care as those of the men; and among the most admired Japanese historians, moralists, and poets are found several female names.' Charles Macfarlane agreed that, 'the condition of women – that real test of true civilisation – is incomparably better and higher in Japan than in any other Oriental country'.

One of the most perceptive accounts of Japanese womanhood was written at the end of the nineteenth century by Alice Bacon. She noticed the key role played by Japanese women in agriculture and domestic production. She found that in the care of horses in the pack trade, in the hotels and tea houses, in the tea plantations and in the important silk industry, women played an equal part with men. Her description of the enormously resilient and hard-working women of Japan, combining child-bearing, child-rearing, domestic duties and work in the fields and forests, reminds me strongly of what I have seen in the relatively egalitarian world of highland Nepal. Yet she also noted the differences and structural inequality: the women's sphere was in the home and they were dependent on men. She also noticed that inequality tended to increase with social ranking.

There have been extensive changes in the relations between the sexes in the last thirty years, yet my impression echoes this double-sided view. In some ways Japan is the most uni-gendered society of which

I know, yet differentiation fluctuates over time and situation. Our friends commented that the interchangeability of clothing and life-styles had been greater in earlier periods. From the 1960s onwards, increasing wealth and the influence of a Western attitude towards women, encouraged by the Americans after the war, confined women to the home and separated them from men, and the clothing and occupations of men and women became more distinct. Recently we noticed in the department stores an increasing overlap in the way young people dress, men adopting flamboyant and colourful clothes while women dress in severe black trouser suits. The genders seem to be blending again.

Likewise the famed differences in men's and women's language are not exactly what they seem. For example, the simplified language used by Lady Murasaki to write the *Genji* was also used by men from the eleventh century for diary writing. And nowadays if women do men's jobs, as sometimes happens, for instance if they are boxing trainers (as some are), or run a sumo 'stable', they use men's language. Everything seems relational, language and costume being adapted to the social context rather than being fixed. Hence in *kabuki* plays, originally women played the roles of men, but now men play women.

Of course, there are times when differences are accentuated, in certain rituals, displays, clothing. Yet in much of daily life and from observation of Japanese boys, girls and adults, I get the impression of a world with little opposition to or stress on gender differences. Context-specific (rather than gender specific) language is used, and there are some elements of difference between men's and women's social roles or status, but there is also a good deal of overlap as far as power, responsibility, clothing and styles are concerned.

I encountered little sense of a macho, 'honour and shame', kind of morality or mentality whether in novels or in the paintings, laws or accounts of domestic life. Today's unisex world of Japanese schools and universities seems to stretch back over time.

In the past, men and women worked side by side, women did

not carefully cover their bodies or live in seclusion, except those at the very highest level of society. Women did not have their feet bound, were not excluded from public religious practices, and became artists, writers and even samurai warriors if the situation demanded.

It would be possible to argue that gender is played down in Japan. The polar opposites we find in many societies – whereby a man is likened to the sun, the woman the moon; men are light, women are darkness; men are right, women are left; men are predators, women the prey – do not exist.

Yet if we try to assimilate the gender relations in Japan to those in the West we obliterate some real differences as well. Women usually need to attend to their 'white faces' before they go out into the world. In the past they served men in the 'floating world' of the sex trade, and some continue to do so in certain contexts. Women still have to use deferential language towards men. They are traditionally considered to be inferior to men. Women and men are not conceived of as the same psychologically or culturally. Many people (especially men and the older generation) probably still believe that men are higher, women lower. Yet the relationship between men and women is more an alliance of unequals – like the relationship between an older and younger brother, for instance – than one where the parties are intrinsically unequal.

In Japan, certainly, it is the women who hold the family and society together through their organisational skills and hard work. It is the young women who are now deciding not to marry and leaving the men stranded. It is the mother-in-law and not the father-in-law who is the major force in many families.

The position of Japanese women is difficult to assess. We talked to a young woman who had just married and was about to join her husband. She would give up work and run the home, but also have a great deal of time for hobbies and interests until children came along.

She would be the family banker and have complete control over her husband's salary. He would probably not even know what he earned. A housewife, she stressed, was thought of as a house-manager in Japan, so this was a much more important and honourable role than in many parts of the West.

Thus we have a mixed, hybrid situation, with a blend of equality and inequality which is distinctive and constantly shifting over time, and depends on class and occupation. After a period up to 1990, when Western models were influential – not only regarding the roles of husbands and wives, but also in relation to feminism and the assertion of female independence – it is beginning to look as if Japan may be reverting to something closer to its older indigenous pattern of interdependence. Again, the Japanese are absorbing parts of the Western model, and rejecting others.

As we have seen, the proverbial propensity for hard work of the Japanese is partly explained by the difficult ecology of their country and by the use of traditionally labour-intensive technologies. Yet necessity is not the only factor. Even nowadays, in the midst of affluence, many people, especially those in large corporations, seem to find much satisfaction in work. 'A job in Japan is not merely a contractual arrangement for pay,' writes Edwin Reischauer, 'but means identification with a larger entity – in other words, a satisfying sense of being part of something big and significant.' The larger the factory or organisation, the happier people appear to be in their work. Working is like belonging to an orchestra or football team, a collab-orative activity which gives mutual satisfaction of a high order.

The Japanese attitude bears some resemblance to the Protestant work ethic, but it is essentially different. It is about sacrifice, self-disci-pline, proving things to others, and represents an always present anxiety, a never-ending debt that must be repaid. Yet, we may wonder, what is the point of this sacrifice? Why is there a debt? For most Japanese there is no God. There is no Afterlife or belief in Heaven and Hell. People are not born as sinners who have to redeem themselves in the eyes of a stern immortal Father. There is just this life.

Here we come across the concept of *on*. *On* roughly means 'the debt or obligation people have to all other humans, particularly to those who have shown them any kindness'. The greatest *on* is to one's parents; this is a debt which at the human level is like the Christian's debt to Christ – it can never be fully repaid. People try to return the gift of life and childhood kindness of their parents throughout their lives. It is often said that in Japan one's obligations to one's parents are 'higher than heaven and deeper than the sea'.

Yet the concept of debt is much wider than this: *on* is incurred by each and every person whenever they meet one another to a certain degree. Not insulting or attacking the other in itself triggers an obligation. Certainly, if a person is helpful in any way, the other becomes deeply indebted. Each person is a permanent debtor, he or she must not forget for a moment that every effort to repay the kindness of others is doomed to be only 'one ten-thousandth' of what one has received. Each repayment only calls forth further reciprocal kindness, not only in the generosity in receiving the offering, but because of the further pressure to mirror kindness. The mutual obligations bounce back and forth and lead people into ever deeper emotional debt.

In most cultures, when a wrapped gift is given, the recipient opens and admires it and thanks the giver. In Japan this would be thought rude. The recipient places the gift unopened on the side, almost not noticing it at all and hence not putting either the recipient or giver in an embarrassing situation. Only when the giver has gone does a person open the gift and then face the universal problem of how to reciprocate in an even more generous way so that the relationship will continue in its see-saw like fashion.

The Japanese are like mirrors facing other mirrors. How can they best please their boss, their workmates, and their family? They can do so by living a life of honest toil, which will incidentally produce material wealth, but more fundamentally need to show their serious intent to do as much as they can.

The Protestant striving to please and thank some 'other' and to ward off the anxieties of damnation; and the Japanese striving to please others, fearing to offend and lose face – both produce effort without any possible limit. The more a person strives, the more there is to do. It is like answering emails. The more one answers, the more there are to answer.

There is evidence to show that Japan was, and still is, one of the most unequal and hierarchical civilisations. Experts tell us that equal relationships are almost impossible there. Japan is, and always has been, what some call a 'vertical' society. Every relationship places a person in either an inferior or a superior position. This inequality is built into the language, the etiquette, and into all of life.

Herbert Passin explains the importance of two terms, *oyabun*, literally 'the father role', that is 'lord, master, boss, leader, employer, landowner, protector, godfather and patron', and *kobun*, literally 'the child role', that is 'underling, subordinate, henchman, godchild, vassal, dependent, protégé, worker, employee, tenant, servant and client'. Any organisation, from family to business, is based on the relations that mix loyalty, obedience, affection and deference in a way that the non-Japanese find unfamiliar. Relations are personal and unbalanced. It is impossible to have two masters in an organisation; each person can be answerable only to one individual above them.

For instance, my Japanese research students continue to refer to me as *sensei*, even though I no longer teach them. Indeed, the very word *sensei*, which is the particular expression of the vertical feature within all crafts and arts (including education), is really untranslatable. According to D. J. Enright it is, 'A magic word, and yet very equivocal. *Sensei* means "teacher" plus "scholar" plus "beloved master"; it means intellect, learning, culture, taste; it means China, *tanka, haiku, Noh* plays, pottery, Zen.' It is part religious guru, part master as in Master of Arts, part patron, and part father.

It looks as if Japanese society is made up of little building blocks of superiority and inferiority between individuals, ties of loyalty between higher and lower status. Men, traditionally, and still nowadays to a large extent, are considered superior to women. Older brothers are intrinsically superior to younger brothers. Parents are superior to children. Bosses are superior to workers. Professors are superior to their students – for life.

The Japanese language has this intrinsic inequality built into it. All Japanese verb endings must denote relative rank. Even if two people are exactly equal in age, social status and gender, they are forced to speak as if the other is their inferior or superior.

Yet before one assumes that Japan is a straightforward hierarchical society, one must realise that it is possible to argue the opposite, namely that Japan is perhaps the most equal of large civilisations and that equality is even built into the system of superior and inferior. The group decision-making or *ringi* process, which we witnessed when we visited the Toshiba factory north of Tokyo, is an illustration of this. There we saw suggestion boxes and heard that shop-floor workers were constantly passing ideas for innovations up through their immediate superiors to the top of the organisation, making superiors dependent on their inferiors as well as the other way round.

Another example is given by Masao Maruyama, who explained that during the Second World War, 'the men who held supreme power in Japan were in fact mere robots manipulated by their subordinates, who in turn were being manipulated by officers serving overseas'. In other words, the Emperor system was kept in equilibrium not only through the effect of 'power-dwarfing' – the transfer of oppression from the Emperor downwards – but also by 'the rule of the higher by the lower'.

The grounds for thinking this is not a straightforward case of hierarchy also lie in the Japanese social structure. Japan is more open to equality of opportunity through its meritocratic educational system than either Britain or America. It is true that there are elites, fed by elite universities, and that increasingly nowadays wealthy parents can help their children into these. Yet compared to the situation in most Western societies, this is not a significant trend.

The degree to which wealth is more evenly distributed in Japan than elsewhere is often debated. This has fluctuated over time. Until the end of the nineteenth century wealth distribution seems to have been more equal in Japan than in most countries in the world. In the forty years up to the Second World War it became as unequal as in many Western countries. The thirty years after the war tended towards egalitarianism. Nowadays there are some signs of increasing inequality and some analysts have argued that income inequality is as high as that in many Western countries, while others believe that this is just a temporary deviation.

Japan appears to have been a surprisingly equal society in terms of status differences, not just recently, but for many centuries. The Japanese believed that a large measure of equality of opportunity and wealth should be available for all well before such an idea was adopted in the West, in the later eighteenth century. For a thousand years it had no instituted system of slavery, though, unlike in many societies (with the particular exception of England), there were many servants. Japan is at the opposite extreme to that system of birth-based difference which we call caste, and there is no evidence that it has ever been a caste society. It has not really had economic classes, or even very strong hereditary ranks throughout its history.

In so far as there were any kinds of 'rank' groupings in the past, they were original and unparalleled in other civilisations. European and Indian civilisations traditionally consisted of four 'estates' or ranks which were aligned on four occupational groupings: lords, priests, merchants, and craftsmen and peasants. Japanese society was also based on four rough categories; lords, peasants, merchants and craftsmen. The absence of priests is notable, as is the high ranking of peasants and the two orders of commercial people.

When the feudal rankings dissolved, unlike England, Japan did not move towards a class society. Historians have recognised that there have always been considerable possibilities for social mobility in Japan in the past. Japanese literature is full of the 'from log cabin to White House' kind of story. The differentiations were porous, allowing people to move between strata on the basis of talent and good fortune.

Status is important, but the sense of class and class antagonism or difference is slight. In almost all recent polls, 90 per cent or more of the Japanese have described themselves as middle class, which is what they seem to me. In most essential ways, Japan today is a very egalitarian society – more so in fact than the United States and many European countries. There is little of the inherited wealth and degrading poverty which characterises supposedly 'equal' civilisations such as Britain or America. Even when Japan was much poorer than it is today, Alice Bacon commented, 'Although there is much poverty, there are few or no beggars in Japan, for both strong and weak find each some occupation that brings the little pittance required to keep soul and body together, and gives to all enough to make them light-hearted, cheerful, and even happy.' Certainly, though I have seen 'homeless' people in Tokyo, they are unusual in Japan as a whole, and a recent visit suggested that, if anything, their number, already very small, is declining further.

In terms of income distribution, Japan has a far better record today than any other large industrialised country in the world, including communist and ex-communist countries. Most of the population are neither very rich nor very poor. As Kenichi put it to me, the most numerous group in Japanese society is the vast middling sort, the equivalent of what the English would once have called the lower middle class: factory, office, shop and other non-professional workers. It is they who hold the power. Consequently, when I ask myself where Japan fits, I find it stands apart as simultaneously the least and the most egalitarian of societies.

A concept central to the Japanese is *giri,* which can be roughly described as the fulfilment of contractual relations. Looking a little more deeply, the word has a bundle of meanings which is peculiarly Japanese and has no equivalent in Confucian, Buddhist or other thought systems. Scholars have found it impossible to decide whether it belongs to the realm of Community or Association.

On the one hand, a *giri* relationship has a form or outward nature which makes it feel like an example of the durable, emotional, committed, total relationship of the Community type. It refers to the enduring obligation to behave towards selected individuals in a special way. It has the moral force, emotional depth and durability that would make Western scholars immediately link it to Community.

Yet there are equally strong indications that *giri* is contractual in the sense that it involves an act of individual will or choice, that a voluntary and conscious decision is taken to enter into such a relationship. It is not given by blood or geography. Thus, in a marriage, carrying out the chosen 'contractual' relations to one's in-laws throughout life is called 'working for *giri*'. We can see that *giri* is the sense of duty which is owed not merely to blood relatives, or fellow villagers, but also to in-laws, superiors and even dependent inferiors, and indeed to all those we meet. It is a sense of duty which definitely has a Contractual or Associational element to it. It falls exactly on the boundary between two types of relation.

The fact that *giri* has an unusual and special flavour can be seen from its history. The notion of abstract justice and reason which is expressed in the two Chinese characters which make up the term *gi-ri* has been transformed as it was absorbed in Japan and does not refer to the universal 'justice' or 'reason' of its Chinese origin, but to the obligations between persons. Your obligations to others are more important than your private opinions. *Giri* is about correct relations with others.

We were constantly told that *giri* is not a contract. Indeed our friends told us that 'we have no contract between human beings'. There can be contracts with things but not with people. 'We cannot contract ourselves out.' Relations between people are recognised in documents or in other forms, but these do not make the relationship, rather they express it. 'We may look like a modern contract society, but we reluc-tantly register marriages, property ownership and so on. We don't care about registration.' Even today there are no binding contracts in the Western sense. 'We think we are modern and have contracts, but in fact we are not contractual. When we buy or borrow things, the human relationship is more important, it is beyond contract, too important for contract.'

This is one reason why there is little civil litigation. For example, divorce is usually arranged by the couple themselves, possibly with the help of friends, but lawyers are only used as a last resort. 'We Japanese have never understood the Western concept of contract,' explained an academic friend. Things and people are very different. Relations with things can have the single-dimensional form of an abstract 'contract', but with people one has to enter into a multi-layered relationship which is based on 'status' – the relative age, gender, social position of the individual and so on.

Another Japanese term used in this context and again falling on the boundary is *ninjo*. According to the *Kodansha Encyclopedia*, this term 'broadly refers to universal feelings of love, affection, pity, sympathy, sorrow, and the like, which one "naturally" feels towards others, as in relations between parent and child or between lovers'. It is the sentiment we associate with Community.

Yet *ninjo* is simultaneously the feeling which people should have, or aspire to, in the *giri* relations. *Ninjo* should be brought into human relationships to turn them from dry, dead things, into living and meaningful ones. This can create a tension, as in the Japanese expression 'getting stuck between *giri* and *ninjo*', a contradiction often explored in the tragedies written by the Shakespeare of Japan, Monzaemon Chikamatsu.

When we look at how the Japanese perceive their family, we find that we are dealing with something which refuses to be pigeon-holed into either Status or Contract. This was observed by the anthropologist Francis Hsu, struck by the difference between Japanese kinship and that of his native China. He found he had to invent a new term to catch the peculiarity, 'kin-tract' which combines kinship and contract.

In the *oyabun kobun* relationship, the basic feature is Contractual, for it is a relation between the patron and the vassal. Yet both kin and non-kin can enter into this relationship, so a close family member can both be in a blood (Status) relationship and a patron (Contractual) relationship at the same time. This is very common in Japan.

Japanese writers have pointed out that there is the concept of contract at the heart of the most Communitarian institution, that is, the family. The parent–child relationship is pure 'Community', but every other relationship begins to have an element of what is called *tanin*, which literally means 'persons with no blood relationship to oneself'. Relationships with brothers and sisters, with one's husband or wife, have an element of *tanin* in them. Hence the Japanese proverb that 'the brother is the beginning of the stranger'.

This double nature reflects the fact that what many people see as the wider kinship group, what is called the *ie*, often translated as the lineage or line, is not really a full kinship group. The word could equally well be translated as a part kin, part stranger, association. It is based on both community and association.

This has been noted by all the leading anthropologists of Japan.

The *ie* or lineage system is modelled on a set of kinship roles; it feels kinship-like. Relations within it take on the parent–child nature of kinship. It feels entirely unlike a modern bureaucratic association. Yet it is also like a business corporation in that, as Takie Lebra notes, 'Biological kinship must be sacrificed, if necessary, in the interest of the corporation'. It is at the opposite extreme to the family groups, the descent groups as they are called, of India, China and elsewhere.

The presence of a relationship which combines the emotional commitment of Community with the flexibility of recruitment implied in Association has far-reaching effects. The nearest a Western person can get to understanding what it is like is to think of a good marriage. Marriage is entered into voluntarily; it is based on a mutual contract. Yet once solemnised it binds the couple together as 'one blood and one heart' for the rest of life. It forms a real Community. This kind of contract does not apply to such an extent with marriage in Japan, but it does apply to many non-kin and non-marital relationships.

This mixture of commitment with flexibility, what Ronald Dore has called 'flexible rigidities', is one of the explanations offered for the phenomenal success of Japanese business. In the business world, neither the pure contractual market principles, nor the pure hierarchy of status relationships completely dominate. This is something which many Western people find difficult to comprehend, and another new term has had to be invented to capture this hybrid, namely 'relational contracting'. A Japanese firm feels 'family-like', workers spending their evenings together, sharing a particularly intense and emotional life, preferably for their whole working life.

In Japan there seems to be a high commitment and involvement in small groups, face to face and with deeply intertwined relationships. Yet they are not units which are given by birth or locality or even blood. Rather they are based on recruitment, an initial contract (as in a feudal oath, or joining a firm, or being adopted into an *ie* or being selected as 'the heir'). This complex hybrid, an intersection between two normally distinct, and many would have thought incompatible, bases for social interaction, is one of the many elements which makes Japan puzzling, intriguing and powerful.

It is as if people live in a constantly shifting set of communities. They are born into one and raised in warmth and great security. They then learn through life to retain the warmth and commitment in a number of different settings, at school, university and in employment. As they move into the middle period, the emotion is at its least intense, but still present. Relations are 'total' and all-encompassing with those around one. It is like living in a series of villages throughout one's life.

I had arrived in Japan thinking in terms of oppositions, a scale on which I would be able to place Japan in relation to other civilisations. These were oppositions such as individualist versus group-based, familistic versus contractual, arranged versus love marriage, egalitarian versus hierarchical, birth and blood ties versus contractual ties. What I have found is that Japan is all of these things and none of them. It does not fit on any continuum. I remain puzzled. Yet since all relations seem to have an element of power it may be that further clues will be found in 'politics' in the wider sense.

5

Power

At first sight an outside observer might think that until after the Second World War Japan was an absolutist Empire, a sort of lesser China. The Japanese Emperor combined divinity with the power that emanated from his court. Japan looked like an imperial and centralised system with unquestioning obedience demanded of its subjects and few checks and balances.

In fact, this kind of imperial system was in place for only a very short period and only in central Honshu, between the eighth and eleventh centuries. Even then, power was devolved down to ministers and subordinates to a far greater extent than in China. The imperial system then dissolved when a split occurred whereby the ceremonial power remained in Kyoto with the imperial family, while political and military power was taken by the leading general or Shogun. Between the twelfth and sixteenth centuries, a form of distributed power, what is often called feudalism, emerged in Japan. It was quite similar to the English feudal system but very different from the centralised system that was found in China.

It is during this period that Japan had its 'middle ages'. This was a disintegrated society. There were many powerful institutions, like the Emperor's court, big temples, shrines, noble houses and the local lords or *daimyo*, each with their own government. It was a mixed situation. The villagers often protected themselves by donating their land to some prestigious institution – for example, a powerful local family or temple, which in turn would allow them to gain some protection as vassals. To strengthen this, they brought their products to their wealthy patrons in Kyoto. The public forces of policing were weak; patronage was important.

The *ie* system became dominant in the later Middle Ages when the Edo Shogunate imported a neo-Confucian ideology for the governing elite. Yet the feudalism of Japan was based on different premises to that of China where the most important Confucian idea was that the family was the foundation for political loyalties. In Japan, the precedence was inverted. Loyalty to the lord came before that to relatives. Politics trumped kinship, just as it came to dominate economics and religion. This is an unusual situation, but quite like what happened in England. Contractual relations established by feudal service or the payment of dues became more important than blood ties based on birth.

Then, with the reunification of Japan in the later sixteenth century by the Tokugawa Shoguns, something similar to the unification of England under the Tudors occurred and a new form of government, what has been called 'centralised feudalism', was established. In contrast with England, however, no parliamentary system based on the middling classes emerged. The Emperor was still almost powerless, but the central power represented by the Shogun became more potent. In theory, the Shogun was a first among equals, but in practice he controlled the country through deals with a powerful set of local lords.

In the middle of the nineteenth century, looking back on the system that had evolved over the previous five hundred years, Sir Rutherford Alcock commented:

> This double machinery of a titular Sovereign who only reigns, and a Lieutenant of the empire who only governs, and does *not* reign, from generation to generation, is certainly something very curious; and by long continuance it seems to have led to a duplicate system such as never existed in any other part of the world, carried out to almost every detail of existence.

❋

What happened after the restoration of the Meiji Emperor in 1868, when the Shogun was defeated and the split between ritual and military power was ended, brings out many of the hidden peculiarities of the relation between politics and religion in Japan. This took place at a time when Japan was faced by the massive imperial might of Western governments who were poised to infiltrate it, as they had done in India, China and much of the Pacific.

In 1912, in 'The Invention of a New Religion', an article which was for long banned in Japan but later published as an appendix to his *Japanese Things*, Basil Hall Chamberlain analysed what he called 'Mikado-worship and Japan-worship'. He commented, 'The twentieth-century Japanese religion of loyalty and patriotism is quite new, for in it pre-existing ideas have been sifted, altered, freshly compounded, turned to new uses, and have found a new centre of gravity.' This invented tradition was 'still in process of being consciously or semi-consciously put together by the official class'. For this purpose, continued Chamberlain, 'Shinto, a primitive nature cult, which had fallen into discredit, was taken out of its cupboard and dusted.' The officials insisted that the Emperor was descended in direct succession from the native Goddess of the Sun, and that all 'such things as laws and constitutions are but free gifts on His part, not in any sense popular rights'.

The new system was enforced in particular through education. History was taught so as 'to focus everything upon Imperialism, and to diminish as far as possible the contrast between ancient and modern conditions'. Much of Japanese history was suppressed. Chamberlain noted that many Emperors had been deposed, assassinated or exiled. There were even rival emperors for fifty-eight years in the fourteenth century, after which point the Emperor had been merely a pawn in the hands of the Shoguns.

As for the warrior code which was supposed to back up this Shinto Emperor ideology, the 'way of the warrior' or *bushi-do*, Chamberlain wrote, 'The very word appears in no dictionary, native or foreign, before the year 1900...*Bushido*, as an institution or a code of rules, has never existed. The accounts given of it have been fabricated out of whole cloth, chiefly for foreign consumption.' It becomes clear that the Emperor religion, and much of the ideology which underpinned the Japanese drive towards modernisation and industrialisation and which led, fatally, into its involvement in the Second World War, was an invented belief.

Following several discussions with leading political scientists in Japan, and from summaries of their recent publications, I was able to piece together a picture of what had happened. The Iwakura Mission of 1871–3 to the United States and Europe was designed to study how Western societies were organised so that the best ideas could be brought back to Japan. On their trip to America, the future leaders of the early Meiji government spent much time discussing what they should say their religion was when questioned by Westerners. They felt embarrassed not to have 'a religion' and annoyed by the thought of the awkwardness ahead.

Buddhism was mainly an instrument of power and most of the religious aspects of Shinto were forgotten by the mid-Tokugawa period, though some of the external ritual remained. The Japanese, who were so secular at the end of the Edo period, were shocked and embarrassed to discover that Western people might really believe in Christianity. From their point of view, to be a Christian was just silly and superstitious. They wondered why intelligent civilised Westerners had adopted Christianity as their religion – there must be some secret. Their assumption was that Western leaders had devised it as a tool for controlling the common people, while they themselves only pretended to believe.

On their return, as they began to draft the Meiji constitution, the future leaders reflected further and concluded that a functional counterpart to religion was needed in Japan to ensure its stability: without this the country would fall apart. They decided that the 'loyal family' system of Shinto was the best fitted for the purpose, but that the role of the Emperor should be emphasised with a kind of Emperor worship, which would provide a functional substitute for Christianity. As a result, the Meiji Constitution (chapter 1, clause 1) as a scholar friend paraphrased it for us, stated that 'Japan was governed by the *Tenno* [Emperor] who had a straight trunk line or connection from the ancient times to the present day'. The 'Rescript of Education' became the equivalent of the Christian 'Lord's Prayer' and had to be memorised by all students. A small chapel was erected in each elementary school where the portrait of the Emperor was placed and the Rescript was read out. It was essential to bow to the portrait, and refusal to bow low enough was considered sacrilegious.

Yet this lead to a dilemma for the Japanese intellectuals. They never believed in the imperial family itself, for everyone knew it was weak and fragile and had little power to attract people. Nor did they believe in the mythical origins of the *Tenno* family. Yet they had to pretend. Probably they thought that although the Emperor myth was silly, it was not as silly as Christianity.

In some ways the Japanese adopted the strategy advocated by the French sociologist Emile Durkheim at exactly the same time. A secularised Jew who had lost his faith, Durkheim had been searching for something that would hold society together when kinship and formal religion had become very weak. He found his solution in the elementary forms of religion practised by the Australian aborigines in their totemic rituals. Society worshipped itself, projecting itself upwards, and then saw its reflection as an external mandate for the social order.

Based on an invented Shintoism, the intellectuals constructed the Emperor as God, a shamanic descendant of the ancient gods. Before the Second World War, many people talked of the Emperor as if he was organically linked to the gods. People were taught that the ancestor of the *Tenno* was the ancestor of the whole Japanese nation.

The Emperor was not just a system but a kind of religion which influenced every aspect of Japanese life. *Tenno* religion, in other words belief in the Emperor, was associated with the ancient shrine at Ise. It was a collective feeling, a focus of affection, warmth and unity, providing social solidarity. Yet attempts to export the system to its new colonies Korea or Manchuria failed miserably. Even in Japan, Emperor Worship ended up as a hopeless and delusory strategy, just as a European fascist ideology finally failed.

When we asked a distinguished political theorist if ordinary people believed in the Emperor myth, he replied that it was very hard to tell. He had questioned his mother about this and she had replied that her head was compartmentalised; 'this is this', and 'that is that'. She did recall that when she was a high school student she had got on a tram car which drove in front of the imperial palace. Everyone on the tram was ordered to bow to the palace, which she did. But inside she thought that maybe the Emperor was in the toilet, so it was a bit silly. Yet she could never say anything. He thought that many people might be in a similar situation to that of the Russian people during the Soviet regime – they knew what they had to say, though there was cynicism and private doubt.

Looked at from afar, Japan has swung back and forth between the two ends of the pole. It has elements of the contractual, feudal, distribution of powers system of England, or the fifteenth-century Italian city states. These are combined with other elements of the divine kingship, court-based, absolutist model of the Chinese emperors, Russian czars or Turkish sultans. Japan pulses back and forth, never really becoming fully one or the other. 'Delegation is practised to such a degree of diffusion,' wrote Kurt Singer, 'that responsibility cannot be located with tolerable certainty. Monarchical, democratic and aristocratic elements are mixed so subtly as to make the body politic shine in every colour of the rainbow.' In some ways, since the Japanese

Emperor was never under the controlling mandate of heaven, he was in theory far more absolutist than even the Chinese Emperor. In practice, his effective power was slight and he was largely a symbolic and empty centre to the vastly interconnected and distributed system of downward and upward flows of power.

The strange style of the contemporary Japanese political system, which has the surface of imposed Western democratic ideas, but underneath seems to be of another world, is partly explained by this tension. In 1917 Yukio Ozaki wrote:

> The customs and usages of feudal times are so deeply impressed upon the minds of men here that even the idea of political parties, as it enters the brains of our countrymen, is influenced by feudal notions. Such being the case, even political parties, which should be based and dissolved solely on principles and political views, are really affairs of personal connections and sentiments, the relations between the leader and the members of a party being similar to those which subsisted between a feudal lord and his liegemen.

Many who have studied the one-party domination in Japan over the last half-century would agree with the anthropologist Fosco Maraini's observation that 'one soon finds that the Japanese version of democracy is very different from what goes under this name in countries with British and American traditions ... democracy has been very much Japanized, rather than Japan having turned genuinely democratic.' For example, our friends told us that most Japanese vote on the basis of very limited knowledge and understanding, and without much interest in relation to political ideology. There is no real basis for democracy, with the opposition parties too weak and compromising to make it a proper democratic system. The closest the political system comes to behaving like a democracy is the alternation of factions within the Liberal Democratic Party, which, certainly until the recent past at least, changed the style of the party without providing a real alternative.

One of the main functions of politics seems to be to funnel the vast wealth of Japan out from the centre to the periphery, a 'pork-barrel' system which exceeds even that of America. 'In return for electoral support,' comments Yoshio Sugimoto, 'members of parliament are expected to bring government-supported construction projects, railways, and trunk roads into their constituencies in order to expand their *jiban* [solid blocks of voters].'

The Japanese political system is another type, which does not fit into any of our classifications. The design is, as the modern economist Robert Ozaki comments, 'neither dictatorial, centralised, nor decentralised. It is more of a collective-mutual-assistance system.' It has worked since the middle of the twentieth century essentially as a one-party democracy, which is a contradiction in terms. Most decisions are taken by unelected officials and policy is made through deals between factions who never come out into the open. Yet Japan is not a dictatorship and it has delivered a large measure of economic and social prosperity.

It is undoubtedly the case that if anything has underpinned Japanese civilisation over the last thousand years it has been political power. Power is everywhere, radiating out like a spider's web from the centre, yet also widely distributed to the lower levels. At times Japan reminds me of the way politics works in societies where there is no formal leader or head of state. Such societies are held together by balanced oppositions between the constituent units based on kinship ties. Japan has traditionally enjoyed a system of 'ordered anarchy', as these systems are often termed. As a Japanese diplomat described it to Singer, 'You will find in Japan what I should like to call "unity in disorder" in more than one sense.'

The paradoxes came out in one of many discussions I had with Kenichi and Toshiko. Japan, we agreed, is like a tribal society, based on quasi-familial relations. It is made up of segments, self-organised. People were traditionally united by facing inwards towards the Emperor. If they faced away from him, it was a sign of rebellion.

The Emperor's position was like that of the Leopard Skin Chief of the Nuer people described by the anthropologist Edward Evans-Pritchard: formally powerless, yet endowed with authority. Before the seventh century, the Emperor's family had not been the most powerful clan in Japan. Yet partly for this very reason it had become ritually and emotionally the centre. It was paradoxically the weakness of the Emperor that held the rest together. For this reason the Shogunate had no need to destroy the Emperor system, but could profit from allowing it to continue alongside the military power as a focus for unity. Likewise, the Emperor system could be revived and manipulated by later politicians to provide a symbolic and emotional focus for the Japanese.

One particularly critical picture of the 'authoritarian bureaucratic state' is provided by Karel Van Wolferen in *The Enigma of Japanese Power*. He describes an elusive and yet all-encompassing system of hidden power. There is no apparent centre; this is a 'Stateless Nation' as he calls it in the subtitle to his book. The 'system', as he terms it, effectively, if somewhat indirectly, controls education, the press, television and much of life. Van Wolferen argues that it stands above law and democratic politics, enforces great conformity and stifles dissent. Yet it is precisely this diffused power which lies behind the amazing achievement of Japan in its peace and prosperity.

When I was shivering in my 'traditional' Tokyo house and wanted to borrow the redundant heater from my university department office, I was astonished to learn that I would need permission, not from the Head of Department, but from a bureaucrat in the university office. I learnt that the university was not full of professors and heads, with free and delegated powers, but that every one of them was a civil servant. It was a bureaucratic organisation with hardly any autonomy.

On my various visits I had frequently been taken to visit rooms full of 'officials' who were stamping and processing documents. I could not recall anything like this in Cambridge, which was, until recently, run by a small handful of administrators together with a large number of academics.

It is well known that nowadays it is the bureaucracy, the powerful ministries, which are central to the running of Japan. It is not so much a parliamentary democracy as a one-party bureaucratic system. As Chamberlain wrote in the early twentieth century, 'Viewed from an Anglo-Saxon point of view, the Japanese are a much-governed people, officials being numerous, their authority great, and all sorts of things which with us are left to private enterprise being here in the hands of government.'

The complex bureaucracy reflects two ancient features of Japanese history. One is the way in which power is always divided and balanced. 'The chief feature in the old Japanese political system was its tendency to dualism', wrote William Griffis, 'The division of the people into soldiers and farmers, and of officers into civil and military ...' acts as a check on power and corruption, even if it slows everything down. Alcock notes:

> Every office doubled; every man is alternately a watcher and watched. Not only the whole administrative machinery is in duplicate, but the most elaborate system of check and counter-check, on the most approved Machiavellian principle, is here developed with a minute-ness and perfection as regards details, difficult at first to realise.

Then there is a vertical organisation of power, starting very early in Japan and reinforced by the feudal ties of loyalty, which means that power is delegated downwards, and then moves up again through the personal links that join everyone in an organisation. Any decision tends to be taken by a group, or a line of people, and hence there is often a great deal of bureaucracy involved – meetings, counter-stamping, negotiation. In some ways, particularly after it incorporated much late nineteenth-century German bureaucratic organisation, Japan feels like the most bureaucratic nation on earth.

Yet if we look at the history of Japan rather than its present organisa-tion, we have a sense of something different and much more akin to the English experience. After all, this was a system of feudal diffusion of power. Japan traditionally had very few, if any, professionally trained bureaucrats, no Confucian examination system, and no class of full-time administrators. Power was wielded in theory by warriors, *daimyo* and *samurai*, who combined their status as men of military prowess and aesthetic discrimination with a certain amount of administra-tion. Decisions were largely taken at the local level and not imposed by a large bureaucracy at the centre.

There was no huge court paraphernalia devoted to writing and collation, as in China. It is true that the beginnings of such a system are described in early accounts of the Chinese-influenced phase of the eighth to eleventh centuries when we hear of the Minis-tries of the Left and the Right, but this was destroyed from the eleventh century onwards and an imperial bureaucratic system did not reassert itself.

We can see this reflected in other areas, for example the justice system, which until the later nineteenth century was largely decen-tralised in Japan. Or again in the economy, which was not centrally planned or monitored in the way which was attempted in France or China. Or even in religion, no bureaus of rites, no Catholic church, which tried to impose a uniform set of beliefs and practices. There was indirect supervision, but not direct control.

For three-quarters of the last twelve hundred years of their history, the Japanese have been a notable example, as was England for roughly the same period, of a deviation from centralised bureaucracy. All this is changing fast in both the West and Japan, yet we cannot understand the present odd mixtures in Britain, America and Japan if we do not recognise how the paths to the present have been different from the majority of centralised states.

Considering the advantages and disadvantages of bureaucratic centralisation, the political thinker Alexis de Tocqueville expressed the conviction that distributed, unbureaucratic power led to far more innovation, spontaneity, involvement in decision-making, and checks and balances to the corruption of power. He saw the French system that had evolved as a nightmare of uniformity and waste which should be avoided at all costs. The ghastly bureaucracies of Stalinist Russia or Maoist China, building on earlier traditions, would have confirmed him in his fears.

In this context it is refreshing to encounter a civilisation at the other side of the world that for long periods sustained an alternative to the bureaucratic systems which seem almost inevitably to have engulfed all empires and all continental nations. Furthermore the way in which it works is different, for, as Singer wrote, 'Japanese bureaucracy is characterised by a much greater freedom from mechanised discipline, abstract and universal rules and rigid unification than most Western counterparts. Every ministry seems to move according to its own house traditions, conserving a large measure of quasi-medieval corporative autonomy.'

In terms of its educational and literary achievements, certain things stand out which can place Japan either at the forefront or as a latecomer. On the plus side is the fact that, from at least the seventeenth century, the literacy rates and the levels of the publishing and reading of books have been extremely high. Compared to any Western country, for example eighteenth-century France or England, Japan was well ahead. It had a network of public libraries and a famous literary tradition.

I remember sitting watching young Japanese children playing a card game which involved them knowing a good deal about the several dozen women writers of the eighth to the twelfth centuries. How many well-known women writers of the period before the fourteenth century (or after) could modern English or French children tell us anything about?

The printing and circulation of books was immense. A dictionary, originally compiled around 1444, went into some 800 editions between the late sixteenth and late eighteenth century. By the late seventeenth century Kyoto booksellers were publishing catalogues of their wood-block printed works, one of which ran to 674 pages, with 7,800 titles listed. By 1720 there were 200 publishers in Kyoto alone. There were numerous private libraries and people went around the streets with huge packs of books for sale on their back, in effect one-man circulating bookshops.

The middle classes were avid readers. Charles Macfarlane wrote, 'It is said that few sights are more common in Japan, during the sunny seasons of the year, than that of a group of ladies and gentlemen seated by a cool, running stream, or in a shady grove, each with a book in hand.' Schooling was almost universal by the early nineteenth century. Macfarlane continues, 'From the highest down to the very lowest, every Japanese is sent to school. It is said that there are more schools in the empire than in any other country in the world, and that all the peasants and poor people can, at least, read.'

This is the background for the high literary skills developed by the middle of the twentieth century when David Riesman reported, 'Eighty per cent of the Japanese, including farmers and workers, write *haiku* [short, condensed poems].' It is difficult to imagine any other society in the middle of the twentieth century, or even today, when four-fifths of the population would be writing poetry as a normal activity.

What is extraordinary, given the proximity of China, is that the Japanese did not use these skills as the basis for administrative and political power. The competitive Confucian examination system, which made skills in reading and writing the classics the criterion for promotion in the Mandarin system, was never imported into Japan.

Unlike with the Mandarins, the Brahmins of India or the medieval church-men in Europe, literacy, though generally valued, was not the badge of a separate ruling elite. Japan, while having one of the greatest literary traditions in the world and the widest use of reading and writing, remained a curiously oral culture in its law and admin-istration, often with a distinctive anti-intellectualism among its ruling elite.

A second feature which may be related to this as both cause and effect is the absence of universities in Japan. Universities were one of the glories of Europe from the Middle Ages, but there was nothing equivalent in Japan. In about 670 a sort of university had been founded, administered by the ministry for ceremonials as an elite school for training top officials, but it never developed into a full university system. There were Buddhist monasteries, and, in the nine-teenth century, a few small technical schools. By the middle of the eighteenth century there were many private teachers and groups of students in the central part of Tokyo where the university would later flourish. Yet institutions with financial endowments, dedicated to the pursuit of knowledge and the teaching of young adults were not to be found. There was nothing equivalent to Bologna, Paris, Oxford or Cambridge.

Literacy was largely confined to the field of literature. The 'liberal arts' and mathematics, medicine, optics and other subjects which became areas of intense study and teaching in Western universities, were left to individuals to engage in. There was no systematic, funded, organisational study. It was only in the later nineteenth century, for instance, with the founding of the first private Western-style university by Fukuzawa at Keio, that this aspect of education developed.

Japan is one of the most peaceful, non-violent, large civilisations of which we know. Buddhism and Shinto demand no shedding of blood in their rituals and teach respect and love for others, as does Confucianism. Meeting individual Japanese I feel far less aggression or threat than I do from people in many other civilisations.

The Japanese took up gunpowder weapons from the Portuguese in the sixteenth century, but then their use was increasingly limited. Between about 1637 and 1837, Japan was the most peaceful, least war-infected of nations. For many centuries the European states were tearing each other apart in almost perpetual wars. They then conquered half the planet with fire and sword, exterminating the majority of the remaining tribal peoples on the way. Meanwhile the Japanese did not have a single war, internal or external.

It is true that at this time the samurai still strode around with their two swords and the martial codes were still emphasised. Yet there was peace. Gun crimes have been practically unknown in Japan in recent years, and even today the Japanese criminal organisations generally forbid the carrying of guns. Japan has officially renounced nuclear weapons. Its present constitution bans the development of an offensive army or navy, although it has developed a formidable self-defence force.

The American visitor Edward Morse tells us in a number of vignettes what Japan felt like in the middle of the nineteenth century:

> For sixty-six miles rumbling along in rather a rattle-trap wagon, not a
> sight or a sound was encountered that was not peaceful and refined: the
> gentleness and courtesy of the country people, the economy, frugality
> and simplicity of living! ... Here I was with a hundred dollars in my

pocket, travelling at night, through dark bamboo thickets and some poverty-stricken villages, having a single *jinrikisha* [wheeled small carriage pulled by hand] man, now and then meeting a traveller, sometimes a crowd of travellers, and I was never spoken to. I had no pistol, no cane even, and yet so assured was I of the gentle character of the people that I did not feel the slightest apprehension.

Yet all of us know that there is a different side to Japan. There is a striking contrast between the widespread gentleness and artistic sensitivity of the Japanese and the well-documented periods of brutality and apparent sadism which have horrified many people in Asia and elsewhere. The Japanese were brutal in early forays. In their war against Korea, in the late sixteenth century, they collected noses from their enemies, pickling them in salt to be inspected by their generals. When they encountered the warships and imperial expansion of Western powers in the nineteenth century, the lesson that they must be tough was reinforced. Griffis summarised how it must have been for the Japanese to be at the receiving end of Western expansion: 'For a land impoverished and torn, for the miseries of a people compelled by foreigners, for the sake of their cursed dollars, to open their country, what sympathy? For their cholera and vile diseases, their defiling immorality, their brutal violence, their rum, what benefits in return?'

As a result, the Japanese emulated the West and built battleships, tanks and planes and became one of the most formidable fighting nations in history. They modelled their army on the Prussian war machine in the nineteenth century, and from the 1930s learnt new lessons from Germany. As Singer writes, 'That Nazi Germany, which adopted Bolshevist terror methods in fighting internal and external enemies, was the teacher of Japanese army leaders would go far to explain why Japanese soldiers could be accused of having committed inhuman deeds on a scale unknown in former Japanese warfare.'

They also learnt a great deal from Britain. While the Japanese army and fighting methods were modelled on Germany, the British Royal Navy was the model on which the Japanese navy was built. British personnel were employed by the Japanese to advise and train their sailors, and a number of the early warships were constructed in British shipyards.

When the Japanese decided to annex eastern Asia in the Pacific war, many Westerners were touched by a violence and brutality which can partly be seen as a boomerang from the violence of the West. Several of my close relatives were involved in the battles against the Japanese troops in Burma and Assam in the Second World War.

From this experience alone it would not be difficult to persuade people that Japan is one of the most warlike civilisations in history. Its core seems to be warlike and it has lived by its famous sword. Yet there is still something mysterious about the rapid switching from extreme gentleness to extreme violence. The contrast is well caught in a description by the early nineteenth-century doctor William Willis:

> In reality the bulk of Japanese are peace loving and very indisposed to violence, but in certain cases a kind of madness for destruction seizes certain individuals. I have seen the following: a quiet man suddenly with slight provocation cuts with a sword severely his neighbour ... then cuts his wife into quarters, then cuts half the head off his child and finally disembowels himself.

Nor is it entirely a 'kind of madness', but rather a tradition of total dedication to the task in hand, including what appears to be an extraordinary level of suppression of all human feeling. Lafcadio Hearn wrote:

> The samurai, before going into a hopeless contest, sometimes killed his wife and children the better to forget those three things no warrior should remember on the battle-field, — namely, home, the dear ones,

and his own body. After that act of ferocious heroism the samurai was ready for the *shinimono-gurui*, – the hour of the 'death-fury,' – giving and taking no quarter.

The Japanese are thus more peaceful or more warlike and violent than almost any other large civilisation. How we regard them partly depends on who we compare them with. If we take China as our vantage point, we can see that there are some similarities between the two nations. China also had a Confucian ethic of harmony, love and, for long periods, almost absolute peace within its vast territories. Yet they differ in terms of their attitudes to war.

The Chinese were certainly warlike during long periods of their history, with huge armies numbering hundreds of thousands fighting pitched battles. Yet for long periods they also tried to contain war. Once the vast Han absorption had taken place, they were notably modest in their imperial ambition. They raided neighbours and those whom they had for long considered to be tributary subordinates, in particular Vietnam, Tibet and Korea. Yet China is the only world civilisation I know of which does not have warriors as one of its major social orders. There is no equivalent to the *kshatrya* of India, the knights of Europe or the *samurai* of Japan. There are only the unarmed Mandarin literati.

Looked at from China, the Japanese seem warlike. Yet measured against the bloodstained and violent history of Western Europe, that of Japan appears relatively non-violent and peaceful.

The Japanese I have talked to find it as puzzling as the rest of us. They know that when they are roused to anger, they can be emotional and irrational. Even without anger, their iron loyalties and conviction of the innate excellence of their civilisation can lead them to treat others as inferior. They find it difficult to apologise for acts that cause deep offence. No one feels personally responsible, and apologies are meaningless. The fact that certain officials in the Ministry of

Education have sought to censor descriptions of Japanese atrocities during the Second World War in history textbooks, is a sensitive issue between Japan and its neighbours, and they appear to show little awareness of the effects of an apparent attempt to whitewash the past. This has been exacerbated by a recent Prime Minister who continued to visit the war-shrine where many Class A Japanese war criminals are remembered.

As Masao Maruyama pointed out very forcefully, because of the system of distributed responsibility, no one will admit that they took the decisions which led to the horrors of the Second World War:

> An uncertain sharing of responsibility was preferred so that no one person could be pointed out as bearing the ultimate responsibility for decisions. It is obvious that the mechanism of the Emperor-system state had inherent within it the danger of developing into a colossal system of irresponsibility.

Maruyama's brilliant essay on the war crimes tribunal gives many examples of Japanese generals and other high-ranking officers who said that they knew from the start that the war was a hopeless venture and Japan would lose.

We are told by Robert Ozaki that 'an expression that widely circulated in Japan right after World War II was the "collective penitence of all one hundred million Japanese" – who were presumably responsible for the crime and tragedy of the war'. The war is also seen as something that was inevitable and to a certain extent externally caused. Van Wolferen quotes from the *Asahi Shimbun*, the leading Japanese newspaper which stated, 'Fortunately at the end, Japan could escape from war.' 'War in this perspective,' he comments, ' is like an earthquake or a typhoon, an "act of nature" that takes people by surprise.' He quotes a Japanese intellectual who wrote of the China war: 'Seen from the outside, Japan appeared to be invading China with imperialist intentions. Seen from the inside, however, most political leaders felt that Japan was being dragged into the swamp of war as part of some inevitable process.'

There is evidence, too, of a rather strikingly unfamiliar view of why Japan invaded China in the first place. A chilling example of this is the deposition of General Matsui Iwane during the war-crimes tribunal:

> It has been my belief during all these years that we must regard this struggle as a method of making the Chinese undergo self-reflection. We do not do this because we hate them, but on the contrary because we love them too much. It is just the same as in a family when an elder brother has taken all that he can stand from his ill-behaved younger brother and has to chastise him in order to make him behave properly.

This is a patronising and arrogant attitude which might well have come out of the mouth of many imperialists through the ages, with some elements of the 'white man's burden' and the schoolmasterly admonition before a beating – 'This hurts me more than it hurts you'. There is also something here akin to the idea, prevalent in some of the new Japanese cults, that it is better to destroy someone rather than let them sink under bad 'karma'.

Yet the Japanese point to the ambivalences of British, German, Italian or Spanish twentieth-century history, where periods of extreme sophistication and pacifism are interspersed with periods of militarisation and the creation of concentration camps. What the Japanese do know well enough is that humans are not one thing or another, neither peaceful nor aggressive. As each of us remembers from our childhood, a thin veneer of reason and kindness can cover deep negative emotions and anger which at times burst through.

The Japanese live in a landscape where the gentle beauties of the blossoms and the moon can suddenly be replaced by chaos and destruction – a *tsunami*, volcano or earthquake. So it has been in their history: long periods of quiet, and then a bloody episode. The quiet contemplation and serenity turn overnight into marauding armies cutting off Korean noses, or the massacres at Nanking, or horrific experiments with germ warfare in Manchuria, or death marches and terrible prisoner-of-war camps. Yet they also suffered nuclear bombs unleashed on two of their cities and the fire-bombing of Tokyo and other cities, with a fortitude and absence of desire for revenge which is surprising.

It is a feature of tribal societies that internally they are often peaceful and people behave gently towards each other. Yet in order to survive in a world without an overarching state, they present towards neighbouring tribes a warlike and ferocious front. The Nagas of Assam are an example of this. Living in a gentle and peaceable way within their own villages, they were also traditionally ferocious head-hunters, their victims often from nearby villages. It is likewise, it seems, with the Japanese, who are internally peaceful, yet outwardly bristling and aggressive.

It is another characteristic of many tribal societies that when they engage in war against foreign tribes, they consider themselves to be real, full, human beings, and their enemies by definition 'non-humans', not part of their tribe, incomprehensible and somehow lacking true humanity. The enormous cruelty and destruction associated with the wandering tribes of the central steppes, the Huns and later the Mongols, are well known. If a city or valley refused immediately to surrender, unimaginable devastation was wreaked on it. This was total war, kill or be killed. There was no room for mercy or for a recognition that real people were being killed or tortured.

At times the Japanese have appeared to behave in the same way when they ventured out of their islands. In the nineteenth century they watched the vicious and, to them hypocritical and cruel, behaviour of Western imperialists and concluded that war was merely a matter of might. The victor took all. There was massive destruction and no surrender. This seemed to be the way of war – and this is how they chose to wage war. They 'cheated', bombing Pearl Harbor on a Sunday and without warning. They starved prisoners of war or bayoneted them in hospitals. They behaved as if the purpose of war was just to win, with whatever method was appropriate.

The Japanese were slow to go to war, but when they did, it was total. Ozaki writes:

> Particularly with respect to wars against foreign states, they long remained almost totally inexperienced ... In pre-modern Japanese history, peace – not war – was the norm. There developed in the Japanese mind a consciousness that a full-fledged war is something extraordinary and abnormal, something that suggests desperation, utmost gravity, and inevitable death.

Or, as our friends explained, 'For the Japanese war is a last resort. They are slow to go to war, but when they do, it is total war, with no quarter given. For Westerners, war seems to be a game. For the Japanese, there is no surrender. They could not understand the limited war of the West.' They starved and tortured their prisoners partly because they thought that those they had captured, particularly if they had surrendered, had thereby betrayed their warrior honour. They had not taken the path of death and had thereby forfeited their humanity and any right to be treated as humans.

Yet they were not unaware of the importance of seeming to abide by Western attitudes to the treatment of prisoners. They built a showcase camp for Russian prisoners of war in Matsuyama and treated them reasonably to suggest to Western diplomats that Japan was a civilised country and Russia was not, but the conditions were far worse in another more secret camp in Sakhalin.

The Japanese did not appreciate the fine and shifting distinctions of Western warfare, of the Geneva Convention, of the idea that you could firebomb Dresden or slaughter innocents in their thousands, but also had to treat prisoners with a minimum degree of humanity. The Westerners who argued that they played by the rules were duly shocked to meet in the twentieth century another set of people who behaved as the Christians had done towards peoples they had enslaved or colonised in the past, or as the Huns and Mongols had done before them.

The theme of inexperience is often stressed by those we talked to, particularly in comparison to other imperial nations in the West. The British learnt over centuries of fighting and Empire how to limit violence and contain it. When the Japanese suddenly erupted onto the Asian mainland they had no such experience. They tried to force their new-found subjects to become Japanese, as in Korea, and to adopt their language and culture as well as their laws and politics. In this way they acted more like the Spanish or Portuguese, and later the French, in earlier centuries.

Islanders tend to think of themselves as a separate race. The English have done so, though the presence of Wales and Scotland has somewhat diluted this insularity. The Japanese, long isolated and with a larger population, have tended to create a strong myth of uniqueness in relation to other peoples.

For many centuries Japan was overshadowed by China. It might have asserted that it was the equal of China, but it was clear where superiority in invention, numbers and wealth lay. By the later nine-teenth century, however, things were changing as China's weakness and divisions under pressure from the rapid imperial and industrial expansion of Europe and America became apparent.

Partly reflecting Western racial categories, Yukichi Fukuzawa first divided the world into four 'kinds'. The lowest were the aborigines of Australia, New Guinea and others. Then there were the nomadic peoples such as those of Mongolia and Arabia. The third were the peoples of Asiatic countries such as China, Turkey, Persia and Japan. The highest kind was the Western nations such as

America, England, France and Germany, whom Japan should aspire to emulate. A few years later he replaced this by a three-level model, 'barbarous', 'half-civilised' and 'civilised'. The Chinese and Japanese were in the middle.

When the Japanese defeated China and then Russia in two wars at the turn of the twentieth century, the ranking was changed. Japan was now in the top stratum, and other civilisations were inferior. It is quite clear from contemporary events and literature that in the first half of the twentieth century the Japanese felt, as the English did, that their imperial ambitions were based on racial superiority, the 'yellow man's burden' to bring civilisation to the inferior peoples of East Asia.

As with almost all racially based empires in history, if the barbarous peoples whose enlightenment and reform was undertaken resisted, they were treated with harshness. This background is, of course, exacerbated during war. If one is going to kill a person, it helps if one regards them as less than fully human. Unlike the French and Germans, who, through their shared Christian faith, could, in theory, remain human to each other when they were enemies, some Japanese could behave towards their enemies as if they were non-human, as the Germans did to the Jews. The difference in the treatment of Westerners and Indians or Chinese in the Japanese prisoner-of-war camps shows racism in action.

Nor was the division of people into 'humans' and 'lesser humans' only applied to those who lived outside Japan. The attitude towards the native Ainu, towards the *hinin* branch of the *burakumin* [outcasts], and even to a considerable extent to the Korean immigrants, showed a continuing set of strong social divisions.

Some older Japanese who lived through the Second World War worry about the fact that many younger Japanese seem to be forgetting what happened. They note the growing arguments of those who wish to increase offensive military capability, or to revise the post-war pacifist arrangements. Yet they also point out that the Japanese constitution is still one of the most peaceful in the world and they have some confidence that Japanese overseas aggression is unlikely, at least in the next generation or two.

If we contrast the confrontational Western legal systems of Anglo-American law with the conciliatory processes to be found in many tribal societies, Japan falls decidedly on the side of the tribal, 'non-modern', reconciliatory, re-integrating, context dependent type. Traditionally, individuals did not have innate rights of any kind, only obligations to others. As the twentieth-century historian George Sansom wrote, 'So unfamiliar was the concept of the rights of the individual subject that in purely Japanese legal writings there is no term which closely corresponds to the word "rights" as expressing something which is due to a person and which he can claim.' Consequently, he continued, the Japanese had to invent a new word to try to match the Western idea of 'rights', the 'compound word *kenri*, made up of *ken*, meaning "power" or "influence" and *ri*, meaning "interest".'

In Japan, reconciliation, mediation and arbitration are more highly valued than court-based decisions. Harmony, not the breaking of relations, is the goal. Law, like the economy, is embedded in continuing social relations. Singer writes:

> Law has not yet emerged from the stream of common life as a sphere of its own ... Between law and custom, habit and convention, order of nature and order of reason, natural inclination and social duty, no rigid demarcation lines are drawn. Everything remains contingent on circumstances, subject to swift transition.

Litigation, criminal or civil, is avoided as much as possible. The small number of lawyers, the relatively low number of civil and criminal cases, the many-year delays by the judges in coming to decisions, are all very different from the West, and particularly

America. The Japanese legal system is based on trust, multi-stranded relations, and different status positions. It is not a competitive battle of equal individuals before the judge. It is a ritual more than a boxing match, joining rather than separating.

Once again, the surface, which suggests an Anglo-American legal system, and what is below, are very different. The surface enrols thousands of young Japanese to train as lawyers in the universities each year. Yet the distaste for legal cases means that there would be nothing for them to do if they qualified. Consequently something like 90 per cent are failed in their final bar exams and are turned away from practising. This is not the end of their career, for there are many other jobs for them. But they are not needed, as they would be in the West, to provide the oil that lubricates a competitive and confrontational system of the kind we are familiar with. The ability to run one of the most sophisticated industrial market economies in the world with an astonishingly low level of law-suits is a singular achievement.

The next time you are stopped by a Japanese policeman, whether you are guilty or not, confess your fault, do not argue, and you will probably be released with a caution. And if you feel that your individual rights have been trampled on by others, bend and do not go to court. Harmony and deference come before abstract ideas of guilt and innocence.

Japan is now one of the leading industrial capitalist countries in the world. It is widely held to be an economic miracle, emerging twice to dominate Asia. Yet this miracle has been achieved without leading to those two banes of almost all other advanced industrial societies: high and rising crime rates and an epidemic of civil litigation.

Starting with the puzzle of Japanese crime, the situation is summed up by Lawrence Beer: 'Japan's system of criminal justice is effective and only rarely severe. The crime rate is very low, and Japan is a physically safe country in which to live.' The case is impressive, as can be seen from comparative figures for Western countries and Japan. For example, comparable figures in the 1980s showed that Japan had around 1.3 robberies per 100,000 people, while the US had 233 and England 65. The Japanese murder rate was just over 1 per 100,000, while that of the US was over 8 per 100,000. For most of the period since 1960 the rate of violent and other crimes has increased throughout the industrialised world, except in Japan where it decreased until about 1990. From then on it increased until about 2003, when it started to drop again.

We might, of course, be inclined to explain away these startling figures by suggesting that there is massive under-reporting. It would appear that this is not so. There have been a number of victimisation surveys which show that in Japan, while many crimes, especially minor ones, are not reported to the police, the official figures are generally achieved with the same margin of error as those recorded in America. The relatively low Japanese rates are not a statistical illusion.

Qualitative evidence bears out the figures. When the American lawyer J. H. Wigmore visited Japan in the 1930s, he found a general peacefulness and happiness of society there, noting: 'One can see in New York in one night such exhibitions of violence, brawling, and abandoned lawlessness as one would not see in an entire year in Tokyo.' When we first went to Japan in 1990 the British Council sent me notes on what I needed to know as a visitor. Among other things, we were told that 'Japanese cities, including Tokyo, are entirely safe to walk in, alone, at all hours of the day and night.' We have found this to be so during all of our visits.

There is other evidence of relative tranquillity. Many local studies throughout Japan bear out the absence of crime. In the 1980s, guns were reported as being present in less than twenty crimes a year in Tokyo. The only legal handguns, apart from those issued to the police, were in the possession of members of the Olympic shooting team. Hard-drug use is a minor problem and has been in decline for many years.

This very low crime rate is not easy to explain. Nowadays it does not seem to result from the fear of harsh legal penalties, though certainly in the past the punishments were savage. Compared to the United States, Japan's sentences are lighter in every category of crime, except for homicide where capital punishment is possible (about three people per year are executed).

Suspended sentences are meted out extensively, as are small fines after cautioning. As a result, few offenders are sent to prisons or juvenile training schools. John Hayley writes that, in the 1980s, 'less than two per cent of all those convicted of a crime ever served a jail sentence in Japan as compared with more than 45 per cent in the United States'. The prison sentences are also very short. Almost half of them are for one year or less, while in America only 4 per cent are for such short periods. It is thus not surprising to find that the Japanese prison population is low and falling.

Nor can the low prison population be explained by the inefficiency of the Japanese police or prosecution system. In both respects, the figures are also remarkable. A survey quoted by Hayley in 1992 suggested that the Japanese police solve 57 per cent of reported cases, as compared to the 20 per cent by the American police, and the clearance rate for violent crimes against the person is 92 per cent in Japan, against 43.7 per cent in the US. Once criminals have been caught, the rate of convictions of those brought to court is extraordinary. Conviction rates are variously estimated at 99 per cent of all cases that go to trial, though this may partly be due to heavy-handed methods by the police.

Yet if a person is imprisoned for a serious offence, he or she is deemed to be cast out of society. There is little idea that prisons should be remedial. Our friends were amazed to hear that English prisoners could take degrees in prison, or watch television. Conditions in Japanese prisons are pretty harsh, with strict discipline and forced labour.

It may well be that the general absence of crime is partly related to the system of mutual surveillance which was developed over the centuries in Japan. This was described by many European visitors. Philipp von Siebold, in the early nineteenth century, commented:

> No one can change his residence without a certificate of good conduct from the inhabitants of the vicinage he wishes to leave, and permission to come among them from those of the street to which he would remove. The result of this minutely ramified and thorough organisation is said to be that, no part of the empire affording a hiding-place for the criminal, there is not a country in the world where so few crimes against property are committed, and doors may be left unbarred with little fear of robbery.

At that time, people were formed into five-household mutual responsibility groups; if one person committed a crime, all the others in the linked households were punished.

Nowadays the system is far less rigorous, but there is still quite a widespread co-operation between the general public and the police. Yoshio Sugimoto writes:

> More than half a million households or about one in fifty, are organised as 'households for crime prevention' and are closely associated with police stations. About 40 percent of Japanese police officers are stationed in small community-based police boxes known as *koban*, or in substations called *chuzaisho* ... Each *koban* or *chuzaisho* policeman routinely visits households and business establishments within his jurisdiction to obtain information about them and to inquire whether any 'suspicious figures' hang around the neighbourhood.

Police supply a liaison card to each household on which they are expected to fill in their telephone numbers, when they settled in the area and other details. Although they are officially voluntary, almost all households do so.

Another key to the very low crime rates and a ramification of the idea that everyone watches everyone may, surprisingly, be found in the curious nature of criminal organisations. For it could be argued that the Japanese equivalent to the mafia or triads, the *yakuza*, constitutes a crime containment, or at least a violence-containing institution.

The Japanese state is not so foolish as to ban all public gambling, sexual services and alcohol-related activities. Yet, like all governments, it finds it peculiarly difficult to police and tax them. If it sends in the ordinary police, as happens in many parts of the world, they are often quickly corrupted; they can become paid agents and protectors of the criminal gangs, tainted by offers of money, women, drugs or alcohol. Yet the state cannot allow this area to go unpoliced. As far as I know, Japan is the only large civilisation to have contained this delicate problem by turning a semi-criminal organisation into a formally recognised and partially accepted agency of the state. The mafia is formally banned; the *yakuza* are permitted to exist.

Yakuza means 8-9-3 in Japanese, a bad combination or curse in gambler jargon. The organisation emerged in the gambling world and then spread outwards. According to the Heibonsha dictionary, it is applied to:

> criminal organisations which have similar characteristics to those of traditional gambler organisations such as a family-like vertical organisation, the absolute power of superiors and absolute subjection of inferiors, highly ritualistic greetings and behaviour at meetings and respect for a special code of conduct and ethics.

This means that only some criminal organisations in Japan fall within the category.

To protect themselves, the Japanese have put in place a set of 'fire-walls' which include the police, who are instructed on how to deal with the *yakuza*. In a number of police stations they have a list of all the local *yakuza* and they keep in contact with them. They have a special division of the police force trained specifically to deal with *yakuza* related work. The police have even been known to arrange parking permits for them when they meet for one of their open conventions, where they arrive in their stretch-limousines, wearing their trademark dark glasses and tattoos.

The *yakuza* are allowed to recruit openly. I remember my surprise when I wandered up to one of their recruiting offices in a Japanese high street, thinking it was a late-night taxi service. My friends suggested hurriedly that I put away my camera and move on.

The *yakuza* normally do not use much physical violence. They almost without exception carry no guns. I remember the enormous storm that was caused when a senior *yakuza* official was found with an unlicensed gun and a few rounds of ammunition in his hotel bedroom. The old-fashioned *yakuza* tend to avoid dealing in hard drugs. They try to keep out the more violent, drug-dealing, Chinese triad organisations. They own many legitimate businesses such as hotel chains and estate agents, which allows them to launder profits. Yet they are clearly involved in serious crimes and cannot be excused as just a rather quirky branch of the police force, a set of lovable hoodlums.

With the *yakuza*, as with Japanese criminality in general, we have the feeling of both familiarity and strangeness. On the surface, the patterns look like those of any other industrial society, with crime and criminal gangs, police and courts. Yet a closer study shows that the motivation, organisations, level of criminality and responses to it are different to those most people are familiar with outside Japan. Our categories do not fit.

I had always thought in terms of binary possibilities with power: absolutist or limited, imperial or balanced, bureaucratic or non-bureaucratic, legal or illegal, centralised or de-centralised, peaceful or warlike. Japan seems to have all of these characteristics. We can make a case for each of them and the opposite. Power is everywhere and nowhere in particular, it is exercised in the most savage and the most peaceful ways, the most and the least formally bureaucratic. While politics is enormously important, it seems to be yet another facet of the mystery which itself needs explanation. I wonder whether the key underlying all that we have looked at so far are mental categories and thought processes specific to the Japanese, which enable them to overcome what we perceive as oppositions or contradictions.

6

Ideas

In a world which is complex, highly mobile, fluid, full of people, one device for carefully ordering relationships is the opposition Japanese make between the inside, internal, private (*uchi*) and what is outside, external, public (*soto*). This is a flexible, contextual opposition, whose meaning shifts with each person and each occasion, rather than being an abstract and fixed grid. It is also linked to other oppositions of a similar kind, between surface (*omote*) and deep (*ura*), front (*tatemae*) and back (*honne*). Much of the meaning and etiquette of Japanese life revolves around these gradations, which are not sharp differences, as between A and B, but the subtle differences between A++ and A+ or A−.

For example, the house, and particularly the central living area, is a safe, clean, special space, from which all the danger, dirt and confusion of the 'outside' is banished. Hence the obsession with not wearing outside shoes and outdoor clothes indoors, washing hands and even mouths on entering the home. This leads to some odd reversals. Ezra Vogel noted, 'One fairly severe form of punishment used in Japan is to lock the child out of the house and require him to apologise before he can come in. A comparable American punishment would be to prevent the child from going out.'

According to *Kojien*, a Japanese dictionary, *uchi* has at least three meanings. There is a geographical and spatial dimension, that is, the inside against the periphery. Secondly it refers to the inside of the boundary of the extended family, my family and my home, and perhaps even human/non-human distinctions. Thirdly it refers to the internal, hidden core, the heart and affection which others cannot see or perceive or observe from the outside. Each strand of meaning is clearly understandable for the Japanese although the subtle changes in different contexts often make the word ambiguous.

Many aspects of life are perceived of as a series of concentric rings, with the very centre being most highly valued, then moving outwards to danger, dirt and otherness. The inner rings include the Japanese and real 'humans', the outer the deities, foreigners or other barbarians or untouchables. Yet what is odd is that sometimes the very centre is empty. The bull's eye, as it were, is without any content.

This is the case with Japanese shrines, which are empty of any spirit, or the tea ceremony, which has no focal point or centre, but is a process. The same, as Roland Barthes commented, is true of Japanese cities: for example, Tokyo 'offers this precious paradox: it does possess a centre, but this centre is empty.' Barthes noted a similar curious feature in Japanese food: 'no Japanese dish is endowed with a centre ... here everything is the ornament of another ornament ... food is never anything but a collection of fragments.'

This gives a clue to what is at the core of the Japanese concept of space. Everything is relational, referring to something other, the inside is defined in relation to the next layer of the outside. It is all about gaps, emptiness, intervals. The meaning lies in the organisation of things in relation to other things and the exact degree of distance or space between them.

Such a system of flexible building blocks helps the Japanese to arrange their highly intense and multi-stranded landscape. In a world where money, urbanism, the written word and advanced technologies normally destroy the integration of face-to-face, multi-level communications, they are able to communicate an enormous amount by the very minimalism which allows others to fill in their own meanings. All options are permanently kept open.

❀

In relation to concepts of time, I expected that there had been a great transformation at some point in Japanese history. I assumed that, whatever vestiges of tribal or peasant life had survived in the past, they would now have disappeared, and that the linear, clock time of modernity would have become more or less universal. At first sight this seems to be true. The Japanese make great watches, their trains work to split-second accuracy. They are generally punctual and their urban lives would collapse without a strong mechanical time sense. Yet when we probe more deeply, something else emerges.

There is the absence of a time dimension in Japanese language itself, a feature it shares with the Chinese. Tenses are rarely used in Japanese, so everything is potentially simultaneously past, present or future. This is completely opposed to the concept of linear time stretched out over things which have happened, are happening, and may or will happen.

Secondly, there is little linearity in the philosophy. Without any afterlife, no second coming or end of the world, no purpose to life, no rebirth, there is no goal to history. We are in the perfect existential society. We just exist, the moment is all. Yet this brings a particular sadness, for the present is constantly vanishing, the perfect moment of the full blossom or the full moon or the waves on the shore is always transient. All is but a momentary dream, soon to evaporate like the morning dew.

Thirdly, the cycle of ceremonies, of changes of dress and food, echoed so strongly nowadays on Japanese television with its seasonal motifs, remind the Japanese of the cyclical world of spring, summer, autumn and winter. Even in the most crowded Japanese city the rhythms of the abruptly changing year are reflected and to catch and feel these changes is very important for most Japanese.

Time does indeed seem to be magical. Certain times are good for doing things, others to be avoided. In the nineteenth century Griffis remarked, 'Even among the educated samurai ... there are many dangerous seasons for travellers, and the number of lucky and unlucky days is too numerous to be fully noted here'. Time varies in quality rather than quantity. It can be speeded up or slowed down; or obliter- ated entirely, as in the tea ceremony where the guests take their watches off before they enter into a space outside time. Time is alive, not dead. The Japanese master time, rather than being mastered by it.

The elasticity or relativity of time is one of the most striking features of traditional time reckoning in Japan. Time literally expanded and shrank, as it does in tribal societies. There was nothing equivalent to a week. The length of an hour was flexible and changed over the year, relative to the season. Although there were a fixed number of hours, it was only at the equinoxes that the actual length of the hours was equal. This made the introduction of the Western clock into Japan a complicated business.

Finally, there is the question of long term time cycles. Here the Japanese combined a conception of mythical, cyclical time – for instance, in the myths of the origin of Japan and the Emperor – along with a linear dimension roughly equivalent to duration. Time both flowed in a cyclical way, but also had length. There were no fixed centuries, but rather the unit used was the 'era' or *nengo*, derived from China, which varied in duration from one year to any number of years.

There are layers to Japanese concepts of time. On the surface we now find Western clock time, but just below is the seasonal, rhythmical, magical time. It has a meaning; it is not dead. Yet, as with everything else in Japan, it does not exist apart from things. The trees, moon, winds and grasses all are clocks which slow or hurry time along. Each person exists in this moment, for an individual has no past or future, except that everyone is caught up in the complete past of the Japanese people, numberless leaves in a great forest.

The Japanese are not slaves to time – they relish, savour, mourn and use it. They manufacture enough of it for their purposes and seldom seem to have too much of it (boredom) or too little (anxiety and guilt).

Time is not separated off as an abstract standard, and it is not made by God. There is, in fact, no such thing as 'time', just being in the here, the now, which mingles with the eternal. All things are negated in the most profound of their aspirations – nothingness.

It is difficult to grasp fully the idea of the past which this generates. On the one hand, without much use of the past tense, with strong circular notions, the past, as in many tribal societies, is part of the present. Rather as I feel in Cambridge that Francis Bacon, Newton and Darwin still walk the riverbanks, so Kenichi often cites in our conversations examples from the thirteenth and fourteenth centuries in Japan as if it was yesterday. The past is not a foreign country. The notions of pre-modern, modern and post-modern do not seem applicable to Japanese history.

Kenichi wrote me a note which explains the simultaneousness of time and the absence of 'stages' into which history can be divided:

> The Japanese sense of the future is, in a way, different from your uni-
> dimensional sense of progress. Simply speaking, Japanese minds live
> simultaneously in the pre-modern, modern and post-modern. It is dif-
> ficult to apply the stage theory which breaks history into things like
> the Kamakura period as pre-modern, Edo and Meiji as modern and
> contemporary Japan as post-modern.

On the other hand, the past is completely past, not to be made too much of, to be covered over. The past, like ancestors, is conceived of as one large lump, simultaneous, not spread out evenly as a trail up to the present. This may be a clue to the puzzling attitude to the war dead, shrines and past history.

The Japanese have well-developed techniques of amnesia, methods of forgetting and forgiving the past. They are very good at reorganising the past so that it is in harmony with the present. One example is their practice of building two kinds of shrines, one for the winners of a battle and another for the losers. This tranquillises the losers, calms down their anger and troubled spirits, soothes the negative side of the past.

There is very little begrudging of the past. For instance, at the Meiji restoration, the defeated side were not punished severely but soon incorporated into the new framework. After the Second World War there was immediate acceptance of defeat and few recriminations. Kenichi thought that this could in part be due to the frequency of natural disasters in Japan – typhoons earthquakes, volcanic eruptions. In order to survive it was necessary to forget the past and rebuild for the future. Whatever the cause, it has been possible quickly to agree to forget and forgive.

In a much-discussed attempt to show that Japan is constantly changing, yet retains a structure which patterns the changes in a certain way, Masao Maruyama developed the theory of the 'deep note' of Japanese history, asking himself 'whether historical changes occurred not in spite of, but precisely because of, some basic continuous factors that underlie the Japanese experience'. He went on:

> In music the *basso ostinato* ... is a recurrent pattern of bass notes. It is an underlying motif that is independent from the treble part and, if the main theme appears in the treble part, it is bound to undergo some modifications by this *basso ostinato*. This metaphor may be applied to the historical development of Japanese thought. Most of the main themes have been imported from abroad since ancient times, beginning with Confucianism, Taoism, Buddhism, and including modern ideologies such as liberalism, constitutionalism, anarchism, socialism, and so on ... If we examine the circumstances in which those ideologies underwent modifications after they arrived in Japan from the Asian continent or from the West, certain patterns of thinking similar in each case emerge, each responsible for subtly changing the original.

These recurrent patterns of thinking are those which I have termed the *basso ostinato* of Japanese intellectual history.

Explaining this metaphor, he wrote:

I do not presuppose the contradiction or exclusiveness of the factor of change and that of continuity ... What I want to emphasise is that ... There exists the same pattern *in the way of changing*, and you can hear the repetitive music phrase in the pattern of changing ... The Japanese history of ideas changes variously and quickly *because* there is the repetitive pattern of ideas and thinking.

This is an important insight. For the Japanese, time is not circular, but there is a certain repetition or similarity of form. I can understand this well as I look around the Cambridge which I have known for thirty-five years and find that it is both greatly changed and yet much the same. Taking a longer time-span, the present-day village of Earls Colne, in England, that I visit today seems very different from, yet also continuous with, the village I have come to know through the records surviving from five hundred years ago.

Maruyama has caught this sense of the 'changing same' which is at the heart of an old civilisation like Japan. He has also given us a clue as to how the Japanese have preserved their distinct 'otherness' in the face of huge external pressures to conform to philosophical models from China, and more recently from the West. Ideas and institutions can change and adapt very fast in Japan, as in England, precisely because there is a repetitive underlying pattern. Rapid change is very quickly absorbed and the new is made to feel old. There is a sense of timelessness which, through the invention of traditions and the rapid covering-over of the new, gives people the illusion that not much has changed.

❖

Usually, people's conception of the universe reflects in some way the structure of the society they live in. Where the social structure has settled down into a fixed, institutionalised pattern, there will be a cosmology to match this, and people will be drawn to the ideal of symmetry. The favourite numbers tend to be even ones, with matched pairs or multiples of pairs. As we have seen, however, for the Japanese, everything is partial, dependent on something else, relational, and it is therefore not surprising to find that they have opted for systems that emphasise the dependency on something else, never specified, to fill the missing part.

Japanese architecture avoids symmetry and balance, as is illustrated in the crooked shapes in tea houses and temples. Whether in *tatami* matting, ceilings or beams, symmetry is avoided. As Singer put it, 'A geometrical array of lines, ideas or virtues makes the Japanese feel as if shut off from the springs of life. He delights in asymmetry, in what seems to be done in a haphazard way ...' There is always some unfinished business, a yearning for the other which would signify the end – death – but also round off things. Leaving things incomplete allows for growth.

We find that three, and particularly five, are the preferable numbers in Japan. I was surprised when I received a present of tea bowls to find five of them – somewhat dismaying since, when we entertain, we try to invite six rather than five guests. Yet I understood this better when I read in Chamberlain that such five-ness extended even into music. He describes how in what he calls the harmonic scale, the fourth and seventh are omitted, 'because, as there are five recognised colours, five planets, five elements, five viscera and so on, there *must* also be five notes in music'.

As Chamberlain notes, the love of lumping things into numerical units is taken to extremes in China and Japan, and in the latter the numbers are usually uneven. There are the 'Three Views' (the three most beautiful places in the Empire), the 'Three Capitals and Five Ports', the 'Five Festivals', the 'One and Twenty Great Anthologies' and the 'Fifty-three stages' on the road from Tokyo to Kyoto.

One final surprise comes from the fact that while in English we speak of *'one* chicken, *two* trees, *three* stars' and so on, the Japanese qualify the numbers according to what they refer to. Scidmore explains how this works:

> After learning the plain cardinal and ordinal numbers, the neo-phyte must remember to add the syllable *hiki* when mentioning any num-ber of animals, *nin* for people, *ken* for houses, *so* for ships, *cho* for jin-rikishas, *hai* for glasses or cups of any liquid, *hon* for long and round objects, *mai* for broad and flat ones, *tsu* for letters or papers, *satsu* for books, *wa*, for bundles or birds.

There is yet further subtlety that adds to the complexity of life: the bundling of objects into a cosmology that seems arbitrary and strange to a Western observer. Sir Rutherford Alcock noted:

> There is one class for all animals – except the flying and swimming species, and insects. Another for birds, in which, however, hares and rabbits are included! A third for ships, and junks, and boats; a fourth for liquids drunk with a glass, as water, wine, tea etc.; a fifth for things having *length*, as trees, pens, sticks, masts, beams, radishes, carrots, fin-gers, brooms, pipes etc. and so on…

Those who have studied the Japanese language are puzzled as to where to place it. There is little link to the neighbouring Chinese-Thai or Sino-Tibetan languages. It has some similarities to the Altaic (Mongol and Turkish) languages. It has a few affinities with Ugro-Finnish. But linguists disagree as to whether its origins can be traced back to any particular region. Although in terms of grammar it is similar to Korean, that in itself is not enough to prove a genetic relationship. The vocabulary cannot be shown to come from a common root and the grammatical similarities may be a matter of chance.

It is important to distinguish here between language and speech. The Japanese language has a rich and complex grammar, a wide range of personal pronouns, ways of indicating tense, negative and positive, whether something is the subject or the object in a sentence – all the elements that are needed to communicate in a clear and direct way. Yet if we look at what is made use of, how people actually communicate in spoken language, we see that most Japanese studiously avoid using many of the resources available to them, and seem deliberately to create an ambiguous, indirect and limited form of speech.

When I first asked how this worked, Kenichi gave me this account:

> The order of the sentence in Japanese follows the Japanese thought process. Firstly, a speaker tries to define the field (as in field theory in physics), the date, space, relations, and finally comes to the movement of the agent. The verb and auxiliary verb come at the end. There is no need for an explicit topic, since it has already been implied by the description of the field. This way of thinking makes structural thinkers like Foucault, Merleau-Ponty and others very popular in Japan. Thus the situation is defined first, and then the subject's action. This is a complete reflection of the way of Japanese thinking, where thought is first directed to the field.

In another overview, this time of the language in the period of the *Genji* (eleventh century), Ivan Morris wrote that the speaker is hardly ever indicated, the subject of the sentence has to be guessed and may change halfway through a sentence without any warning. He added:

> The mutually exclusive categories that we take for granted in European languages – past and present tense, affirmation and question, singular and plural, male and female (as identified by personal names

and pronouns), doubt and certainty — have little relevance in Heian Japanese; sometimes it is not even clear whether the sentence is positive or negative.

As Arthur Koestler commented, the text often 'describes events that somehow float through the air without naming the subject, gender, person and number to whom they happen.' Chamberlain explained that 'Japanese nouns have no gender or number, Japanese adjectives no degrees of comparison, Japanese verbs no person.'

I do not find it easy to imagine how I would speak without the use of tense, subject and object or degrees of comparison. In Japanese, the complexity is increased by the fact that words can have several meanings. The spoken language has many words which sound alike but in fact mean something different, and the written characters can be read to mean entirely different things depending on the context. A nice example is given by Fukuzawa when he analyses a *haiku*: 'Since the first line may signify either *gourd* or *warfare*, the second has the idea of *the beginning*, and the last may equally be taken for *cold* or *rocket*, the whole verse may be read in two ways: 1) The first drink from the gourd, we take it cold. 2) The first shot of the war, we do it with the rocket.' This ambiguity makes Japanese a wonderful language for riddles and puns, for allusions and double meanings.

Japanese speech is deeply contextual and changes with the relationship between the speakers. This is a very marked feature of this hierarchical society although it is found to a certain degree in all societies. Robert Smith writes, 'The level chosen by each speaker, who is compelled to make a choice before uttering a verb form, is based on calculation of social distance, largely conceived in terms of a complex combination of age, sex, social position, nature of previous interactions and context.' Thus males will tend to speak down to females, or younger people use honorific terms of address for older people or bosses. This is changing today, with less emphasis on hierarchy, but much of it remains.

Speech appears to sacrifice objective solidity in favour of subjective subtlety. Maraini notes:

> Indo-European languages possess an objective logic: they set great store by variations of being, by number and (often) gender, by who does what to whom, and when. The Japanese language could not care less. *Ikimasu* can mean a dozen different things: I go, but also I come; he, she, it goes or comes, or they go or come; it is going; I will go; I shall go, and so on.

In fact, there are separate words for 'come' and 'go', and it would be possible to specify all the subtleties which Maraini found wanting. Yet often, in speech, the distinctions and variations are omitted.

For example, there may appear to be no subject in a sentence, so that we wonder who is doing the action, yet the subject is in fact contained in the honorific verb used, which tells us that 'an honourable person does something'. This indicates that the subject is someone other than the speaker (who would never exalt themselves by using such a verb).

The effect of all this is that there is no confrontation, no abstract exchange, but rather a binding together. The communication should never lead into confrontation or disagreement. Interpersonal harmony is essential, and argument or debate avoided. I found this puzzling when I taught in Tokyo University, for I could not get the students to debate or argue with me. Unlike my British students, these post-graduates sat quietly and refused to express opinions or disagreements or even ask questions.

In fact, most binary thought is an abomination, especially when it has the potential to polarise opinion. It is in line with this that we find the particularly intriguing absence of negative and positive in Japanese speech. As we have seen, the grammar does provide ways of indicating positive and negative, but, in practice, these are hardly used except between people in a very close and long-term relationship.

Following an early discussion with our friends, I had noted:

> The word for 'yes' in Japan, hai, can be taken to mean yes, but can also mean anything from yes, through maybe, to no. Really it is reflecting the other's words and intentions and saying 'you know' or 'you decide'. A person must not say no directly in Japan. Rather they must leave it to the other's discretion to pick up the negative signals that underlie a 'yes'. The word for 'no' is much heavier than in the West. It is only possible to say no to very close friends. With others, only very occasionally can one say no. If one does so, it precludes all future intimacy and communication, and is tantamount to a declaration of war.

This leads to the avoidance of a real distinction between positives and negatives, things that are and are not. Because of the relational nature of Japanese thought, many things are both one thing and another simultaneously in a way which is not allowed by the binary logic of the West. The Japanese have always steered clear of contradiction. It could truly be said, to paraphrase Lewis Carroll, that this allows them to believe six impossible things before breakfast.

The effect of all this is that it is often difficult for a Japanese to fully understand a piece of writing, or to communicate unambiguously with another. Very early on, before I went to Japan, I was amazed when a Japanese friend of our daughter gave us a 'lucky horse', enclosing a sheet of paper with a few lines of explanation regarding its history. I asked her to tell me what it said. She looked perplexed and said that she could not easily read it, but would need to go away for a few days and try to work it out before she could tell me. This might, of course, have been due to unusual or antiquated calligraphy.

But I have had many similar experiences of people unable to translate texts without a great deal of effort and consultation of dictionaries.

On another occasion, I went with a group of friends to a Japanese restaurant. Our Japanese interpreter spent twenty minutes puzzling over the menu with the waitress, trying to work out what the dishes were before making the order. What arrived bore no relation to what we thought we had asked for.

Written Japanese takes more time and effort to learn than any other language in the world. Scholars have said that to master the language takes from twelve to thirty years, and it certainly takes many school lessons for children just to learn the two or three thousand Chinese characters and the two phonetic Japanese scripts which they need in order to be deemed educated. In many ways written and spoken language proficiency is as high an art as the tea ceremony, calligraphy or Zen meditation.

Yet, after this huge effort, language is relegated to a partial form of communication. Chie Nakane comments that 'the essence of pleasure in conversation for the Japanese is not in discussion (a logical game) but in emotional exchange'. It is not the voice which communicates, but the whole body, including the eyes, smile, hair, gestures and clothing.

The aim is to use the language to achieve perfect communication with the minimal number of signs, as in the tiny verse form of the *haiku*. Kenichi believes that the collaborative poem known as *renga* used to be the highest form of communication, the most intensive emotional exchange, and a kind of ecstatic oneness or empathy. The ideal is silence. All language, the Japanese proverb has it, is a barrier to real, deep, exchange. For into silence can be read whatever the other wishes, as a person can read what they like into the emptiness of a shrine or Zen meditation. The individualistic English, who are also sometimes thought of as understated and reserved, will partly understand this. They often sit in companionable silence. The Japanese take this to an extreme.

The Japanese listen for the pauses, the silences between words, to what is not being said rather than what is. 'We prefer the soft voice, the understatement,' comments Tanizaki. 'Most important of all are the pauses.' The silence is greatest where what is being communicated is the deepest. Herbert Passin writes, 'In the most intimate of relations explicit statement is not necessary: wordless understanding is the mode; or hints and fragments of sentences may serve as pointers, even though outsiders may find them completely incomprehensible.' For Inazo Nitobe, 'Speech is very often with us, as the Frenchman defines it, "the art of concealing thought".' And Hearn was told, 'We Japanese think we can better express our feelings by silence.' This is certainly true in some situations, but it should be balanced by the fact that anyone travelling in Japan can see people chatting amiably and establishing and maintaining contacts through speech.

Vocabulary and the selective use of grammatical and syntactical devices allow speech to act as glue between almost any people and in any situation. They become a mirror of relative status, of the other's intentions and desires, a tool for fudging oppositions, ripe with ambiguity, nuance, and hybridity. The Japanese appear to know what the signs mean because they already know what the other will say before he or she says it. This makes the Japanese able to inhabit their interconnected world, for all the language is relational. It has few intrinsic meanings, but great subtlety when interpreted by the listener.

It is worth stressing again that many other languages share features with Japanese. Thai also has pronouns that reflect social differences and many Asian languages have the Japanese word order. Korean has honorifics similar to Japanese. It is therefore hard to pin down the peculiarities of everyday speech on to the language itself. What is important is the pattern of communication rather than the structure of the language.

In some ways the Japanese represent the opposite of the linguistic hypothesis (Sapir-Whorf) that language defines what we can think. In fact, in Japan the language allows many things to be thought and said, but the Japanese, always reluctant to throw away anything, keep a huge array of linguistic tools in their grammar which they hardly use. Social relations determine how language is used and how the world is conceived rather than the other way round.

In Japanese, there are perfectly good ways to distinguish between active and passive, between being an agent doing something or a passive part of a process to whom things happen. The grammar allows you to say 'I do'. Yet, in practice, passive forms are preferred. Some say English is a 'do' language, agents do things, while Japanese is a 'becoming' language, describing process and change without focus on an actor. For example, an Englishwoman might say to her boss, 'I have decided to get married', while a Japanese woman would say, 'Things have evolved in such a way that a marriage is happening.'

The indirect mode of speech can have a significant impact when personal responsibility for an act is disputed. After 1946, what the Japanese said was not so much 'We chose democracy' as 'It has become the world of democracy.' As the reports on the trials of accused war criminals at that time show, many refused to acknowledge that they had played an active role in events. While German generals said they took the decision to go to war, many Japanese portrayed the process as an unrolling, external, set of events which swept them up, and over which they had little or no control. They believed that they were as much done to as doing.

Before considering Japanese logic, I should emphasise that I am not suggesting that the Japanese are pre-logical or non-logical. Nor do I believe that they are, or have ever been, uninterested in how the real world works. 'A late writer', approvingly quoted by Morse, commented, 'No people on earth is keener in search of exact knowledge ... No people on earth excels the Japanese in clarity or subtlety of logical thought.' It is rather a case of different logical procedures.

One feature of the alternative logic is the normal avoidance of absolute and binary thought. The oppositions which are deeply embedded in monotheistic and Greek-derived systems are not popular. We have seen this in relation to 'yes' and 'no'. Maraini sums up the Japanese approach:

> In Japan one is rarely confronted with those cleaving dualisms that typify Western thought: God and man, creator and creature, spirit and matter, body and soul, good and evil, nature and supernatural reality, the sacred and profane. In Shinto, men, the world and the gods all belong to what is essentially a single vital continuum.

The highest goal is not distinctions, but synthesis and harmony. 'Harmony consists in *not making* distinctions; if a distinction between good and bad can be made, there *wa* [harmony] does not exist.'

Many writers have noted that in Japan context is more important than an abstract or absolute set of logical laws. Matsumoto explains that situation takes precedence over reason, what Japanese call 'reason beyond reason' (*rigai no ri*). 'The Japanese do not seem to possess principles, if the word "principle" is to be defined from the logic-oriented Western perspective', he comments. 'Logic is considered to be "cold" or "unemotional" in Japan and certainly not identical to the truth.'

As in many non-divided worlds, social relations come first. The Japanese are encouraged to put social coherence before universalistic and sceptical observations. Individual rationality and perception of the world becomes moulded by the social structure. Social relations are more important than dispassionate cognitive truth. Nothing is absolute. Everything bends and depends on the relationships.

If two ideas clash or contradict each other according to strict logic, that can be overlooked, for reason is fallible and inferior to emotion and intuition. A Japanese is able to hold contradictory views without conflict. As the philosopher Hajime Nakamura remarks, there is 'a tendency toward an absence of theoretical or systematic thinking, along with an emphasis upon an aesthetic and intuitive and concrete, rather than a strictly logical orientation.' The parts may clash, but the whole still works, as with a work of art, where irregularities and imperfections are made whole in the final synthesis.

One effect of all this has been to avoid metaphysics and those kinds of speculation related to religion which are so popular in the West. The questions people ask tend not to be of the 'why' kind, for a situation exists as it exists and there is no point in asking why. Reason is less important than emotion and intuition. The social relationship is more important than abstract principles, as we would expect in a hierarchical society. Logical contradictions are not a threat to the system. The powerful tools for constructing causal chains based on either induction or deduction are not favoured.

The Japanese think that it is not they but Westerners who are irrational, for two reasons. Firstly, Westerners constantly allow 'religious' truths of a non-verifiable kind to enter into their metaphysics, assuming a creator God, hidden rules and 'laws' behind phenomena which cannot be proved, and making other leaps of faith such as believing in miracles. They see us as very superstitious, almost magical in our thinking.

Secondly, we may strive for logical consistency within our spheres, for example within an instituted economy driven by the rules of the market, where we make the implausible assumption of perfect knowledge of the choices to be made. Yet the price we pay is a form of higher irrationality, for we have to pretend that there really are separations when all we have done is to construct them for our own convenience. In real life, parts of our world are not separated off in this way and everything is interconnected.

The Japanese behave in a manner not dissimilar to the codes

enshrined in the English Common Law, that is to say they do not try to set out rules and laws of a detailed, universal kind, which they feel would be bound to become rigid and unworkable as contexts change. Rather, the system is *ad hoc*, unprincipled, case-by-case, flexible, based on 'common sense' or 'intuition', of a kind whose reasons are beyond reason. They may not be able to explain how their system works, but, like riding a bicycle, they learn instinctively how to use it.

The Japanese often find themselves in a situation similar to that of the English curate asked by the Bishop's wife at breakfast whether his boiled egg was nice. The egg was in fact rotten, but, if he said so, the displeasure of the Bishop's household might seriously damage his career. If he told a blank lie, his immortal soul would be at risk. So he answered that it was 'good in parts' — an illogical, but socially and spiritually satisfying way out. The Japanese live in such a predicament every hour of every day, with intertwined social structure and power relations. Their language and logic is full of 'good in parts'.

The Japanese communicate ideas through manners as much as through language. What is at first remarkable in the world of Japanese etiquette is the extreme self-discipline, stiffness and reserve that are displayed. No single person (except for very young babies) is singled out by demonstrative gestures by an adult or even an older child. Husbands, wives and lovers traditionally did not kiss in public, though customs are now changing and younger people do so. Parents do not embrace and hug their children once they are over the age of about six. Infants, it is true, are held in close physical contact with their parents, being carried around, slept with, touched frequently. But once aged about six or seven, they are physically distanced, literally kept at arm's length. Thus there are few outward signs of particular favouritism or closeness. More or less everyone is treated with respect and equality.

What strikes me is the highly ritualised and formalised inter-personal etiquette, most immediately noticeable in the frequent bowing, where the whole body is used to communicate in a society where there is otherwise little obvious body language. There is not much waving of arms or other gestures, and I cannot ever recall seeing a Japanese wink, though that may be my lack of careful observation. Behaviour generally seems very deferential, even defensive and obsequious; people are warily avoiding any sign of aggression, but also trying to ingratiate themselves with each other. Relations are very 'sticky', entangled when people become close, ultra-careful.

Much of the greeting etiquette does, indeed, seem to be a way of binding strangers together into a mutually acknowledging and inter-dependent relationship. Tentative harmony, trust, relationality, desire to please and be pleased, all these are stressed purposes. The whole body becomes a symbol, by its bent shape, of the inner intention which is to strike up a non-threatening and sincere relationship. This is in line with a society where differences and divisions are down-played and mutual respect, trust and conformity are emphasised.

Hence there is hardly ever any direct confrontation between people. Minimal gestures and very few strongly positive or negative signs allow people to keep as low a profile as possible. They are like wary ballroom dancers, trying not to step on each other's feet. Everything possible is done to keep the emotional tone of interactions as muted as possible. This is one of the reasons why a visitor who travels on the packed subways or walks through the crowded streets of a big Japanese city feels safe, relaxed and almost alone. Harmony, fitting in, careful adjustment and awareness of the other seem to be central.

The learning of the complex code which governs every gesture and word starts early. It is under way as soon as a Japanese child can speak, and by the age of ten almost all of the code has been learnt. The aim is to absorb the rules of composure and calmness, to mute and control one's feelings. The young Fukuzawa spoke for many Japanese when he wrote: 'One day while reading a Chinese book, I came upon these ancient words: "Never show joy or anger in the face". These words brought a thrill of relief as if I had learned a new philosophy of life.' It has been observed that Japanese have very neutral expressions; they do not get excited and passionate – except, sometimes, when they have relaxed with alcohol and, nowadays, while watching baseball or football.

Politeness and etiquette come before morals and before law, for, as we have seen, interpersonal relations are more important than abstractions of a religious or legal kind. It is more important to be polite than to tell the literal truth. This is a view which most of us partially subscribe to when we refrain from making truthful remarks about our friends which will hurt their feelings. But it is taken to extremes in Japan, and indeed politeness and courtesy become a form of the deepest love.

The immensely careful negotiation of a respectful, trusting relationship in a civilisation where almost everything is about interpersonal harmony, was explained to us. When starting a conversation, the first remarks are of a very general establishing kind. One starts by using the highest distance/ranking words, extreme politeness, 'I am a very poor, humble person', 'I know very little about this subject' and so on. But gradually the language becomes less humble and less formal. If one maintains the original distanced language, it is a sign that one dislikes the person and does not want to get any closer in the relationship. It might take up to thirty minutes of conversation to negotiate the right level.

All of this elaborate behaviour puts an immense strain on each individual since negotiating with strangers, in particular, is very tricky. I have noticed that when I talk to many Japanese, even when I get to know them quite well, this puts them into a stressful relationship, and they are frequently mopping their brow, for perspiration stands out even in cool weather. It is as if they are constantly on their guard, not merely trying to avoid embarrassing signs of lack of bodily control, but much more deeply overseeing themselves so that the other's happiness and self-esteem is protected.

All of this means that much of life is an avoidance of saying or doing anything out of the way, too immediately different, critical or competitive. This is made more tolerable by fairly frequent inversions, when the ridiculous, direct and confrontational are allowed and encouraged. Much of this happens in fantasy – in the Japanese television games and their displays of 'bad behaviour' watched by millions, or in the popular comic books or films.

The imaginary world of the Japanese is richly catered for by the widespread availability and use of visual imagery. More than nine-tenths of Japanese watch television every day for an average of almost three and a half hours. The generic category of *manga*, literally meaning 'funny pictures', covers cartoon, comic strips and caricatures, and comprises about 40 per cent of publications in Japan, a far higher proportion than in any other society in the world. They have become very popular outside Japan in recent years and within Japan have evolved in the last three years into a new phenomenon, the *manga-kissa*, or *manga* tea-bar. This is a combination of capsule hotel, self-service tea and coffee shop, video parlour, internet café and library of *manga* cartoon books.

Because of the great difficulty of overcoming the normal distance and etiquette, companionable drinking is very important in Japan. It provides a kind of sacred space and time for relaxation where 'impolite is all right'. One can reveal one's true feelings at this time, for instance a cleaner can talk frankly and even criticise their boss. It has the feeling of liminality. Thus, for instance, professors will sometimes go off with their students and drink *sake* and a sort of 'ceremonial community' of drink will be established.

The most complete forms of relief from the strain of maintaining the very high standard of interpersonal ceremonial behaviour are found in silence and non-communication. The Japanese wrap themselves in sleep whenever they can. Travelling with large numbers of slumbering Japanese on a train or underground, their keys and mobile phones left trustingly on their laps or nearby shelves, is an odd and striking experience.

Even more extraordinary are the *pachinko* parlours where, drowned in the sound of heavy rock music and the crashing of millions of steel bagatelle balls, reputedly over twenty million Japanese find themselves alone and free from all pressure to talk or interact. The craze originated after the Second World War in Nagoya where the many military aircraft manufacturing firms had to find a profitable way of using millions of surplus ball bearings. A *pachinko* parlour might be seen as strangely like an extreme form of an upper-middle-class English gentlemen's club; there, another reserved and hyper self-disciplined people, hiding behind their newspapers, also sought peace from the stress of the delicate and ceaseless manoeuvring of interpersonal relations.

The Japanese are perhaps the most polite, ceremonious and formal people on earth, though these features are also widespread in East Asia. Their reserve is proverbial. The purpose of all this seems to be to make it possible to manage a world where structuring social mechanisms such as class or caste are absent, and where all relationships are potentially very deep.

This immense care to preserve friendly and non-conflictual ties with the other, I have observed, for example, among the Gurungs of Nepal. The Gurungs are studiously courteous and considerate, and dance the social dance with great care. It does not do to alienate people with whom one has a possibly permanent and on-going relationship. Co-villagers are to be treated as moral beings, ends in themselves, and not merely means. The relationship cannot be merely an economic, social, religious or political one; it is a multi-level one in that undivided village world.

It is similar in Japan, yet the situation there is even more challenging for its inhabitants, since the potentially multi-stranded relations of any Japanese to another take place within a rushing, busy, highly mobile modern society. Much of the time a person does not interact with others in the crowd. But when a significant and necessary encounter does take place, it cannot be treated in the somewhat single-stranded way familiar in the West. It becomes a much more elaborate ceremonial, which engages the whole person.

It is difficult for a Westerner to understand the weight of ceremonial formality. Yet it makes sense if we know that in Japan there are one hundred and twenty million people living in an imagined community which basically resembles a small village. Certain parts of the 'village' – school friends, co-workers, neighbours – are clearly demarcated and heavily emphasised as important close contacts. Multi-stranded relations with them are not too difficult. Yet these havens are constantly being invaded by others. Each new encounter must be negotiated with care, not damaging the sensitivities of the other, and in turn finding one's own highly fluid being honourably reflected and respected.

The categories of dirt and cleanliness and the boundaries between them are important in Japan. I vividly remember being amazed that every matchstick dropped on the station platform was immediately swept up, that every surface and even the train windows were spotlessly clean. If dirt is 'matter out of place', the Japanese devote huge efforts to separating and confining such matter so that it is firmly placed where they consider it can be safely contained.

As we noticed on our first visit, garbage is very carefully sorted into categories, collected and recycled. The outdoor and the indoor worlds are kept apart, and it is a grave breach of etiquette to wear one's outdoor shoes inside the house. Special shoes are provided for the toilet. Many of the ceremonies and leisure activities have a purifying element in them, such as the salt sprinkled in the Sumo ring before contests, the careful wiping and cleaning of each item in the tea ceremony.

None of this is new. If we look at the descriptions of Japan from the very first European contacts, it is clear that the Japanese were far cleaner than even the cleanest of Europeans, the Dutch, who were considered by the Japanese to be quite filthy in their behaviour.

Any visitor to Japan will gradually realise that life is made up of boundaries, spaces and times and things, which should be kept apart or cleaned. There has long been an obsession with cleaning one's body, bathing, washing, shaving the head and eyebrows, even cleaning the eyes very carefully. Toilets were supplied with flowers to freshen them, paper for wiping, and systems to take away the waste very frequently. Nowadays, many hotels and flats have elaborate toilets with a wide range of gadgets to warm the seat, wash various parts of the body. All these are operated by a daunting control pad which is a new hazard for the non-initiated.

At first, such a focus on cleanliness may appear to be linked to religion and to concepts of ritual pollution. Anyone familiar with belief systems where there is an emphasis on purity, and where the distinction between clean and unclean is a strong feature – for instance Judaism or, in a more extreme way, Hinduism, where concepts of dirt and contamination are intrinsic to the caste system – will sense some overlap with Japan.

There is clearly some deep association between purity and the early Shinto rituals. The founding creator-divinity of Japan, Izanagi, takes a bath of purification on the first page of the mythical history the Kojiki. The Japanese have always intertwined religion and cleanliness. As Hearn wrote, 'From the earliest period Shinto exacted scrupulous cleanliness – indeed, we might say that it regarded physical impurity as identical with moral impurity, and intolerable to the gods.'

It seems that purity has both a physical and an ethical dimension, a clean environment and clean thoughts and emotions are linked, at least indirectly. According to Maraini:

> The ethical expression of purity was conceived as sincerity (*makoto*), which has been a cardinal virtue in Japan down the centuries and which is still highly admired today. Sincerity can be defined as the outward manifestation of an inner purity ... Sincerity is the antithesis of duplicity and cunning. Its symbol is the mirror, which harbours nothing within itself. As it reflects all phenomena without a selfish heart, there is never an instant when the forms of right and wrong, of good and evil, fail to show up.

The connection seems rather similar to that in puritanism in the West where godliness, simplicity, cleanliness and order were all interrelated at an often implicit level.

In Shinto shrines, cleanliness is of the utmost importance, for if the purification has not been thorough the *kami*, the shrine spirits, will not enter. Likewise houses need to be cleaned so that the entities which live in the various shrines and god-shelves will not be displeased. Yet there is also something different at play here. To wear one's shoes inside a house or fail to bathe leads to no danger of supernatural punishment. A person who crosses one of these boundaries is not breaking a taboo in the strict sense. They do not by their actions release an avenging force that will cause sickness or death. They do not put their spiritual well-being into peril. And consequently there are few specific cleansing rituals.

When we inadvertently forgot to take off our shoes while watching a young *geisha* dancing in Kyoto, our friends were evidently shocked and distressed. But they prescribed no cleansing ritual and would clearly have thought us mad if we had suggested that the angry gods would punish us in some way. The menace is at the worldly level: it is in the breach of social norms, of self-respect, of what it is to be a decent human being.

There is some overlap with the Dutch or English middle-class concern with 'cleanliness being next to godliness' as a virtue. It is possible to understand the disgust and disapproval somewhat. Yet there is more than the obsession with dusting, cleaning and polishing. Japanese life is in some ways reminiscent of the A. A. Milne poem about the bears which pop up if one inadvertently treads on the borders between squares. There seems to be an immense grid which divides the world into invisible compartments and the Japanese make their way carefully and nervously across it, trying to avoid arousing the bears.

When I first went to Japan, a professor from England who had studied and lived in Japan and spoke the language fluently told me of the presence of innumerable boundaries which constrained life. He said he kept a card index in which he wrote down cases where he had trodden on one of the lines and a bear had threatened. He claimed that he was adding a card or two each day, even after several years in the country.

Yet, as with everything in Japan, things are not straightforward. For while it is generally true that no one is considered impure, there is one exception: a group, almost invisible since they are seldom mentioned, who have been treated as defiled. These are people known as the *burakumin* and they tend to follow certain occupations.

There are estimated to be about six thousand *buraku* communities in Japan, with a total population of about three million. There are two types of *buraku*. The first are known as *eta*, which literally means the polluted or highly contaminated. They include people once associated with butchery and leather work, who may have acquired the stigma with the introduction of Buddhism. The second category is called *hinin* and includes entertainers, beggars and executioners.

When I first heard and read novels about them (for instance Shimazaki Toson's *The Broken Commandment*) I immediately classified them as similar to an Indian caste. They had all the features of a caste. They were thought to be impure because they dealt with blood, animal slaughter and leather. In the past they did not marry outside the group. They lived in segregated areas away from the rest of the population, and were discriminated against in employment and education. Their literacy rates were much lower than those of other Japanese.

Yet some of the *burakamin*, named the *yase no doji*, carried the Emperor (the purest person in Japan) at the time of greatest ceremonial importance, his funeral. Consequently they became sacred for this moment in time. I was told that sometimes the *burakamin* group lived around the entrance of a village and would lead its inhabitants in processions. It was suggested that this was because their special talent was to purify and to placate the spirits of the earth for the rest of the population.

Equally odd was the fact that they seemed rather invisible, even to themselves. When we visited one of the centres of *burakumin* peoples, near the town where Toson lived, we met a group of women, some *burakumin*, others married to *buraku*, and they told us about the discrimination they endured and what they were trying to do to overcome it.

One woman, whose marriage had been arranged, had come to live in the town to be with her husband. She had thought she was marrying an ordinary Japanese and for a number of years had interacted with people in the area and with other Japanese without sensing anything was amiss. Then one day her daughter, aged about eight, came back from school saying that the other children were being rude to her and calling her a funny name. It was only when she questioned her husband, that she learnt that she had married a *buraku*.

There has clearly been deep stigmatisation, yet this is declining. Inter-community marriages have increased, so that more than half the marriages where the *buraku* husband is under thirty are with non-

buraku and discrimination in the workplace is gradually becoming less frequent.

A particular case of racial marginalisation concerns the Ainu peoples of northern Japan. 'Ainu' means 'man', 'human being' or 'male' in the Ainu language. Ainu origins and connections to other racial groups are hotly debated. Some say that their size, eye shape and particularly their quite abundant body hair, which distinguishes them from other Japanese, suggest a Caucasoid or Australoid derivation. Others argue that they have strong affinities with the Tungus, Altaic and Uralic peoples of northern Russia. The Ainu language is very different from Japanese, and is again difficult to place.

The Ainu originally inhabited much of the island of Honshu, as well as Hokkaido and the Kuril Islands. But in the competition for land, they were driven north out of Honshu. By 1807 there were supposedly only some 27,000 Ainu left in the whole of Japan and the number had dropped to 16,000 in 1931 as a result of disease and persecution. There is now estimated to be about 25,000 Ainu, only a few dozen of whom are supposed to be 'pure' Ainu. Seven thousand Ainu households are now to be found in Hokkaido.

The Ainu were originally a hunter-gatherer group, with a rich folklore and complex mythology. They practised a shamanic religion, worshipping the bear. Their kinship system is very different from that of the Japanese, tracing descent through males and females separately and hence creating both male and female clans. Nowadays most Ainu have given up their old beliefs and language and follow a mainly Japanese lifestyle.

The tale of their marginalisation is a sad but familiar one, though not as extreme as the destruction of the Tasmanians by British settlers. Until quite recently the national government and the local Japanese regarded the Ainu as uncivilised and inferior, and much of their culture was destroyed. There were changes in the twentieth century, though it is only very recently that the Ainu were given full protection against discrimination.

As we have seen, the Japanese are greatly concerned with keeping themselves clean. This is to do with a desire for some kind of order, rather than with medical knowledge. Young children are taught to fear dirt, which is 'bad'. They are taught the meaning of *bacchii* [dirty] by being shown items such as shoes, which are considered unsanitary. Dangerous and dirty places in the outside world are brought to their attention in a way found in many cultures, but perhaps particularly stressed in Japan.

Outside the house are found all kinds of 'people dirt', which is deemed to be dangerous in some rather vague way. Emiko Ohnuki-Tierney describes how, 'In the case of children returning from the outside after play, the mother often comes to the entrance with a bucket of water and washes their feet.' Yet we should also recall that for most of their history, the Japanese have largely been farmers and both children and parents were constantly dealing with soil, which was not seen as polluting. Nowadays, the Japanese feel strongly that food should not be touched directly even after the hands have been repeatedly washed.

Finally, it is worth remembering that this careful concern with the inner and the outer worlds extends to the whole of the Japanese experience. It applies not just to things, but also people. We have seen this in relation to the almost invisible *burakumin*, but it is also the case with others.

Being islanders, the Japanese often see their country as in many ways a safe haven in an impure and hostile world. Those who go outside or abroad have traditionally been seen as dangerous when they returned, contaminated by various kinds of 'dirt'. The attempts of outsiders such as the Portuguese or Dutch to infiltrate the country were very carefully regulated with strict quarantining on the island

of Deshima in Nagasaki Harbour. It is reckoned that in 2001 there
were about 1.7 million foreigners resident in Japan, but while they are
tolerated and left to themselves, they are more or less invisible.

We may wonder how the apparent contradictions in Japanese
society, when looked at from a Western point of view, can possibly
be ignored. One way to resolve them is to approach them from a
Japanese perspective and bear in mind that all aspects of the world
have a surface and an inner depth, a front (outside) and an inner
truth. One's real, natural and inner desires are one thing, while the
outside rules or principles are entirely different, and people need to
discriminate very carefully between them. Insiders and close associ-
ates are shown one side of a person, outsiders another. Of course, this
is a feature of all societies to a certain extent, but in the Japanese case
it is taken to the extreme.

Another way is to consider that in Japan, all things, thoughts,
actions and objects are carefully prepared and wrapped up so that
they have a protective covering which can conceal their inner self.
Enormous attention is paid to wrapping. This is clearly something
which keeps options open, for there is the outside meaning and the
inner meaning. This is related to the strong theme of concealment,
of masks, silences, absences, which is particularly strong in Japanese
culture. It is present in many novels, and in the Noh drama where
there is a great deal of darkness, concealment and masking.

Yet, paradoxically, while there is concealment, great stress is also
laid on honourable, sincere, deep feelings. It is not actions which
matter, but motives, 'true heart', sincerity, being true to oneself. To a
considerable extent, the supreme moral virtue is 'sincerity'. Yet what,
exactly, is 'sincerity'? In the West, we might equate it with truthfulness, honesty, directness. Yet this is not the meaning. Arthur Koestler
notes, 'A man may be pretending and yet be "sincere" if his pretence
conforms to the code of manners; and it is "insincere" to be too

outspoken and direct.' Thus the word seems to mean 'behaving with courtesy and empathy'.

A final way to understand Japan is to overcome the Western distinc-tion between reality and invention, or fact and fiction. Just as we know that art, religion, games and ideas can be 'true' in a way that is different to provable scientific truth, so the Japanese have long lived in a world where imagined and actual worlds are not separate. The way in which blurring this boundary allows the Japanese to keep contra-dictory pressures in perpetual balance was explained to me in a note from Kenichi:

> Whenever I use the term 'pretend to be modern', you might think that we just cheat you and we follow the way of democracy, capitalism and modernity only with superficial forms and we do not do so in reality. It is partly so but partly not so. It is true that Japanese regard these imported institutions as designs just as clothes or plays. But it is also true that the clothes and plays are essential (substantial) parts of the body. Without them the system we belong to is not workable and not complete. Therefore democracy, according to Professor Maruyama, should be chosen by the Japanese as an 'essential fiction' which he would take a gamble on himself. The term identity and authenticity opposed to false and fiction is difficult for the Japanese to feel.

In relation to concepts and categories, I had assumed that a modern society would lie on one side of certain divides, that there would be linear rather than cyclical time, uniform rather than qualitatively differ-entiated space, decontextualised and stable as opposed to embedded language, logical reason above intuitive emotion. Yet the Japanese cannot be placed on one side or another. They are not pre-, anti- nor non-logical. Their language can convey anything while their speech often has little content. Their bodies often convey more information than the sounds from their mouths. The categories I am familiar with are reversed, inverted, and largely unfamiliar. What lies behind all of this and the absences of familiar divisions throughout Japanese culture? Our elusive prey appears to seek refuge in what seems to be the middle of the maze, what is often termed 'religion'.

7

Beliefs

A visit to Japan, even in the early twenty-first century, suggests a religion-soaked society. All towns and cities have temples and shrines, and they are increasing in popularity, attracting millions of visitors every year. The Shinto and Buddhist shrines are full of religious symbols – altars, gongs, incense, numerous effigies of gods, and priests in splendid robes. The settings are frequently dramatic, with raked sand or pebbles, gleaming lacquer, wooded hills and charming gardens.

The shrines are full of people. A pilgrimage to the main Shinto shrine of Ise is essential for almost every Japanese. A visit to the Shogunate shrines at Nikko is another favourite destination. Religious processions with men carrying portable Shinto shrines (*mikoshi*) occur at times of festival. These are occasions when shrine deities are taken out and paraded around the streets, rather similar to the parading of saints in Catholic countries.

Nor is the religious activity confined to public places. Many families have small Buddhist ancestor cabinets (*butsudan*) where food and incense are placed. In a number of surveys in the 1980s it was found that between 60 and 80 per cent of houses had a Shinto 'god-shelf' which is associated with the imperial ancestress of Japan, Amaterasu. When we went round a reconstruction of nineteenth-century houses in a Tokyo museum, we found that on average they had four shrines apiece, including one for the 'gathering-luck god', a Shinto shrine or shelf, a non-Shinto kitchen god, and a *butsudan*.

It is thus not surprising to find that while in a 1981 survey only one third of the Japanese claimed they had a 'personal religion', over half prayed in times of stress and almost everyone visited ancestral tombs. A Japanese friend had done a survey of her students, who had stated that they were not interested in religion, but found that nine out of ten had recently been involved in some kind of religious ceremony.

We learnt that every company, every factory, every *sumo* 'stable' and organisation had a shrine; even the *yakuza* had Shinto shrines in them. In the Japanese countryside, wherever there is an unusual or striking feature, such as a huge rock or waterfall, there will tend to be a shrine or temple.

When I talked to a young Japanese friend she said that there was a child god living in many houses, which only children could see. She did not have one in her very modern flat, but many people in the countryside had such spirits and they were to be found in older houses. Although she had never seen any of these spirits, many of her friends had done so and she commented, 'I believe we are surrounded by such things though I cannot see them.' In a newspaper article, the Honorary Chief Priest of Osaka City's Imamiya-Ebisu Shrine, Takao Tsue, stated, 'Mountains, animals, trees, weeds … everything has divine spirits inside them … In Shinto, we say "*yaoyorozu*", which means there are eight million gods and goddesses, but that is just an expression. There might be many more.' These beliefs inform the work of *anime* film producer Hayao Miyazaki, and in particular that of his film *My Neighbour Totoro*, which is about local spirits.

Almost all activities, from painting and drinking tea to *Noh* drama and *sumo* wrestling, and even opening a new building or tunnel, is given a 'sacred' feel, often with Shinto priests in attendance to perform a ceremony. I have a stronger sense of a living religion in Japan than anywhere else I have been in the world, including Catholic and Hindu societies. Hearn seems to be right in saying, 'No more irrational assertion was ever made about the Japanese than the statement of their indifference to religion. Religion is still, as it has ever been, the very life of the people, – the motive and the directing power of their every action.'

Yet, as we investigate further, we begin to enter unfamiliar territory. None of the apparent religiosity of Japan has any developed theology or sacred text. Like the early missionaries to Japan, we find it impossible to translate the Western idea of a God into Japanese. They had to invent a special term for God, *Tenshu* ('Lord of Heaven'). This was because *kami*, which is the word sometimes taken to mean 'gods', is very different indeed from the Western monotheistic concept of 'God'.

Kami, W. G. Aston explains, 'are superior, swift, brave, bright, rich, etc. but not immortal, omniscient, or possessed of infinite power'. A *kami* can be good or bad, and there is no morality attached to it. Their strange parallel world is not in some 'heaven' but here, there and everywhere. They are by your side when something shocks or surprises or moves you deeply, when there is a feeling of the sublime. As one friend put it, she sensed a *kami* when she first saw an original Leonardo da Vinci painting. Another time she felt one was present when she was knocked off her bicycle. A great *kabuki* actor can be a *kami*.

'Anything which was beyond the ordinary, other, powerful, terrible, was called *kami*', wrote Motoori Norinaga. 'Thus the emperor, dragons, the echo, foxes, peaches, mountains and the sea, all these were called *kami* because they were mysterious, full of strangeness and power ... In all of these things there shows through, as though through a thin place, an incomprehensible otherness which betokens power.'

I was somewhat prepared for understanding alternative ways of conceptualising religion after I had worked for a number of years in a Nepalese village. There I learnt to my surprise that the functions of religion, such as to provide an explanation for suffering, a way of communicating with supernatural forces through ritual, and a moral code, could, to a large extent, be split apart and be dealt with by different ritual practitioners. Furthermore, many of my own assumptions, in particular notions of sin, heaven and hell, were put in doubt.

In Nepal, the death rituals and questions of the afterlife are dealt with by shamans or lamas. The everyday rituals to protect crops, animals and humans consist of a mix of shamanism, Hindu pujas and Buddhism. Ethics are not informed by strong ideas of heaven and hell or by a set of religious commandments. Rather, what underpins morality is a mixture of vague Buddhist ideas, such as receiving merit from good acts and losing merit from bad ones, combined with a strong desire to 'do as you would be done by' and to aspire to harmonious social relations. Yet even with my experience of this 'cafeteria' approach, I was unprepared for the enigmatic situation I have encountered in Japan.

For example, what was I to make of the fact that when I asked a young Japanese friend what idea she had of heaven, she replied that she had none. In relation to religion, she said, 'we don't have religion'. Yet she and her friends went to shrines and engaged in rituals to relieve their anxieties, though she did not really believe that this had any efficacy. Perhaps the nearest thing I have experienced to this is our desire not to walk under ladders, the instinct to 'touch wood' if we feel threatened, to avoid spilling salt or cracking mirrors. None of these is necessarily related explicitly to God or gods, but these behaviours show that we are not immune to some feeling of spiritual danger.

In a Shinto shrine, there is no God as such. 'When you stand, therefore, in front of the shrine to worship,' Nitobe writes, 'you see your own image reflected on its shining surface, and the act of worship is tantamount to the old Delphic injunction, "Know Thyself".' 'All the dead become gods,' wrote the Shinto commentator Hirata. In Buddhism there is no God. As Kato commented in the seventeenth century, 'He that is honest, is himself a God (*kami*), and if merciful, he is himself a Buddha (*hotoke*). Know that man in his essential nature is one and the same with God and Buddha.' There is no difference; humans are gods, gods are humans.

With the exception of the few Christians and Muslims, there appear to be no believers in God in Japan. Nor are there gods who control people's lives. Neither Buddhism nor Confucianism mentions a God or gods. Nor is there a Devil or an Evil power. In Shinto there are *kami*, but these non-human powers are capricious and the priests cannot negotiate with them, just hope to welcome and placate them somewhat.

There is no belief that humans have an inner spiritual essence given by God. There are no souls, immortal or otherwise. When a person dies, their memory lingers and is respected, but their spirit goes nowhere and they gradually fade into nothingness as the people who remember them die off.

There is no afterlife, no heaven or hell, though there are traces of such beliefs in the Buddhist art of the thirteenth and fourteenth centuries. There is no strong opposition between Good and Evil, no set of commandments about behaviour given religious endorsement which everyone subscribes to. Shinto is just a ceremonial system. I was told by one Shinto priest that in order to have views on ethics he had taken a course in Western philosophy, studying Kant and Hegel to learn about morality.

Confucianism, or the inverted neo-Confucian form in Japan, prescribes certain types of correct social behaviour in comportment, manners and inter-personal relations. But it hardly provides a deep ethical code. Nor can the Japanese find a full moral code in the multiple schools of Buddhism, each preaching a contradictory and partial message and often, in their extreme forms, negating even the Buddha or the reality of existence.

If the Western reader is confused by this account, this is not surprising for the shape of the area we call 'religion' is unfamiliar. It should also be noted that many of the Japanese themselves are confused. I talked to a friend who had been educated in a Jesuit school. He commented, 'In terms of religion, I myself am struggling to understand the society, for example the millions who descend each New Year's Day on the Meiji shrine to apparently worship the Emperor. Most people do not care, yet they do descend upon it.' He could not understand why people went to shrines generally; nor could he make up his mind as to whether the Japanese are religious or not, believe in gods or God, or in souls. 'I'm not sure,' he concluded.

The indecision is related to several factors. The strength of belief has fluctuated over time. The one period when the Japanese could be said to have had some sincere religious belief, or at least a considerable interest in spirits and the possibility of another world, was between the twelfth and fifteenth centuries. This interest then died away, but not completely. As Kenichi put it, if one puts 'religiosity' on a scale of one to ten, with 'very religious' at ten, then the Japanese have moved from roughly six to two on the scale. He thought that Europeans had moved from nine or ten to zero (at least for atheists).

Clearly, the fact that there are multiple paths adds to the confusion. To the question 'Is Japan religious or not?' one informant answered that there is multiple dependency: Shinto for life, Buddhism for death. There is no opposition between them, and between them and Confucianism. This is linked to the absence of absolute logic. 'There was a multiple party system, so to speak, which gave some freedom', he said. 'We have a multiple, vague system to maintain animism. This is what makes Japanese ethics so illogical, as opposed to the logical ethics of the West. Ours is contextual and bending. Affection is more important than logic or ethics. If one is too logical, it will destroy the other. Buddhism, Shinto and Confucianism continued alongside each other. If logic had prevailed, there would have been religious wars.' A word for religion, *shu-kyo*, literally means 'sect' (subgroup) and 'teaching'. Thus Christianity is 'sectarian teaching'. Just as there are many schools of tea ceremonial, flower arranging or calligraphy, so there are many paths in relation to the rituals of life or explanations of misfortune.

How is one to reconcile these two apparent views: the prosaic, secular, this-worldly materialistic view, on the one hand, and that which is enchanted, 'religious' and interpenetrated with spirits, on the other? The only way is to accept the contradictions. 'In Japan the vision of the other world is riddled with ambivalence, like a piece of shot silk,' writes Carmen Blacker. 'Move it ever so slightly and what we thought to be red is now blue; another tremor and both colours flash out simultaneously. It is the same with the other world ... no sooner have we caught sight of the *kami* there, in their own world, than they are here, in ours, hidden invisibly within certain suggestive shapes.'

I think one of my mistakes was to assume that *kami* were like Western spirits, in other words that they were like fairies, overlapping with humans. This is wrong. *Kami* are forces, powers. They are in lightning or earthquakes, in nature bursting in upon humans, but not in any way similar to godlings, elves or other human-like entities. This resolves the paradox of how they both exist outside the usual perceived dimension of life, but at the same time do not live in some supernatural world. Film-maker Miyazaki's depiction of *kami* as abstract dancing lights in *Princess Mononoke* captures their nature.

Thus *kami* have no intentions, no morality, they are not linked to ethics or to human behaviour. They are just part of the unpredictable and strange world in which humans live but do not understand. Their shape and nature probably helps to explain how and why they have managed to survive secularisation. They are wrongly classified as religious in the Western sense, or even spiritual. Kenichi tried to see if they were similar to the concept of 'the sublime' in the West – but this is not right. They are Edgar Allen Poe's '*outré*', things that do not fit in.

Science and rationality pass them by, since they are not on the same plane. They cannot be disproved any more than a rainbow can be disproved. They just exist and constantly intrude. A curious synthesis of shamanism from the north and *tabu* from the Pacific, they are in a category of their own.

The nearest approximation to *kami* is radio waves or electricity. We know these are there and we have learnt to capture them for our benefit, yet they are not visible except through monitoring devices. *Kami* are like a huge electrical force field whose temporary 'homes' are the *kami* shelves and shrines which dot Japan and to whom the Japanese pay wary attention, while loudly proclaiming their disbelief. Children can see and describe them, but for most people they are just a 'rumour of angels', and a reported tale of something bizarre, unfitting, powerful and disturbing.

Not only do the Japanese walk through a social minefield, where enormous attention must be paid to smoothing social relations with other humans, but they also walk through a magical minefield where there are a host of highly volatile forces which, if touched, may explode. The difficulty of comprehending this in a monotheistic Christian context is very great since our distinctions between natural and supernatural, spirit and matter, human and divine do not apply.

In an early conversation with Kenichi and Toshiko, we discussed the attitude to punishment by spirits or gods. I recorded that there is apparently no idea of such punishment. The Japanese 'devil' is depicted as rather ridiculous, half-funny and far from diabolical. The little spirits which are expelled in the New Year house-cleansing rites are mischievous (stealing food and drink) rather than dangerous or evil.

On the question of why misfortune or suffering occurs, an explanation is that it is a punishment that falls on a person for some earlier uncharitable or unethical act. For instance, a person's child might suffer because the parent has earlier in life done something bad. But I did not get the sense that this explanation was often invoked, and most Japanese have no idea of what the punishing force was.

A striking fact is that the Japanese have almost entirely managed to do without personal, human-like causes to make sense of their world. As far as I know, this is the only civilisation with no trace of witchcraft beliefs in its recorded history. Unlike China and Korea, it also largely dispenses with malevolent ancestors. Dead kin do not tend to afflict the living.

Furthermore, there is no set of small human-like spirits or fairies that haunt and harm the living. Indeed the so-called fairy-tales of Japan, as Chamberlain noted, are really not about fairies at all, but rather about animals like foxes, cats and badgers. There are vague beliefs concerning the 'evil eye', which have historical roots, so that in the early nineteenth century von Siebold could write, 'The Japanese children are very meanly clad ... This, it is said, is to preserve them from the blighting effects of the admiration which, if well-dressed, their beauty might excite ... the *evil-eye*.' Yet anyone watching the frequent parading of beautifully dressed Japanese children at shrines and elsewhere can see that such beliefs, if they exist, are tempered by others.

In terms of wider religious phenomena, there is also a curious absence. There is little equivalent to the idea of *karma* or destiny at birth, found both in Hinduism and in a different form in ideas of predestination within Calvinist Christianity. Nor is there anything similar to the Hindu idea of rebirth where a person's present troubles can be explained by sins committed in a previous life. Even the idea of sin itself, so central to the monotheistic religions of the West, seems absent. There is no single punishing and rewarding God. Confucius, the Buddha, the Shinto spirits do not weigh up a person's actions and then punish him or her in the way the Christian or Judaic God is thought to do.

The Japanese seem to be in a strange position. Almost none of the usual explanations for suffering found in other societies are used by them. Consequently the spiritual techniques to ward off future pain which accompany such explanations are also absent. Witches are not hunted or kept away by magical charms. Ancestors do not receive offerings and sacrifices, just a greeting and a small symbolic piece of fruit or flower to express respect and gratitude. Wandering spirits are not directly addressed or warned off. There are no sacrifices to a God or gods.

Instead, people visit shrines and hang up small requests for success in examinations or for good health, or sprinkle salt when someone dies, or in front of their houses, with only the vague idea of attracting good fortune or avoiding suffering from an unspecified power that may exist.

It is true that there is magic. As Chamberlain wrote, 'Astrology, horoscopy, palmistry, physiognomy, foretelling the future by dreams – all these forms of superstition are current in Japan; but the greatest favourite is divination by means of the Eight Diagrams of classical China.' Official diviners were attached to many of the great cults of Japan in the past, using bones, birds, rice, footprints, rods and other methods, and it is probably still the case that most of these old methods of divination are in use.

There is a widespread use of good-luck charms by many educated, urban Japanese, for instance an *omamori*, a little charm sold in temples. I discussed their use with Kenichi. 'Our attitude to religion is in charms,' he said. 'They are not important, but it is good for us. Chance is widely accepted as a cause, but charms may help. Some things are beyond my control. I cannot protect my family by myself. I need some strength from the science of chance.' Consequently he often buys charms, for example when his children are about to take exams or some other major event is happening in the family.

Yet there is no universal or accepted system, each person chooses and half-believes in many techniques. What kind of explanation does this leave to the Japanese? Nowadays a certain amount can be explained by natural laws, by science. Before the later nineteenth century, however, this was not really available as a strong explanation. What did the Japanese do?

What seems extraordinary is that they accepted the randomness, capriciousness and meaninglessness of suffering, the role of chance and fortune, in a way that I have not encountered elsewhere. The volatility of their physical world – the earthquakes, tidal waves, volcanoes, floods – were accepted as natural, ultimately caused by non-spiritual powers at work in this material world.

Adjusting one's behaviour towards others might help, but in the end Japanese philosophy appears to a Westerner to be most like that of the Stoics in Greece. Life is full of pleasure, but also suffering. There are no evil people or spirits or ancestors we can blame for this. There is no punishing God. There are no inevitable rules in the stars. We are just creatures, subject to chance, by the random and immensely complex working out of forces around us. This is a practical, non-mystical and in many ways very modern philosophy. Yet it also stretches back hundreds of years.

Humans engage in a huge amount of behaviour which anthropologists label as 'ritual', that is standardised, repetitive, formalised, communicative behaviour. Japan is full of such ritual, from the formal bowing and exchange of name cards to the numerous ceremonies and leisure activities such as the tea ceremony. It is perhaps the most ritualistic society in the world.

Yet speaking more precisely, the special function of ritual is to communicate not just or even primarily with other humans, but with supernatural or divine power. Through sacrifice, the intoning of powerful words, the use of symbols, humans can move out of this material world into another dimension. When we look at this kind of ritual, Japan poses a problem. There is no God or gods and there is no other separate supernatural world. With what can ritual communicate? When thousands visit the Ise shrine or go to Buddhist and Shinto shrines and wash their hands, clap, make little monetary offerings, write up their wishes and hang them on trees, what are they doing?

There is a widespread attempt to communicate with something spiritual; giving fruit or *sake*, praying, chanting, processing through the streets, abstaining from things. But it is difficult to find out what exactly is happening. 'We discussed ritual,' I noted after a conversation with Toshiko and Kenichi, 'and I explained what anthropologists meant by it. They could think of no rituals in the proper sense in Japanese society. They partly put this down to the absence of a duality between man and nature. Hence there is no need to break through to a spiritual dimension using ritual.'

More concretely, I also wrote:

They described about a dozen annual rituals, for ancestors, good luck and so on. They admitted, however, that they only did a few of them and that they were hazy about the origins and meaning of most of them. Furthermore, if they did not do them, it would not matter, marriage could be as formal/ritualistic or simple as one liked. When we saw someone doing a small ceremonial act, they commented that the boundary between formalised custom and intercession with some other power is unclear. They explained that here there is no other world and so we cannot imagine another world fused together by human behaviour.

Perhaps the best one can say is that Japan is highly ritualistic, but does not have Ritual. Almost every action has great symbolic implications. Yet it all exists in a here and now, non-deistic context, where nothing very concrete can be addressed. Practices obey the laws of aesthetics – purity, simplicity, balance, harmony more than the laws of good and evil, right and wrong.

Writers on Japan agree that the concept of the afterlife is rather weakly developed. The two main Chinese influences which might have led towards beliefs in an after-world were transmuted to have the opposite effect. The widespread Chinese faith in Heaven as a transcendental entity that governed human destiny, which became an important element of Confucianism, was never developed in Japan. In most forms of Japanese Buddhism, human beings have this world and this life and no other. As Yamagata Banto put it, 'There is no hell, no heaven, no soul, only man and the material world.' Yet those who know Japan will remember the veneration that Japanese are supposed to feel for their ancestors – the shrines, graveyards, *butsudan*. How are we to resolve the apparent contradiction?

There is some feeling that even without an individual soul, something continues after death. The graves of the recently dead should be carefully tended and annually visited. But once the person has been dead for some time, the grave is often neglected. The dead are first worshipped as *hotoke*, or spirits, but eventually, the spirit of the dead person becomes fused with the spirits of the ancestors in general. This seems different from the classic accounts of ancestor worship.

I asked an elderly lady where the spirit of her dead husband resided, but she didn't know. She asked a priest who answered, 'He exists wherever you pray' – the implication being that he will no longer exist when she forgets him or dies, thus the spirit has no separate existence. In the summer festival of *bon*, an equivalent festival to All Souls in the Christian calendar, the spirits of the recently dead are led home.

She felt that he was actually coming home. She believed that as her husband, he protected her and the house. If she didn't have a *butsudan* for her husband, his spirit would be free from the duty to protect her. She stressed that this was not an 'ancestor shrine' but a 'husband shrine'. It was for a particular person, not a general category of ancestors. A grave was for 'general ancestors'.

Spirits of close relatives are important. Buddhist monks now sell names for the dead – if you pay more, you get more precious characters. These are inscribed on a wood or stone tablet which stands in the *butsudan*. In a friend's *butsudan* there are tablets for her father and her father's two brothers. She doesn't believe that their spirits are here since 'it must be the first son's job' to look after them. In an earthquake, people are supposed to take with them the tablets (at the risk of their own life) before escaping, but she doubts that they are of any value. To her, they are just tablets. She does not really believe in the Buddhist rites. Survival is much more important and therefore she would advocate just running out of the house.

We asked a young Japanese friend what happened after death. She said she didn't so much believe in a surviving spirit, as in a return to nature in some way. She thought her grandmother had gone through a ritual to bring back her grandfather's spirit at the *bon* festival as a kind of commemoration and for her own satisfaction, but considered that death rituals were for the living and not the dead. She believed that all the individuality of a person dies and just goes back into some sort of mass. She continued by explaining that there is no other world. Some people think that the Shinto spirits or *kami* have some relation to dead spirits, others believe that the *hotoke* or Buddhist spirits go to another world but also inhabit graveyards. This is why graves are cleaned and spirits welcomed from the graveyard at the *bon* festival.

As can be seen, there are many different elements here, with doubt, belief and, to a degree, ancestor ideas. There is clearly great variety between different people, the same person at different points in their life, different groups of people and in different parts of Japan. 'In most rural communities,' Robert Smith writes, 'people say that the ancestral spirits are passively benign or altogether powerless, but we have accounts of some places where they are regularly charged with causing misfortune.' The fragmentation of belief in Japan is one of its most conspicuous characteristics, but makes generalisation very difficult. It could be argued that the Japanese are ancestor worshippers, or not; that they believe in dead spirits, or are very sceptical; that they fear the dead, or ignore them. All are simultaneously true.

As with the living, the relations with the dead are formal, ceremonial and depend on the context. Because the Japanese trace their family through both males and females, it is difficult for them to establish the strong ancestor lines which are reported for male-dominated lineages in China and parts of Africa. Dead individuals soon disappear into a general category of ancestor and the past closes up behind the living. There is no particular interest in them when they disappear into that nebulous space and one will never meet them again. They are not waiting as in heaven, as is conceived in Western monotheism. They become part of nature and nothingness again. Dust to dust, ashes to ashes, but no resurrection at the Last Trumpet and no return to this life. This life is all we have.

It is impossible to say categorically that any particular thought or action is always wrong in Japan; it all depends on the context. Truth and morality are socially constructed in relation to the specific situation. Actions and thoughts are pragmatic, guided by reciprocities, 'do as you would be done by', codes of beauty and respect. Japanese aesthetics and ethics are intimately related.

Observers have contrasted the 'guilt' cultures of the monotheistic West to the 'shame' culture of Japan. Guilt occurs when people feel an internal pressure from an invisible force (God) who watches our every thought and controls us through a fear of eternal damnation. This is very different to a 'shame' culture, where only a fear of loss of 'face' or respect in the eyes of others will guide people's actions.

Actually, this is a half-truth, but it does capture the social nature of Japanese thought and the absence of God-driven guilt, particularly that found at its extreme in some Protestant versions of Christianity. This contrast, if it gives the impression that the Japanese are not constantly weighing their motives and actions in line with deeply internalised standards, is a distortion of a complex situation.

A better distinction would be between ethics and morality. The Japanese are completely absorbed by ethical, or human-to-human standards. Yet, without a transcendent God or gods, there is no concern with morality. It is important not to confuse this with an internal and external distinction between guilt and shame.

Every Japanese operates under a very heavy weight of obligations and pressures to behave by the highest standards. If he or she fails, whether another person notices or not, the person feels the failure deeply. It is not just a matter of external 'face'. Curiously, even without an observing God, many Japanese have a strong sense of internalised anxiety. Yet it is not sin towards God that is involved, but a failure to live up to other people's expectations, and hence, since we mirror others, our own expectations as well. This is a kind of guilt, but not of the usual religious kind. It is human guilt, not God guilt.

In such an ethical system, which has nothing to do with religion, all actions and thoughts become relative. There are no absolutes. As a Japanese lady explained to David Riesman, 'There is a lack of understanding of universalistic rule; justice is tied up with status, and there is no right or wrong, that is, no transcendental rightness, and there are no rigid attitudes in the religion.' Whether it is a matter of truth, honour, life, death, cruelty, kindness or anything else, all behaviour and thought becomes fluid. There may well still be a struggle within each individual between true desire (*honne*) and moral obligations to others (*tatamae*), but not between human desire and divine commandments.

❀

Christians, Muslims or Hindus, members of most religions and civilisations, have perpetrated many horrors on those they considered infidels or semi-humans. The Germans on the Jews, the Turks on the Armenians, the Arabs on Africans – there are too many examples of atrocities just to single out the Japanese, and often there is the same denial of the cruelties.

Yet there is a special feature of situational morality that helps us to understand a little the great contrast between the courteous, harmonious and peaceful ethics of much of Japanese life and the moments of great brutality and apparent loss of control. If behaviour is not underpinned by a notion that humans have an immortal soul, that there are absolute standards of behaviour towards everyone, then there may be unexpected consequences.

We could argue that Japan is at once the most highly moral and the most immoral large civilisation. All of life is a mixture of the social, moral and aesthetic; there are no divisions. Economic and political behaviour, often seen as outside the moral sphere in the West, are bound up with morality in Japan, but not of a transcendental, religious kind. As with religion, morality is everywhere and nowhere simultaneously.

This universal fusion of morality with all aspects of life is a central characteristic of some of the tribal societies that I have studied. Every action, whether economic, political or social, has a moral dimension to it, in other words it changes human relations. Exchanges between people and social contacts are moral, as well as practical. Human beings are always ends, as well as means to an end. Nothing is split apart.

In this sense Japan feels like an ethically interwoven tribe, yet one where millions are caught up in the web, not just thousands. Because morality in turn is affected by kinship and politics, it is always situational and contextual. There can be no absolute rules, just as there cannot be in law, for everything depends on the relationship and the circumstances. The proclaimed absolute morality of a God-based and deeply separated modern world is neither possible nor desirable. Morality is like bamboo, strong, yet bending with the winds of power and sentiment.

I asked a Japanese friend if there is any concept of absolute evil. 'No. There is no absolute right or wrong. No sense of absolutes – good, beauty, etc. No absolute ruler. No transcending authority, no such ideology ... How do the Japanese explain the world? It's unanswerable. It needs no answer. We have no world view. With all human effort there must be some unanswerable questions. We are very small and nature will overwhelm us in the end. In fact 99.9 per cent of things we can't answer.'

The essence of the undivided situation in Japan is that everything is partially fused with everything else and no sphere is either dominant or entirely separate. The only way this can work is if all aspects of life are very flexible and every gesture, action, thought, can be interpreted in a number of ways, multi-level symbols with extreme dependence on the context in which they are used.

Everything has to be relative, not absolute; time, truth, space, personhood, status – each, rather than being fixed, absolute and external, is fluid, non-absolute, contextual. Likewise all thought and all morality must be situational and relative, adapted to each situation, negotiable, provisional, unfinished, evolving and never completed.

While principles may appear to be reasonable, they are quite likely to cause obstructions and blockages since, like rocks in a stream, they break up the flow of the ever-changing reality of life. In the absence of any God or absolute moral authority, it is easier to ensure that such fluidity is maintained.

All forms of behaviour and thought may be inappropriate or appropriate depending on their context. Analysts have called this morality based on social relativism by various names such as 'situationalism', 'situational ethic', 'situational morality' or 'contextualism'. The essence of it is that nothing is fixed, and the external world is unstable, floating, changing and everyone has to constantly adapt themselves to it.

Other people from whom, in a relational culture, a person draws his or her own sense of self, are constantly changing and hence make the 'I' into a different shape. The mirror changes as in a hall of magical mirrors and what appears is thus shrunk, stretched and distorted. There is no 'true', uncontextual self.

Yet it is not just other people and the notoriously shifting and unpredictable ecology that make life somewhat like white-water rafting, a constant avoiding of chaos and disaster, but also the capriciousness of the spirits. Matsumoto comments, 'The Japanese feel comfortable with the notion that nature is situational and that man is situational, and at the same time, "kami" (gods) are situational towards both man and nature.'

The plasticity of power, an exact equivalent to the elastic morality and notions of the self and reality, was described by Fukuzawa. He wrote:

Power in the West is like iron; it does not readily expand or contract. On the other hand, the power of the Japanese warriors was as flexible as rubber, adapting itself to whatever it came in contact with. In contact with inferiors, it swelled up immensely, in contact with those above, it shrivelled up and shrank.

When I visited Japan I made certain assumptions about the necessary relationship between religion and ethics. I believed that one of the central functions of religion is to tell us what is good and what is evil. Religion warns us of the consequences of evil actions, tells us that there will be punishment in the afterlife and disasters in this one. Religious beliefs also tell us that human nature is divided, almost equally split between a 'good', and a 'bad' side.

We have seen that much of this connection is missing in Japan. There is no God or gods to endorse morality. Consequently, moral behaviour cannot be derived or deduced from religion. Ethics are a social, aesthetic matter, nothing to do with Spirit or spirits. This is emphasised by the absence of an afterlife. There is no punishment, no heaven and hell, no punishing ancestors, no external sanctions.

Japanese looking at the West are uncomfortable about systems that assume an intimate and necessary connection between morality and religion. For them, there has never been a single religious organisation or church which has been in charge of morality, and so the teaching of ethics is left to the family and to the education system. There was no original Fall from grace or loss of innocence. The prevailing attitude is that humans are neither angels nor devils, but somewhere in between and intrinsically changeable. There is no eternal war between two sides of our nature, our mind and our body, our ideals and our lusts. There is no soul in jeopardy. There is no living Spirit watching to see if we behave well or what our inner motives are. There is no absolute Good or Evil.

One fruitful way of approaching the puzzling world of Japanese religious belief is to use the framework developed by Karl Jaspers. In his late work on the concept of the 'Axial Age', Jaspers draws attention to those civilisations that went through a great shift in their philosophical and religious foundation, turning like a wheel on its axis, in the period between the eighth and second centuries BC.

Before this Axial Age, the natural and supernatural worlds were entangled with each other, not seen as opposed. As in most tribal religions, the world of spirits was largely a reflection of this world and intermingled with it. Humans and animals, this life and the afterlife, were blended together. This was often a world of shamanism and witchcraft, of animism (material things have spirit in them) and of attempts to put pressure upon spirits through sacrifice and magical spells. The divine world was not a separate ideal order against which we measured this life, but a continuation of the sensory world in an invisible form.

For reasons as yet unexplained, in much of Europe and Asia over a period of six hundred years, a number of great religious and philosophical figures emerged who changed this. They created a dynamic tension between this world of matter and another world of spirit. They set up ideals against which our behaviour should be judged. New philosophical systems provided a reorganised relation between a God, or ideal system, and this corrupted world.

In China this is manifested in the work of Lao-tzu and Confucius; in India in the Upanishads and the teachings of the Buddha; in Iran, with Zarathustra or Zoroastra; in the Middle East in the books of the great Old Testament prophets, including Elijah, Jeremiah and Isaiah; in Greece, the fount of Western thought, in Homer, Heraclitus and Plato. China found its Confucian template, by which it has lived ever since; much of India and Central Asia its Buddhist salvation, and the Western end of the continent the firm foundations for the monotheistic religions of Judaism, Christianity and Islam which were to dominate that world, combined with Greek philosophy.

An aftershock of this philosophical *tsunami* occurred about two thousand years later with the religious and scientific revolutions of the sixteenth and seventeenth centuries. This took the first separation to its ultimate conclusion. The radical dissociation of the natural and supernatural worlds, which was at the heart of Protestantism, was combined with the separations which are associated with Descartes and the seventeenth-century scientific revolution. This disenchantment of the world included the separation of the human world, based on discoverable natural laws of physics and chemistry, from the spiritual world, which is somewhere else.

It appears that Japan is the one great civilisation that has never gone through the Axial Age. Its geographical isolation has meant that it has been protected against the religious tidal wave which swept over the rest of Asia and Europe. The Axial divisions triumphed in the monotheisms of the West, deeply altered the pluralistic systems of India and China, yet had spent their force by the time they reached Japan. The Japanese have long been aware of Axiality, however, and therefore cannot be called pre-Axial, but rather non-Axial.

Evidence for this is to be found throughout the descriptions of Japanese attitudes towards God, Heaven, Hell, Sin, Nature and Man. At the centre of it all is the absence of dichotomies. There is no split between body and soul, flesh and spirit.

The oppositions created by the Axial philosophers are absent. 'Intellect itself was considered subordinate to ethical emotion,' Nitobe writes. 'Man and the universe were conceived to be alike spiritual and ethical'. In Japan everything is interconnected, unseparated, relative and impermanent. Nothing is absolute and there is no contradiction between the here and now and the Eternal, between the 'ought' and the 'is', between man and god.

The sociologist S. N. Eisenstadt has argued, with a great deal of supporting evidence, that Japan managed to subvert the Axial philosophies as they came into the country so that they lost their basic tension between the Ideal and the Actual. He comments:

> The distinctiveness of Japan lies in its being the only non-Axial civilisation that maintained – throughout its history, up to the modern time – a history of its own, without becoming in some way marginalised by the Axial civilisations, China and Korea, Confucianism and Buddhism, with which it was in continuous contact.

What is particularly startling is that this should have been possible in one of the great literate world civilisations which, on the surface, embraced the great traditions of Confucianism and Buddhism. Eisenstadt continues, 'The transformation of Confucianism and

Buddhism, and later of Western ideologies, in Japan … constitutes the de-Axialisation of Axial religions, ideologies, and civilisations not in the local or peripheral arenas of "small traditions" but in the very core of the "great tradition".'

Japan rejected the philosophical idea of another separate world of the ideal and the good, a world of spirit separate from man and nature, against which we judge our actions and direct our attempts at salvation. This is an extraordinary situation and one which explains a great deal about the strangeness of Japan. It suggests that what underpins Japanese philosophy and cosmology is a set of premises that are radically different to those of the Axial systems of mainland Europe and Asia.

In his recent book, *Imagining Japan*, Robert Bellah stresses that Japan has remained a non-Axial civilisation up to the present. He argues, 'Japanese culture and society in the Tokugawa period can still be characterized as nonaxial'; and, after the Meiji restoration, 'nonaxial premises survived, though reformulated in a complex mixture with axial principles, but with the nonaxial premises still retaining primacy'.

'Through all these enormous changes,' Bellah maintains, 'the basic premises of Japanese society, though drastically reformulated, have remained nonaxial. That is, the axial and subsequent differentiations between transcendent reality and the state, between state and society, and between society and self have not been completed.'

How did Japan manage to remain the one non-Axial modern civilisation on earth? To start with, there was a widespread animistic belief and a system of purification rites. This was later modified, and it became very recently codified under the name 'Shinto'. This is largely a system of ritual, etiquette and respect; it has never been abandoned or completely overlaid.

This animistic faith was strong until the arrival of the reformed

Buddhist sects in the fourteenth century and then it was submerged, to be revived as part of the Emperor system at the end of the nineteenth century. Shinto shrines are now to be found all over Japan, often nestling inside or encompassing in a friendly way the Buddhist temples which one might have expected them to be at war with. Shinto is not a religion in the modern sense of the word, but it has clearly something to do with guiding humans in a spirit-filled world.

When Buddhism was introduced it was soon transmuted into something that again did not bring a radical Axial change. In the reformed sects of the fourteenth century such as Nichiren and Zen, the Japanese took the idea that Buddhism is not a religion to its extremest forms. The Buddha had taught of the vanity of God and gods, and so the Japanese Buddhists took him at his word and proclaimed an anti-religion. 'If you see the Buddha, kill him.' He does not exist, indeed nothing exists. Japanese Buddhism has little oppositional tension with this world, it is just a set of practices to help the individual seek salvation in this life.

It is this Japanese transformation of Buddhism, the great Axial world philosophy that is closest to a religion, which is most extraordinary. In an article on the crucial period of the introduction of Buddhism, the thirteenth and fourteenth centuries, Kazuo Osumi explains, 'The Japanese adaptation of Buddhism made it diverge in several ways from its original form. From the beginning the Japanese fused Buddhism with Shinto and with their own long-held cosmology of the spirit world.' Because of the pre-existing situation, and the political and philosophical climate of the time, the Buddhist sects split and diverged from each other and from mainland Buddhism so that 'the tenets of Kamakura Buddhism were often framed in opposition to established Buddhist doctrines. These doctrinal divergences only heightened the reputation of the new Buddhist schools as opponents of ecclesiastical authority.'

A detailed account of what happened is given by Hajime Nakamura in a systematic analysis of the difference between Indian and Chinese Buddhism on the one hand, and the various schools of thought in Japan. Given the primary loyalty to small, closed groups and social ties, he writes:

> It is easy to understand why Japanese Buddhists have tended to dis-regard the Universalistic Buddhist Precepts ... Buddhism, we note, has thus been completely transformed for the sake of practicability. Japanese society as the ground of Buddhist practice had rejected the religious practices of India and China ... [It] was within the frame-work of their own peculiar nationalistic standpoint and orientation that the Japanese accepted Buddhism. They were inclined to utilize it as a means and an instrument to realise a certain socio-political end. They were not converted to Buddhism. They converted Buddhism to their own tribalism ... [The] Japanese accepted Buddhism without changing their own original standpoint an iota. That was why Bud-dhism spread with such speed.

By the standards of the universalistic world religions of India and China, he concludes, 'Religion, in the true sense of the word, never deeply took root on Japanese soil.'

The different sects of Buddhism received support from different groups in Japan, the samurai, urban aristocrats and others. Japan not only hosted divergent traditions – Shinto, Buddhist, Confucian and, later, Western philosophies – but each tradition was fragmented, teaching fundamentally different things. Buddhism actually reinforced previous beliefs and rituals by providing explicit doctrines to explain the world of spirits and by strengthening local rituals. Bellah describes how early Buddhist thinkers in Japan have 'used the materials of an axial tradition (in this case Buddhist, but in many cases Confucian as well) to justify a nonaxial position ... This might be called using the axial to overcome the axial.'

The 'adaptation of Buddhism to local circumstances, its de-Axialisation' is unique, Eisenstadt argued, as in the case of Japan 'its

pagan premises, a basically this-worldly religious outlook, have transformed those of a "great" religion in shaping the tradition of an entire
civilisation, bracketing out, though certainly not obliterating, its more
transcendental or other-worldly premises'. In Japanese Buddhism,
human beings only have this life.

Likewise, when Confucianism entered Japan it was not in the strong
and all-embracing form which dominated China and spread to
Korea. It was muted, became what is called neo-Confucianism, and
soon adapted to fit alongside Shinto and Buddhism in the relativistic
world of Japan. It provided some norms of behaviour, particularly in
the relations between human beings, but it was not a religion or even
a widespread set of principles which set up an ideal against which
a person should measure his or her life. It has profoundly affected
much of Japanese life, but, as with Buddhism, it lost its Axiality as it
was absorbed. Confucianism did not transform the basic premises of
Japanese social organisation.

An important aspect of the de-Axialisation of Confucianism
was the way in which the relation between religion and politics was
transformed when the philosophy was imported into Japan. If the
Japanese had replaced their idea of a direct divine descent of the
emperor's line from the gods, 'this would have been for the Japanese
to move from an archaic to an axial conception of rule'. Yet, as Bellah
notes, 'Such a move, though available ever since Confucian doctrines
were first understood, was never made.'

How Confucianism was transformed as it developed through
history in Japan was explained to me by Professor Hiroshi Watanabe.
He described how Confucianism in China did contain some idea
of transcendence, of a supreme heaven, even if the strong opposition
between this world and the other was missing. When the doctrine was
first expounded in Japan, the judgement of heaven was stripped away
and the ruler was not subject to the mandate of heaven. Furthermore,

in the second great wave of Confucian influence in the eighteenth century there were further transformations.

In particular, the highly influential thinker Sorai Ogyu turned another tenet of Confucianism upside down. He argued that the masses could not become better human beings, whereas the Chinese emperors ruled by encouraging the humanising process in what they considered were basically good people whose virtues they reflected. Sorai thought more along the lines of the cynical Machiavelli and exhorted the Shogunate to rule the ignorant and restless people through force. As others put it, might is right, the ends – order and discipline – justify the means.

Another transformation was in the balance between affection and logic within the Confucian tradition. Another scholar explained to us that the reason why Japanese ethics were 'affection-strong rather than logic-strong' was due to the Confucian emphasis on affectionate benevolence. 'When it [Confucianism] was imported from China it put off the logical and accepted the affectionate.' While the Chinese system was in some ways as syncretic as the Japanese, mixing Taoism, Confucianism and Buddhism, it emphasised logic as the most important part of the system of philosophy. 'In the Japanese case logic was replaced by affection – there was no logic. Our system is not axial but permeated by affection.' If there is a clash between the head and the heart in Japan, the heart wins.

Through the last two thousand years Japan never made the radical break between the natural and the supernatural. No single God whose worship would encompass all the strands – ethics, ritual and ideas about suffering, the afterlife and the purpose of things – ever dominated. No wonder the Japanese cannot understand what Westerners mean when they talk of 'a religion'.

Yet the asceticism, purity and simplicity of much of Japanese life, including the temples and crafts, do remind me of the Protestant reformation. This is why some leading experts see a similarity between what happened in Japan with the Buddhist sects and what happened in Europe in the sixteenth century with Calvin and Luther. There is something familiar about the calm and empty religious buildings of Kyoto. Something 'other' than the human is present, but I cannot put my finger on what it is.

What we have in Japan is a hybrid, something which falls into neither of the two main categories of religious systems. Everything is imbued with 'spirit' or *kami* – pots, computers, goldfish, buildings, space, time, tea, stones, *sumo*, peaches, echoes, even the *yakuza*. This civilisation feels 'enchanted'.

Yet on the other hand nothing is fully 'religious' in the Axial sense. There is no other world. There is no God. There is no Heaven. There is no need to appease God or gods with animal or other sacrifice. Shamanism is held at the margins. Individual ancestors only last as long as they are remembered personally and then are merged with all the ancestors. They do not tend to trouble the living. There are no curses, no witchcraft, nothing in particular to believe in.

Japan does not feel like god-crowded India. Nor is it like the West, still living with the ghosts of monotheistic religion. Japan is neither sacred nor profane, secular nor religious, neither enchanted nor disenchanted. It lives along other dimensions and with a mix that our nets of understanding do not help us to capture. Japan is a synthesis which gives people many options.

To the more traditional approaches of earlier Shinto, Buddhist, Taoist and Christian frameworks there have been added a whole set of new religions, often combining what are thought to be the best of science and religion. 'New religions' is a general term used to refer to various movements since the eighteenth century. Their number and strength has grown dramatically in the twentieth century. They are described in the *Kodansha Encyclopedia* by such terms as 'messianic, nativistic, millenarian, utopian, revitalistic, eschatological, faith healing, or crisis cult'. They have drawn on all the previous beliefs and rituals in Japan, including Buddhism, Shinto, Confucianism, folk religion and shamanism, renewing various elements from them. Often they are founded by a charismatic leader, frequently a woman who has a vision or visitation, and then the followers set up an organisation to spread the word. The two largest, *Rissho Koseikai* and *Soka Gakkai*, each number many millions among their followers.

The new religions are sometimes criticised as their leaders often assert that character-building is a key to happiness in life. It has been pointed out that by attributing all problems to the philosophical attitude and control of the mind, this approach tends to divert attention from social problems and to lead to a conservative view of life. The emergence of such religions could be seen as a symptom of the breakdown of society. Yet it can also be interpreted as another example of the way in which new hybrids are created in the attempt to revive and adapt older beliefs to changing circumstances, keeping the core of something old within the shell of something new.

The philosophy behind the new religions is compatible with intuition, emotion, and reason beyond reason. One must sincerely try to do what one feels one has to do. In the end, all calculations, principles, absolute commands fall away and the individual has to follow his sincere and true beliefs. They promise to make accessible a way of dealing with all needs and requirements in spiritual and material terms, with full or partial commitment.

At first sight the claim that the philosophical system in Japan is almost totally different from that of all other large civilisations on earth seems an exaggeration. For what is being argued is that Japan is not just different from the rest in the way that, for example, Islam is different from Christianity, or Hinduism is different from Judaism. Rather, the difference is at a more fundamental level. Japan has avoided the whole axial shift which would have underpinned it with a world religion.

Yet the evidence for a profound difference permeates all spheres of Japanese life. Only something on this scale can provide the key which will simultaneously unlock the series of mysteries which I have tried to explore. Only when we realise that the Japanese are still living within a shamanic, 'tribal', world, can we begin to understand the very simple explanation lying behind the immensely contorted and contradictory surface which is so baffling not only to outsiders, but also to the Japanese themselves.

That Japan has evolved in a direction which separates it off from all other world civilisations becomes less implausible if we consider the historical and geographical forces which have played themselves out on these islands over the last two thousand years. Furthermore, if we place the philosophical story within the wider context of the influences from the outside which have been deeply modified as they entered Japan, we can see the de-Axialisation story as just one among a number of transformations. We can see that the Japanese have reshaped, and continue to reorganise, the forces which press in upon them so that they do not fundamentally destroy what is felt to be the quintessential unifying force which holds together their undivided world.

Japan has been inhabited by many different peoples for thousands of years. By the sixth century the economy, society, politics and religion were still intermixed. The myths of the founding of Japan were tribal, with the rulers said to descend from the female goddess Amaterasu. The Japanese were a large and mixed tribal community who already had an unusual language, little related to any known form on the mainland, a set of local customs and a pantheistic approach to life.

By the seventh century, when the first major influx of Chinese institutions started to infuse Japan, the local culture was already so strong, and the distance the ideas had to travel from China so great, that the new systems did not completely take over. They were filtered as they arrived, and over time a good deal of the Chinese world-view was modified.

This subverting of the waves of outside thought happened repeat-edly. The Confucian, Buddhist and Imperial systems of the Chinese were inspected, adapted and fitted into a strong pre-existing Japanese mould, so that they took on new and different meanings. Likewise, Chinese administrative practices, city forms and technologies were altered. For example, the Mandarin system was not adopted and the city walls of China were not copied. Chinese written characters (*kanji*) were absorbed, but then altered in their meaning and gram-matical forms as a parallel simpler writing system was developed.

In the fourteenth century another wave of imports, particularly new agricultural and other technologies, as well as philosophies, entered Japan. Yet the reformed Buddhist sects of Japan were different from varieties on the mainland, for they became absorbed into the powerful animist and Confucian mix that pre-existed their arrival.

By the time the Europeans, first the Portuguese and then the Dutch, added their influences in the sixteenth century, Japan was able to absorb what it wanted without itself changing entirely. As a result, it experimented with gunpowder weapons, European animals, wine and glass, Christianity and Western scientific ideas. Yet after a short investigation, it rejected much of this. By 1700 it was much the same cultural river as it had been two centuries earlier, but strengthened by the new flows from outside.

In the next two hundred years Japan absorbed further Chinese and Western ideas, but this increased its otherness. As a consequence, when the most massive challenge presented itself, in the middle of the nineteenth century in the outward imperial expansion of Europe and America, Japan was in a position to do what it had always done. The Japanese absorbed what they needed, transformed certain parts of society and politics and adopted Western technologies and science.

By 1920 Japan looked on the surface as if it had become the first Asian industrial capitalist society modelled on the West. Yet deeper down, much of the old river still flowed on under the superficially Western surface. Structurally Japan remained quite different from the democratic, capitalist West.

After the Second World War, Japan took an American turn and a powerful new stream flowed in so that it looked for a while like a copy of America. But again this was a colouring, mainly on the surface, the effect of selective borrowing. Although there were dramatic changes, many social attitudes and practices remained largely unaltered.

It is this rejection of the rigid divisions that exist in most civilisa- tions, the Axial dichotomies, which has been one of the secrets of Japanese flexibility and ability to change rapidly when required. 'One reason why Japan entered the modern industrial world with relative ease compared with China and other Asian nations,' writes Van Wolferen, 'lay in the very lack of any strongly held precepts, based on transcendental beliefs, to block the changes of mentality that were required to cope with the material changes.' Van Wolferen uses the term 'ideological chameleons' to describe the Japanese, a metaphor which captures the rapid surface changes, but also implies that the animal itself survives beneath its ever-changing skin.

It might reasonably be argued that all countries do this. The French pride themselves on remaining French while absorbing influences from the many invasions and outside pressures. The English on their island see their culture as a long river originating from the Anglo- Saxons, with various smaller streams joining it along the way. What makes Japan an extreme case is that it is such a large and diverse culture, with a very ancient history of separateness. It is also a long way from any mainland. The gradual leaking in of outside influences over the last fifteen hundred years has inoculated it against complete and revolutionary change, giving it greater power to reject and adapt. It has successfully filtered outside influences more often than any other nation.

Throughout Japanese history, there has been a tension between closeness and distance from Asian neighbours. This middling position explains a great deal. The presence of China, the greatest, most ancient and most creative of civilisations only some hundreds of miles away has been a powerful factor, for Japan has always been both influenced and eclipsed by its neighbour. The flow of high culture both from China and, to a considerable extent, from Korea, has put it in a fortunate position.

Imagine if Japan had been in the Indonesian archipelago. Thousands of miles away from the Chinese mainland, it would not have become a rich mirror of all those early and hugely impressive technologies and cultural artefacts which we associate with China. For much of its history, Japan has lived in the shadow of a mighty tree that constantly shed new fruit and seeds: pottery and porcelain, silk, tea, weapons, a writing system, governmental systems, religions and philosophies. What it learnt to do was to take the Chinese inventions and to adapt them, often reversing them and improving them even further. Thus it refined the pottery, the tea ceremony, the armour and swords, the gardens, the Buddhism, the writing. This art of screening influences stood Japan in good stead when it was subjected to a new onslaught of outside pressures.

At the same time, Japan's distance from the Chinese mainland has protected it. Had Japan been, like Korea, linked by land to China, it would have been overrun by its dominant neighbour, and would now be as sinicised as Korea became. Closer to China, it would not have struck off in its singular way. The four hundred miles or so of dangerous sea, combined with the inward turn in Chinese culture after it gave up its great maritime adventures in the early fifteenth century, saved Japan from being invaded. Along with Western Europe, Japan is the only part of the Eurasian continent not conquered by the Mongols. It became like some other islands: ideas and institutions originating from many different outside sources formed a new mixture.

According to Japanese myth, the adapted imports set into a unified and largely uniform 'Japaneseness'. Yet it is important to remember how varied these imports are in their origins. I remember well a conversation with the Japanese demographic historian Akira Hayami, who summarised for me the results of his major project on the social structures of Japan over the last three hundred years. He explained that north-east Japan was a 'Jomon' culture area, of Siberian origin, features of which were early marriage, low fertility, stem families and primogeniture; this was a kind of hunter-gatherer culture. In the central part of Japan were people of Chinese origin, characterised by late marriage, a mix of stem and nuclear families and a high degree of urbanisation. In the south-west were people of Polynesian origin, via the Ryukyu chain of islands; late marriage, high illegitimacy, divorce and remarriage rates and stem families, together with a high social status for women, were the features.

We know that even until the end of the nineteenth century the social structures, marriage systems and folklore of parts of Japan show that there were at least three great waves of in-migration. Strong traditions and peoples came from the shamanic north through Sakhalin and to the centre through Korea. Much of Japanese culture and some Japanese clearly migrated from China. From Malaya, Polynesia and other parts of the Pacific, peoples island-hopped to inhabit southern Japan. All these peoples and influences coalesced into a unique mixture whose diversity can be attested by a glance at faces in any crowded street.

As with England with its mongrel population, Japan's island-hood gave an early sense of national identity and difference. Japan contained many civilisations, but directly mirrored none of them. There were strong dialect and cultural differences, yet there was also an unusually unified national language, literature, religion and administration for more than a thousand years. With its size and diverse population, Japan was able to develop and experiment with what worked best within the particular ecology and geography of this long set of rocky islands.

The Japanese have devoted huge energy to quarantining them‐ selves. They want to be seriously bounded, but also to allow in a certain amount, having discovered that this is the most satisfactory way to live. Controlled immigration, not so much of people but of ideas, technologies and influences, has been at the heart of Japanese history.

In the light of this, what I experienced as strange on encountering many aspects of Japanese culture and society begins to make sense. The refusal to fit into the categories of thought and action which were developed in either the West or the East, especially in China and India, becomes comprehensible.

As with Britain, almost all the elements in Japanese civilisation were imported from abroad. We have seen that there have been very few macro‐inventions in Japan to rival the scope of the great inven‐ tions of China, or, from the seventeenth century, the philosophical and technological macro‐inventions of the West. But to all the inven‐ tions that they have adopted, the Japanese have added value.

Just walk a few paces from the Chinese gallery in the Victoria and Albert Museum in London into the adjacent Japanese room. You will immediately feel that you are in a vaguely familiar yet different civilisation. In many ways Japan inhabits a more delicate, sensitive and playful world. It has the quirky, irregular feel of real creativity, all the more surprising since most of it originated from the hall next door. Beneath the surface of restless small changes, Japan has, like a miraculous Australia, maintained a unique set of cultural flora and fauna which enriches us all.

8

Out of the mirror

When she was little, my grand-daughter Lily jumped out of a large wardrobe through which she had visited a magical land. She looked round and said gravely, 'The whole world has changed!' In a similar way my world has changed after travelling within the Japanese magic mirror. One effect is to make me wonder whether it is my own world or that of the Japanese that is 'normal'. I understand what a number of those who went to Japan in the nineteenth century meant when they reflected on this question.

William Griffis asked, 'Why is it that we do things contrariwise to the Japanese? Are we upside down, or they? The Japanese say that we are reversed. They call our penmanship "crab-writing", because, say they, "it goes backward" … Which race is left-handed? Which has the negative, which the positive of truth? What is truth? What is down, what is up?' Edward Morse put his money on the Japanese being the right way up, and the West being upside down:

> The first observation a foreigner makes on coming to Japan is that the Japanese in certain things do just the reverse from us. We think our way is undeniably right, whereas the Japanese are equally impressed with the fact that we do everything differently from them. As the Japanese are a much older civilised race, it may be possible that their way of doing some things is really the best way.

❧

One of the most extraordinary features of the world of the Japanese is what a well-kept secret it is. Like any parallel world, it is more or less invisible, but just shines through occasionally. Many visitors have sensed there is something strange, but in the absence of any sustained mapping it has not been possible for a wider public to know what is there. The mirror is not one which people can look into.

If we confine ourselves to just the period since Japan was 'opened up' to the West in the 1870s we can see how far various Western writers on Japan have gone in their understanding of this enigmatic civilisation. Isabella Bird was an experienced travel writer but without any training in comparative analysis. Edward Morse was a wonderful observer, but had no background in social theory. Lafcadio Hearn had to rely on the somewhat inappropriate Herbert Spencer for his theoretical framework. All wrote before the anthropological break-through in the early twentieth century. Nor had they systematically investigated the West – against which Japan can be measured – or even China, the other essential comparison. The deeply observant generation of 1860–1920 are full of insights, but cannot reach much beyond the room on the other side of the mirror. They describe the inverted world most sensitively, but cannot really understand it or relate it to ours.

The generation between 1920 and 1960 – Kurt Singer, Fosco Maraini, Norman Jacobs and Ruth Benedict – were equipped with anthropological and comparative sociological perspectives so that they advanced a little further into a landscape that was still outwardly very different from that in the West. Yet there are reasons why they were unable to attain the deepest understanding.

Benedict never went to or experienced Japan. Singer was an economist and there is little evidence that he had any formal training in comparative social analysis, or systematic knowledge of Europe or experience of China. Jacobs used a Weberian framework, but the sociologist Max Weber never fully understood Japan. As an anthropologist who knew Italy and Tibet among other countries, Maraini was the best equipped. His writing is both insightful and, at times, beautiful and, like Singer and Hearn, he sensed the other side of Japan. Yet he did not attempt to put Japan into a universal frame which would bring it back into our comprehension.

After the Second World War there were a number of excellent sociologists and anthropologists, including Ronald Dore, Chie Nakane, Robert Smith and Ezra Vogel, as well as general writers like Edwin Reischauer. All of these increased our understanding of some aspects of Japanese civilisation. Along with some very good historians such as Thomas Smith and George Sansom, they provided much of the detail for a new reappraisal of Japan. More recently, there have been a number of interesting insights into particular aspects of Japanese society by anthropologists and sociologists such as Joy Hendry, Emiko Ohnuki-Tierney, John Clammer, Takie Lebra and Dorinne Kondo, although these writers find it difficult to maintain the sense of strangeness which the earlier writers possessed. The vision is fading, and Japan is being 'normalised' and fitted into Western categories.

Then, towards the end of the century, our understanding of Japan was again invigorated by a number of wide comparative sociological studies, especially those of Robert Bellah and S. N. Eisenstadt. Both applied theories from German sociology, and particularly Karl Jaspers. They showed something of the deep, non-Axial, otherness of the Japanese. What they have not yet done is fully to integrate their new discoveries with the contradictions and puzzles revealed by earlier writers.

While the world within the mirror is difficult for outsiders to penetrate, those within the mirror also find it hard to understand Japan and hence to provide us with guidance. There have been a number of deeply insightful analyses, for example by Yukichi Fukuzawa, Kunio

Yanagita, Masao Maruyama and Yoshihiko Amino. Yet the fact that only very little of their work has been translated makes it difficult for non-Japanese specialists to have access to it. Furthermore these works have proved puzzling to many highly educated Japanese.

Part of the problem lies in the surface of the mirror, which is full of Western influences and 'modernity'. Most Japanese think that they are very modern and more or less like Western people, give or take a few differences. They are taught that the Meiji restoration and industrial development in the later nineteenth century created a revolutionary change from the feudal to the modern. This was what made the Japanese successful. But this self-image is not entirely convincing.

The Japanese are as much hampered by unquestioned evolutionary frameworks as outsiders are. Their encounters with foreign theories lead them to accept that Japan is a successful 'modern, capitalist, industrial' society. However, if this is so, why do many still seem to feel so different? A number of those I have met have told me that they find it difficult to understand Western religion, the emotions of romantic love, the meaning of individualism, how capitalist ethics work, the significance of legal contracts – all of which they are constantly told are central parts of being 'modern'.

The Japanese feel that they have mastered the language of the West and assume that they should be fluent in understanding it. Yet for some unaccountable reason they still feel somewhat confused and insecure. They do not dare to ask for help for fear of revealing their ignorance. Asking might show that other things are seriously misunderstood; they tend to suffer in silence.

Hence a sense of frustration builds up. People on the outside describe and analyse Japan, but all their analyses are rejected as missing the point by the Japanese. And when asked what the point *is*, the Japanese answer with bewilderment that they do not know; all they know is that it has been missed.

One way of thinking about this dilemma is to picture the gap between the surface of the mirror and the interior. The Japanese have constructed an almost impenetrable protection against foreign interference, which includes intrusive attempts to understand Japan. Those who look at Japan have tended to see their own world reflected there. If they come from an industrial capitalist society, they see such a society in the Japanese mirror. Those traces of something other tend to be brushed aside as meaningless, or relics of a former age. There is no way they can be comprehended for they are too far from anything that the ordinary visitor has ever experienced.

Meanwhile the Japanese are faced with an equally large problem. They sense that while their world is somewhat like that in the West or China, a great deal is fundamentally different. Yet they are too close to their own society to be able to make sense of what seems contradictory and beyond analysis.

It is only through the patient teasing out of the difference between surface and inner essence through prolonged discussions that Kenichi, Toshiko and I have begun to see what the problem is. A recent article by Toshiko on Yukichi Fukuzawa, on whom we have worked together over the years, puts the situation well:

> In Fukuzawa's thinking, Japanese family relations had to be kept whole. But outside the family circle, i.e. in the economic and political fields, Japan had to become as capitalistic and liberal as the west. Japanese people tried to imitate those outside social systems since the Meiji restoration without changing much of their close human relations. So we always have this double layer social structure. The outer structure of society is western, but the inner Japanese. We can see this double layer structure, in various combinations, in every aspect of social life in Japan. Perhaps this is what makes foreigners rather confused when they try to understand Japanese people and society. But this was the way in which Japan accepted western influences from the outside.

My own attempt to understand the Japanese has long been hampered by the simple, but erroneous, evolutionary assumptions touched on at the start of this book. For most of my adult life I have implicitly accepted that all civilisations on earth followed a similar route to the modern world. First, there were hunter-gatherers, then tribal societies, some of which developed into peasant civilisations with recognisable world religions based on 'axial' oppositions. Finally, in the last two hundred and fifty years, industrial societies emerged.

I believed that the Japanese fitted in this framework. If an alternative kind of civilisation did exist, and not just the lingering vestiges of those worlds still to be found in small remote tribes, then surely this would be obvious and we would know of it? It could not be hidden away out of sight.

All that was to be argued about was what stage or branch of the route Japan has reached. I had a hunch that, like England, it was at the forefront of its region and hence far advanced on the modern route. It could be fitted quite neatly within the grand theories of 'development'.

Trying to force Japan into this scheme occupied much of my thoughts in the 1990s, yet it never fitted. It was only when I let 'Japan' be itself, when I began to listen more carefully, that I realised that my whole framework was too rigid and ethnocentric.

Depending on definitions, it now appears that Japan is not modern, pre-modern nor post-modern. Rather, it lies on a trajectory where these terms do not apply. Nor is it capitalist, pre- or post-capitalist, but a mixture that does not conform to Marxist definitions. Furthermore, if we mean by 'scientific' roughly what Einstein described as the essence of the scientific revolution, a mixture of Greek philosophy (particularly geometry) and Baconian empiricism, then Japan is again neither scientific, nor pre-scientific. The Japanese types of causal chains of reasoning and their idea of what constitutes proof do not fit into the Graeco-Renaissance framework of the West. On the difficult question of religion, Japan does not wholly reject it, but nor does it see it as necessary.

❀

It is not easy to see the world inside the Japanese mirror. Even when we do glimpse it, what we see is difficult to interpret. After fifteen years of visits, conversations and thinking, the Japanese do not seem to me to be just trivially different from the West and other civilisations, but different at such a deep level that the very tools of understanding we normally use prove inadequate. The Japanese do not fit within our set of distinctions.

This has been recognised by some of those who have tried to understand Japan. One of these is John Clammer, who believes that 'Japanese society does indeed challenge in major ways many of the perspectives of Western social theory' and that it has developed 'a unique form of modernity which challenges like no other the assumption and pretensions of the West and the social theory, one of its intellectual glories, that it has developed to explain itself and the world of which it is a part.' How, then, can we understand Japan?

It is worth remembering that scholars have been dealing with the challenge of comprehending radically different social systems for over a century. When anthropologists went to South America, Africa, New Guinea or South East Asia, they found themselves unable to apply their Western grid of categories to the tribes they encountered. It would have been fruitless to ask if such tribes were based on Status or Contract, Individualism or Holism, or any of the other Western-derived oppositions. Instead they tried to form a notion of the inter-connections, the relations between parts of a culture.

Anthropologists came up with a method which focused on the whole first, and then the elements. They stressed the functional interdependence of the parts and the impossibility of understanding any feature except in relation to others. They looked at the structural homologies between different aspects of tribal life. Their resulting monographs were placed within a comparative framework which, rather than merely classifying societies, saw each as a variant, a different, yet in some ways comparable, entity. Their new analytical approaches reflected the vast difference between the tribal worlds they had encountered and the societies from which they had come.

What characterises a tribal society is that everything within it is inter-connected. It is not possible to divide off an aspect or institution and call it 'art', 'the economy', 'the family', 'the political system', 'the ideology' or 'the religion'. Each of these domains is simultaneously nowhere and everywhere. Almost all thoughts and actions have an aesthetic, economic, familistic, political, ideological and political dimension. When a gift is bestowed, for example, all these dimen-sions will be present to varying extents.

The world from which the anthropologists had come had taken the rigorous division of functions to an extreme so that, at least in theory, each area became a separate sphere. Art is for art's sake; the economy is for production and consumption; the family is limited to near kin and should be kept out of politics, economics and religion; there is a state and political institutions; there is religion. The anthro-pological problem was how to abandon these assumptions and to explain how 'seamless' societies work.

Looking back over what we have discovered in Japan, we can see that it fits in much better with the 'tribal' than with the 'modern' or 'divided' kind of structure. There is an aesthetic component in many activities and much of life is concerned with the pursuit of beauty. It was only very late that the Japanese, under outside influence, began to be aware that there was something called 'art'.

The desire to produce objects which will improve the material comfort of humans is very strong and efficiently managed in Japan, yet human relations cannot be subjected to the rules of abstract market forces, of short-term profit and loss. As a result, there is no separate economy. The family as a bundle of sentiments and as a template for interpersonal relations pervades much of daily life, including all social interactions and much of the economy and religion. Yet blood relationships between blood relatives are very weak. It could be argued that there is no real family system at all in Japan, just a series of artificial, family-like, constructed groups.

The flow of force and compulsion, what we call political power, envelops everyone so that all are caught up in a web that exerts upwards, sideways and downwards pressures which an individual can hardly resist. Yet there is no real state or developed political system. Ideas and thoughts are highly sophisticated, and there is a magnificent literary tradition. Yet logical thought is downplayed in relation to emotion and intuition. There is no absolute truth, everything bends within constantly shifting contexts. Religious rituals abound and there is a pervasive sense that something other than human force and dead nature exists. Yet individual religions are weak, and theology, dogma, rituals and morality are not developed as powerful and separate systems.

Obviously Japan is not a tribal society, since it has many of the characteristics of an industrial world – literacy, cities, factories and sophisticated technology. Below the surface, however, it seems somehow to have prevented any single sphere either separating off or becoming the dominant and determining infrastructure. This is what I think Singer means in the epigraph at the front of this book when he describes Japan as 'so simple'. The civilisation is structur-ally simple, with no divisions or elaborate architecture; it is like a single-cell creature. This simplicity is puzzling to us since we cannot easily comprehend a system of integration where there are no conflicts between the different elements; we are used to a world of separations and hence of clashes of loyalty and interest.

Once we have grasped the fact that Japan, like all societies on earth before the advent of the Axial Age, does not exist with a set of watertight compartments but is more like swirling currents in a rushing stream, or a cloth where all the colours seep into each other, then we are in a position to understand its vitality and superficial paradoxes. Japan is no more 'another planet' than one of the many tribal societies described by anthropologists. It is just the shock of finding technological sophistication combined with deeper non-divisions that halts our comprehension for a while. What is inside the mirror is perfectly logical and beautifully integrated, but it does not accord with Western logic; nor is it partitioned in the way that has come to dominate other world civilisations.

The simple interconnectedness of what lies below the surface in Japan cannot be easily perceived if we use the individualistic, functional approach of much Western social science. This approach did not serve us well in the quest for understanding. If we try to grasp Japan as a 'modern' civilisation where there are things ('individuals') or discrete institutional forms ('economy', 'religion', 'politics', 'society') we remain baffled.

In the Japanese context, the basic entity is not a thing or an institutional sphere, a molecule or an individual, as might be assumed in much of Western thought. Rather it is a *relation*. Everything is situational, symbolically linked to something else. This is how Japan works and how it has to be understood. Gardens, ceremonies, people cannot be understood in themselves, but always in relation to something else. We are in a hall of mirrors, all reflecting each other, all empty in themselves. We have to approach Japan as an undivided civilisation, taking account of the fact that there are over one hundred million people rather than a few thousand. If we do this, many of the 'both/and' contradictions which first puzzle us make sense.

Like many others, I have frequently been struck by the hybridity of Japan, the way in which it seems to combine opposite things, violence and peace, innocence and pornography, and many more. As we have seen, the Japanese do not divide things which we hold apart in Western thought. Natural and supernatural, individual and group, mind and matter – all the dichotomies stemming from Greek thought onwards, and indeed of all monotheistic and even, to a considerable extent, Hindu and Chinese philosophies, vanish.

Of course each nation and civilisation is unique and different. To understand Italian or French culture can be difficult if you are English. Yet, in these cases, the grid we apply fits to a greater or lesser extent, and then we tend to be able to explain what does not fit. What is odd about Japan is that almost nothing fits. There is hardly any congruence. From the very beginning we are in an unfamiliar landscape, where the set of connections with which we are familiar do not work. We are in a relativistic world such as that envisaged by Einstein or Escher, as bizarre (to us) as that of the most exotic of anthropological tribes.

The fact that Japan is the one great world civilisation which cannot be divided into segments has an effect on how we come to understand it. Like a photograph or painting, Japan is a *gestalt*; it is a place we have to take in with one glance, or not at all. In this sense it is like the standard undivided society studied by anthropologists. We cannot understand a tribal society by breaking it into bits. The pieces of the jigsaw mean nothing away from the whole. It has to be comprehended with one rapid sweep of the mental eye.

This is one reason why the portrait so quickly sketched in this book, while necessarily superficial in relation to any one part, is an attempt to capture Japan as a whole. My hope is that this approach will give a truer sense of what it is like than if one lingered longer on any one area at the expense of others. While it makes sense to approach America or France by studying them bit by bit, Japan eludes us if we do so. If we want to understand a central thread of Japanese culture, we have to trace it through all aspects of life. 'It is in this spirit penetrating every detail of life in peace and war, poetry and archery, ritual and leisure', wrote Singer, 'that we may find the true measure of the Japanese mind. For it is not to be discovered in an abstract idea, or system, or work of art, or institution.' To dissect is to lose this meaning.

What I found in Japan was a third type of modern civilisation. Up to my encounter with it, I thought there were only two types: the Western open, institutionally divided type, represented by present-day Europe and America, or the more closed type where one sphere dominates – for instance, politics in fascism and communism, religion in Islamic societies. Japan is neither fully open nor closed.

It is mainly for this reason that I have found 'Japan' is good to think with. Surrounded by my own culture, cocooned by advanced technologies, flooded by images and assumptions, it is very difficult to stand back and see my world as the accidental, constructed, non-inevitable place that it is.

When Europe was at its most triumphalist, at the end of the nine-teenth century, one of anthropology's main contributions was to present alternatives, pockets of 'otherness'. Anthropologists brought us tales from distant lands which challenged Western assumptions. There were descriptions of witch doctors, bizarre sexual customs, belief in strange spirits and taboos. Yet all of these came from small groups, at the most two or three hundred thousand people. Such practices, which might challenge basic assumptions, could be ignored. The societies where they were found were so small, technologically unso-phisticated and different in every way that they seemed relics from another age, even if they coexisted with us in time. It was assumed that such societies were about to become extinct and that, anyway, they could not possibly survive the modern environment.

Japan is a civilisation of over 120 million, hyper-efficient, econom-ically successful people, and although in theory it has only a 'defence force', this is very large and well equipped. Japan cannot be ignored. If it is based on premises and principles that are different to those in the West, it constitutes a real alternative for our exhausted imaginations. Japan helps us realise that the central features of Western modernity, the divisions between mind/body, natural/supernatural, the institutional spheres of the economy, polity, society and belief, may not be needed to become a world power. The divisions which happened alongside the scientific and industrial revolutions in the West may have been a necessary pre-condition for these great transfor- mations. Their absence may help to explain why science and indus- trialism did not originate in the East. Yet Japan also shows us that a modern society can exist without them.

In some ways Japan is Utopian in the strict sense of that word, which literally means 'Nowhere' in Greek. It is relatively egalitarian, with little disorder and high artistic standards. Such characteristics often describe non-literate societies. Yet in Japan they exist alongside a modern industrial production system and urban way of life.

The situation in Japan contrasts with the picture I had developed in relation to my own society. As the modern world emerged in the West, it impressed people with its productiveness (industrialism), its technical efficiency, its discovery of hidden laws (science) and its tolerance and democracy. Yet these came with costs.

One cost was spiritual. The void created by the separation of mind and body, of fact and value was felt and explored by genera- tions of poets and philosophers, most notably by Blake, Words- worth, Keats, Tennyson, Ruskin, Arnold and Yeats. Life might have become more prosperous and more secure, yet it seemed to have lost much of its meaning. Head and heart were split apart, the world had become disenchanted; materialism was rampant. The deeper numinous essence was gone. The world had become a psychological and spiritual wilderness.

The second cost was social. With the withering away of religion and of kinship groupings as means to integrate and give their lives a purpose, people are often adrift and alone. Such rootlessness may have set individuals free, but as a result they have no deep link to others. I believed that lonely individualism is the inevitable consequence of the powerful forces of Western modernity, which break down all groups and hierarchies and creates an empty world of selfish individuals who, in Tocqueville's phrase, touch one another, but do not feel the other's presence.

If we compare the other alternatives to Western capitalism, Japan seems rather attractive. Islam shares many of the features of intolerance that characterise the other 'religions based on a text' written. Although there are many variants, there is often a tendency toward anti-intellectualism and anti-feminism, towards bureaucratic corruption and economic inefficiency. Such societies do not appear to me to be intrinsically better as a total package than Western capitalism.

Likewise, the communism derived from the teachings of Marx and Lenin, despite its high ideals, has weaknesses. It does not work effectively as a way of organising the economy. It often leads to other forms of absolutism and to savage brutality towards minorities and dissidents. It does not even banish inequality. It has lost its allure.

The example of Japan shows that, as John Clammer writes, 'there is not only one trajectory to modernity', which he thinks explains why 'Japan seems to be in the world, but not of it'. Japan's modern history indicates that the technological modernisation of a country does not necessarily imply its full 'Westernisation'.

We can either turn away from the Japanese experience, or we can learn something from it. Some have done the former. As Robert Smith comments, 'We seek to reassure ourselves by denying the implications of what we see, for otherwise we should be forced to concede that a system different from our own, without becoming like us, has achieved goals we have long taken to be uniquely ours.'

We may not wish to be like the Japanese, yet we cannot but admire their struggle to create a decent, beautiful and meaningful society along different lines to our own. Japanese attitudes to ecology, polity, society and religion suggest that we do not have to consume so much, to empty our life of meaning, to become ever more unequal, to believe in a single God, to have high crime rates or become a litigation dominated society. They provide us with choices.

Maraini sums this up:

> By looking carefully at Japan we learn not only about an unfamiliar part of the world or culture, but about ourselves. Comparison gives wings to eyes; it takes us up into space and permits us to look at the planet Earth from a new distance, from a point where backgrounds and positions can be seen in lights of revealing wavelengths. If Japan did not exist, Japan would have to be urgently invented.

It is important to think about this at a time when inherited models are being seriously questioned. Many people are looking for a philosophy which will give them both economic wealth and meaning. It is not possible to emulate the Japanese solution. Yet Japan does show that there is an alternative, that history has not ended. 'Their ways cannot become ours,' Singer comments, 'but they show, as in a reducing mirror, the nature of a civilisation that has achieved integration.'

This is not the Confucian way; indeed, it is anti-Confucian. Yet it is an alternative, reintegrating a shattered experience. I am interested in it not only because of our growing awareness of global inter-dependence, but also because we feel increasingly dissatisfied with the artificial separations of modernity. We are moving towards what is often loosely called post-modernity. Yet the shape of this move in the West, from modernity to something else, is very different from what is happening in Japan. Japan is thus a fascinating experiment in a different way of structuring society.

❧

To seize the opportunity to escape from the assumptions of our own culture is especially important now, at a time when the world's centre of gravity is reverting back to Asia, after a brief few hundred years of Western superiority. As India and especially China participate in the construction of a new world order, it is important that they have more than the current set of models – capitalist, communist, Islamic – to consider. They can learn from a civilisation which has equalled the West at its own game – capitalist production – yet refused to be pressurised into abandoning its core cultural values.

Not only has Japan learnt to subvert modernity, as represented by Europe and America, but it has refused to be browbeaten by Confucianism, Buddhism or other world philosophies. It has done what all self-respecting nations would like to do, which is to retain its identity while accepting useful things from outside.

On the one hand, imports have often been magnified and improved, the technologies have been sharpened and made more effective and the Japanese production of objects, utilitarian and aesthetic, is unsurpassed. On the other hand, the rejection of the underlying philosophical frameworks is more absolute. It is not just a matter of making Confucianism, Buddhism, Western industrial capitalism, a little less forceful; they are subverted almost entirely so that they do not destroy the undivided nature of Japanese life. New words are added to the cultural language all the time, but the grammar remains largely unchanged, or, rather, changes quite rapidly but not merely to reflect outside pressures.

Japan gives us simultaneously hints of a distant past – of a world of undivided, tribal life, or of our own childhood – and of our future. It may partly foreshadow a world where the dominance of the Western heritage has faded. The best residues of Renaissance thought and of the scientific and industrial revolutions will have become a legacy for all mankind. But the political, philosophical and social frameworks originating in a peripheral part of north-western Europe and then exported to the United States will have again assumed more appropriate proportions – and become just one variant among many. New unities and integrations will have occurred, based on both the postmodernities of the West and the more ancient traditions of the East.

There is a danger of overstressing Japanese uniqueness. Whenever I discuss or lecture on Japan, members of the audience remind me of this. It is worth stating clearly what I am and am not arguing or implying by approaching Japanese civilisation in this way.

Japan is so interesting because it is an industrial civilisation fundamentally different from ours. The tools of social science based on Western experience are helpful in showing what Japan is *not* – but they do not exactly capture what Japan is. This is better done through a more localised anthropological description.

The historical conditions which have led to the unusual features of Japan are fairly easy to understand. The isolation, islandhood, position near China and a set of accidental events explain what has happened. It has nothing to do with race or DNA, or with innate cultural strangeness.

Japan is not uniform (there are huge geographical and social variations); it is not static (there are changes taking place all the time); it is not everlasting (much of it was invented in the later nineteenth century). It is, however, 'the changing same'. It is as absurd to think of it as ancient as it is to think of it as entirely new.

There is absolutely no superiority in 'the Japanese way'. It offers the Japanese many good things (integration, affluence, beauty, peacefulness), but many less attractive things as well (conformity, amnesia, racism). Many of their less attractive traits are also found in another island people, the British. There is absolutely no licence for the Japanese to forcibly impose their way of life on others any more than there has been a right for other imperialists – for instance the British, French, Germans or Americans – to do so.

❖

An exploration within the mirror reveals many delights. Yet there are also costs. There is the high suicide rate among children, who often feel they cannot achieve the success that others expect of them. There are the estimated 100,000–400,000 *hikikomori* or shut-in young people who stay locked in their rooms unwilling to go out for years at a time. There is a widespread fear of the strange and unknown. There is an unwillingness to accept responsibility for past mistakes or to apologise in a straightforward and recognisable way. There is sometimes too great a distrust of logic and rationality.

Women and some almost invisible groups, such as the *buraku*, Ainu, Koreans and migrant workers, are often marginalised and treated as second-class citizens. There is enormous pressure to conform to the wishes of those above, to the side and below. The consumption of violent and pornographic fantasy is widespread. Sometimes reality and fiction are confused. There is a largely unquestioning acceptance of power. There is sudden despair and self-hate.

Many of those who have written about enchanted lands more generally have stressed the seductive perils. One is that beauty gets mistaken for either truth or virtue. In fact, ethics become contextual and double standards are common. Deep love can turn to anger very easily. Outsiders are treated as non-human and often as demons or 'gods' (*kami*), and attacked or quarantined. Any questioning of the order which challenges the conformist accord and the enchantment that upholds it is stamped upon. New ideas are frequently considered dangerous.

It is often difficult to tell illusion from reality in this entranced world. Reason and logic are seriously downplayed in favour of emotion, intuition and feeling. These are positive traits when they result in happiness, but they can very easily evolve into mass emotion and fascism – a sort of childishness, group frenzy or crowd ecstasy where the individual, always fragile, gets completely submerged.

Those living within enchantment find it difficult to understand the disenchanted, hence the Japanese bafflement with the West and how the West views Japan. Furthermore, what interests and amuses enchanted people is often of no interest to others, and vice versa. It is impossible for those living outside the enchanted area either to enter it, or to see it behind its protective mirror. Glimpses of what is going on, as with fairyland, are accidental and usually fleeting.

It is very difficult for a foreigner to become integrated in Japanese society and lose their foreignness. Whereas a sustained effort may enable you to become part of French, American or Chinese society, for instance, many foreigners have found that no matter how long they have lived in Japan, or how hard they have tried to fit in, they always remain outsiders. Indeed, some of my friends tell me, the closer they become in language and manners to the Japanese, the more the Japanese reject them. I doubt whether any other nation can now imitate Japan, even though they may envy it and copy elements. This inner, non-Axial, undivided social model is not the sort of thing that can be transplanted or transported anywhere else in the world.

It is difficult for me to tell whether I am attracted or repelled by Japan; indeed most outsiders who know Japan feel both these emotions. At times it all seems so beautiful, meaningful, attractive, a return to paradise, Eden, childhood and security. It fulfils the romantic longing for a lost world, Paradise, Atlantis, the Lands of the Grail, fairylands forlorn. Then when one awakes from the dream, Japan seems a savage, childish, conformist and aggressive land, clogging, sticky, regressive, a trap, a siren song leading to shipwreck for the Enlightenment and reason. Japan is full of hybrids, ambiguities, full of attraction and repulsion simultaneously, absorbing people and also rejecting them.

How are we to leave the Japanese mirror? One good way is to recall another departure from a magic island, Prospero's farewell at the end of Shakespeare's *The Tempest*. As a German Jew, the economist Kurt Singer was forced out of Japan in 1939 after eight years of teaching in Japanese universities. He wrote his book *Mirror, Sword and Jewel* a few years later, knowing full well what the Japanese behaviour in the Second World War had been, just as he knew that his own country had provided part of the model for Japan. Yet in recalling his experience, he concluded: 'But this awakening, recalling Prospero's *Epilogue*, does not detract from the magical charm of the dream as long as it was dreamt, nor from the value of a style of life which shapes out of this world of change, squalor and pettiness a realm of light and sweetness, harmonious flow and persistent gentleness.'

As I sit typing these last words in an English garden, surrounded by roses, honeysuckle and gently falling rain, my visits to Japan seem like a dream. Yet I know that spending time within the magic mirror of that other island civilisation has changed me. I hope that this looking-glass journey will also help you to experience a little of the strangeness of that fascinating parallel world, so difficult to understand because it is so simple.

Major eras in Japanese history, conventions

50,000 BC	Palaeolithic
11,000 BC	Jomon
300 BC	Yayoi
AD 300	Kofun
552	Late Yamato
710	Nara
794	Heian
1192	Kamakura
1333	Northern and Southern Courts
1392	Muromachi
1568	Momoyama
1600	Edo (Tokugawa)
1868	Meiji
1912	Taisho
1926	Showa
1989	Heisei

(Based on Martin Collcutt, Marius Jansen and Isao Kumakura, *Cultural Atlas of Japan* (Phaidon, Oxford, 1988), 8–9. Early dates are obviously approximate)

Conventions

In this book Japanese personal names are written in the English order, i.e. the first name is given first (e.g. Yukichi Fukuzawa). The Japanese order is the reverse; the surname comes first (e.g. Fukuzawa Yukichi).

Although the use of the macron in such terms as *inrō* or *kyōsō* is often adopted when transcribing Japanese, since it represents more closely Japanese pronunciation, many books do not apply this convention, as it does not necessarily help the reader (macrons are also usually omitted in words such as *sumo* and *judo*) and I have chosen not to use them in this book.

Frequently cited early visitors

Alcock: Sir Rutherford Alcock, British diplomat. Visited Japan on two occasions between 1859 and 1864. Travelled in various regions.

Bacon: Alice Bacon, American visitor to Japan in the late nineteenth century.

Bird: Isabella Bird, British traveller. Toured through central and northern Japan for seven months in 1878.

Chamberlain: Basil Hall Chamberlain, British teacher. Lived in Japan for most of the period 1873–1911 and travelled widely.

Griffis: William E. Griffis, American teacher. Visited Japan in 1870–4, travelling to various places.

Hearn: Lafcadio Hearn, author and educator, of Irish-Greek parentage. In Japan for much of the period 1890–1904.

Morse: Edward L.Morse, American zoologist and art expert. Visited Japan on three occasions between 1883 and 1887 and travelled widely.

Scidmore: Eliza Scidmore, American visitor to Japan in the late 1880s.

Sources for quoted passages

(Full titles of books are in the bibliography)

1. Into the mirror

'Japan offers ...', Bird quoted in Yapp, *Travellers*, 601; 'existence in the moon', Arnold, *Seas*, 357; 'A double pleasure ...', Griffis, *Mikado*, II, 417; 'As first perceived ...', Hearn, *Interpretation*, 10, 12, 14; 'What we regard ...' Lowell, *Soul*, 2–3; 'A stranger landing ...', Singer, *Sword*, 90; 'Japan's closed doors', Benedict, *Chrysanthemum*, 1, 2; 'considered it impossible', Yoshino, *Nationalism*, 117, 116; 'a culturally and socially homogeneous', Dale, *Myth*, 1; 'a foreigner cannot understand', Tocqueville, *Memoir*, II, 365, 304; 'all laws originate', Tocqueville, *Journeys*, xviii.

2. Culture shock

'What amazes one ...', Morse, *Day*, I, 261, 259; children and drawing, Morse, *Day*, I, 56, 55; 'Japanese taste in painting ...', Chamberlain, *Things*, 449; 'When we gaze ...', Tanizaki, *Shadows*, 20–21; 'the lacquerware of the past ...', Tanizaki, *Shadows*, 13; jet-black *inro*, Morse, *Day*, I, 259; 'no doors or windows', Morse, *Homes*, 7, 108; 'floating Japanese house', Singer, *Sword*, 145–6, 147; 'built like a ship', Maraini, *Meeting*, 75; 'A Japanese city ...', Hearn, *Kokoro*, 14; 'machine for living', Enright, *Dew*, 148; shrines and cryptomeria,

Bird, *Tracks,* 65; gardens and flowerpots, Morse, *Day,* II, 330; chrysan-
themums in pots, Benedict, *Chrysanthemum,* 207; flower-fever, Lowell,
Soul, 140–41; Oliphant, *Elgin Mission,* 164; gardening necromancy,
Scidmore, *Jinrikisha,* 12; 'At first sight you might be …', Maraini,
Meeting, 27; garden more human than house, Lowell, *Soul,* 128–9;
'No civilised nation …', Morse, *Day,* I, 253; 'dances of North-east
Siberian shamans', Singer, *Sword,* 130; 'concealed shamanic rituals',
Blacker, *Catalpa,* 36; 'Never nude', Lowell, *Soul,* 144; 'scanty loin-
cloth', Elgin, *Mission,* 18–19; 'sit half nude', Griffis, *Mikado,* II, 529;
'the open bath-houses …', Bacon, *Girls,* 217; 'In their eyes a state of
nature …', Lowell, *Soul,* 145–6; 'it is a fatal mistake', Lowell, *Soul,*
144–5; 'Japanese ideas of decency', Bacon, *Girls,* 216–17; 'people in
low-necked dresses', Morse, *Day,* I, 99; 'the erotic aspect of nudity',
Maraini, *Meeting,* 60; 'the nude is seen …', Chamberlain, *Things,* 60;
'nine or ten neat houses …', Kaempfer, *History,* 3, 53; 'free sex life as
bad' Van Meerdervoort, *Five Years,* 112–13; sold into prostitution,
Alcock, *Tycoon,* II, 95; prostitutes go to church, Van Meerdevort,
Five Years, 113; a custom-house and 'brothel', Griffis, *Mikado,* II, 364;
'a cuisine to be looked at', Tanizaki, *Shadows,* 15; miniature garden in
shallow box, Morse, *Homes,* 63, 274–75.

3. Wealth

'Twenty-five synonyms for rice …', Scidmore, *Jinrikisha,* 294;
'Curiosity to a great length', Thunberg, *Travels,* III, 256; 'Perhaps
in nothing …', Chamberlain, *Things,* 255, quoting Alcock; 'In the
expositions …', Griffis, *Mikado,* II, 603; 'so many toy-shops', Griffis,
Mikado, II, 453; 'that astounding ingenuity …', Hearn, *Gleanings,*
57; 'We examined the toy-shops …', Oliphant, *Elgin Mission,* 218;
'competitive society *sans* competition', Koestler, *Lotus,* 222; 'I began
translating it …', Fukuzawa, *Autobiography,* 190–91; 'politico-
spiritual guidance …', Singer, *Sword and Jewel,* 58; 'A man may be
descended …', Saikaku, *Storehouse,* 144; 'In order to survive …',
quoted in Hane, *Rebels,* 82.

4. People

'As soon as a child is born ...', Thunberg, *Travels*, III, 266; 'The Japanese never live ...', Endo, *Samurai*, 164; Three Little Pigs, Hendry, *Understanding*, 47; 'The millions of Japanese ...', Fukuzawa, *Civilisation*, 160; 'The wealthy brother ...', Nakane, *Japanese Society*, 6; 'Nowadays a marriage-broker ...', Saikaku, *Storehouse*, 29; marriage sponsor or negotiator, Sugimoto, *Japanese Society*, 169; 'Our society novels ...', Hearn, *East*, 72; 'If the wife dies ...', Bacon, *Japanese Girls*, 277; 'I never saw people take ...', Bird, *Tracks*, 80; 'so perfectly docile and obedient', Bird, *Tracks*, 80; 'Japan is the paradise for children ...', Morse, *Day*, I, 41; 'lacking in all discrimination', Saikaku, *Storehouse*, 84; 'subjected to no jealous seclusion', Siebold, *Manners*, 123; 'the condition of women ...', Macfarlane, *Japan*, 293; the key role played by Japanese women, Bacon, *Japanese Girls*, 90–92, 206–9; 'A job in Japan ...', Reischauer, *Japanese*, 133; meaning of *oyabun*, Passin, 'Japanese Society', 144; the meaning of *sensei*, Enright, *Dew*, 24; 'The men who held supreme power ...', Maruyama, *Japanese Politics*, 16, 18, 107; 'Although there is much poverty ...', Bacon, *Japanese Girls*, 199; 'universal feelings of love, affection', Kodansha, *Encyclopedia*, under 'giri'; 'Biological kinship ...', Lebra, *Japanese*, 172; 'relational contracting', Dore, *Flexible*, 77, quoting Goldberg.

5. Power

'This double machinery ...', Alcock, *Tycoon*, I,228; 'Mikado-worship ...', Chamberlain, *Things*, 531–9; 'Delegation is practised ...', Singer, *Sword*, 57; 'The customs and usages ...', Singer, *Sword*, 78–9, quoting Yukio Ozaki; ' one soon finds ...', Maraini, *Patterns*, 180; 'In return for electoral support ...', Sugimoto, *Japanese Society*, 224; 'neither dictatorial, centralised ...', Ozaki, *Japanese*, 151; 'unity in disorder', Singer, *Sword*, 24; a 'Stateless Nation', Van Wolferen, *Enigma*, *passim*, and especially ch. 2; 'Viewed from an Anglo-Saxon ...', Chamberlain, *Things*, 219; 'The chief feature in the old ...', Griffis, *Mikado*, II, 608; 'Every office doubled ...', Alcock, *Tycoon*,

I, 228; 'Japanese bureaucracy is characterised ...', Singer, *Sword*, 80; number of editions and publishers, Donald Shively in Hall, (ed.), *Cambridge History*, IV, 721, 731; 'It is said that few sights ...', Macfarlane, *Japan*, 313, 294; farmers write *haiku*, Riesman, *Japan*, 182; 'For sixty-six miles rumbling ...', Morse, *Day*, I, 56, 196; 'For a land impoverished ...', Griffis, *Mikado*, II, 377; 'That Nazi Germany ...', Singer, *Sword*, 41; 'In reality the bulk of Japanese ...', Cortazzi, *Dr Willis*, 202; 'The samurai, before going ...', Hearn, *East*, 210; 'An uncertain sharing of responsibility ...', Maruyama, quoted in Van Wolferen, *Enigma*, 396; 'collective penitence of all', Ozaki, *Japanese*, 158; 'Fortunately at the end ...', Van Wolferen, *Enigma*, 557; 'It has been my belief ...' General Matsui Iwane quoted in Maruyama, *Japanese Politics*, 95; 'Particularly with respect to wars ...', Ozaki, *Japanese*, 90; 'So unfamiliar was the concept ...', Sansom, *Western World*, 471–2; 'Law has not yet emerged ...', Singer, *Sword*, 72; 'Japan's system of criminal justice ...', *Kodansha*, in article on 'Legal Systems'; rates of crime in 1984, Van Wolferen, *Enigma*, 255; 'general peacefulness and happiness ...', Wigmore, *Law*, I, 43; 'less than two per cent ...', Hayley, *Sheathing*, 273; clearance rates for crimes, Hayley, *Police*, 182; conviction rates for crimes, Hayley, *Sheathing*, 270; 'No one can change his residence ...', Siebold, *Manners*, 254; 'More than half a million households ...', Sugimoto, *Japanese Society*, 276;

6. Ideas

'One fairly severe form ...', quoted in Lebra, *Japanese*, 151; 'offers this precious paradox ...', Barthes, *Empire*, 30; 'no Japanese dish is endowed with a centre ...', Barthes, *Empire*, 22; 'Even among the educated samurai ...', Griffis, *Mikado*, II, 471; 'In music the *basso ostinato* ...', Maruyama, 'The structure of *Matsurigoto*', 27; 'I do not presuppose ...', Maruyama, 'Proto-type, Old layer....' [italics in original]; 'A geometrical array ...', Singer, *Sword*, 114; 'as there are five recognised colours', Chamberlain, *Things*, 341; 'After learning the plain cardinal ...', Scidmore, *Jinriksha*, 294; 'There is one class

...', Alcock, *Tycoon*, I, 179; 'The mutually exclusive categories ...', Morris, *Shining*, 290; 'events that somehow float', Koestler, *Lotus*, 216; 'Japanese nouns have no gender ...', Chamberlain, *Things*, 276; 'Since the first line may signify ...', Fukuzawa, *Autobiography*, 146; 'The level chosen by each speaker ...', Smith, *Japanese*, 77; 'Indo-European languages possess ...', Maraini, *Patterns*, 29; 'the essence of pleasure in conversation ...', Nakane, *Japanese*, 130; 'We prefer the soft voice ...', Tanizaki, *Shadows*, 9; 'In the most intimate of relations ...', Herbert Passin, 'Japanese Society', 247; 'the art of concealing thought', Nitobe, *Bushido*, 107; 'express our feelings by silence', Hearn, *Gleanings*, 70; 'No people on earth is keener ...', Morse, *Day*, II, 435; 'In Japan one is rarely confronted ...', Maraini, *Tokyo*, 39; 'Harmony consists in ...', Ono Seiichiro, quoted by Smith, *Japanese*, 41; 'the Japanese do not seem to possess principles ...', Matsumoto, *Unspoken Way*, 43,8; 'a tendency toward an absence of theoretical ...', quoted in Smith, *Japanese*, 111; 'One day while reading ...', Fukuzawa, *Autobiography*, 19; 'From the earliest period Shinto ...', Hearn, *Interpretation*, 160–61; 'The ethical expression of purity ...', Maraini, *Patterns*, 26, quoting Chikafusa; size and nature of *buraku* communities in Japan, Sugimoto, *Japanese Society*, 3; marriage with *non-buraku* person, Sugimoto, *Japanese Society*, 190; 'people dirt', Ohnuki-Tierney, *Illness*, 22; Ainu rights, Sugimoto, *Japanese Society*, 202; 'A man may be pretending ...', Koestler, *Lotus*, 219.

7. Beliefs

Surveys of god-shelves, cited in Hendry, *Understanding*, 29; Honorary Chief Priest of Osaka, article by Judit Kawaguchi in *The Japan Times*, 28 March, 2006, 17; 'No more irrational assertion ...', Hearn, *Interpretation*, 507–8; 'are superior, swift, brave ...', Aston, quoted in Maraini, *Meeting*, 145; 'dragons, the echo, foxes', quoted in Blacker, *Catalpa*, 34; 'Know thyself', Nitobe, *Bushido*, 13; 'All the dead become gods', quoted in Hearn, *Interpretation*, 33; 'He that is honest ...', Kato, a seventeenth-century thinker, quoted in Bellah, *Tokugawa*, 76;

'like a piece of shot silk', Blacker, *Catalpa Bow*, 69–70; 'The Japanese children are very meanly clad …', Siebold, *Manners*, 126; 'Astrology, horoscopy …', Chamberlain, *Things*, 121; widespread use of good luck charms, Hearn, *Interpretation*, 167; 'There is no hell …', quoted in Hall, *Japan*, 183; 'In most rural communities …', Smith, *Japanese*, 95; 'There is a lack of understanding …', Riesman, *Japan*, 251; 'The Japanese feel comfortable …', Matsumoto, *Unspoken Way*, 89; 'Power in the West is like iron …', Fukuzawa, *Civilisation*, 155; 'Intellect itself was considered …', Nitobe, *Bushido*, 17; 'The distinctiveness of Japan …', Eisenstadt, *Japanese*, 14; 'The transformation of Confucianism …', Eisenstadt, *Japanese*, 260; 'Japanese culture and society …', Bellah, *Imagining*, 23,32; 'Through all these enormous changes …', Bellah, *Imagining*, 59; 'The Japanese adaptation of Buddhism …', quoted in Yamamura, *Cambridge*, III, 581; 'the tenets of Kamakura Buddhism …', quoted in Yamamura, *Cambridge*, III, 565; various quotations from Nakamura, *Ways of Thinking*, 415, 528–30; 'using the axial to overcome the axial', Bellah, *Imagining*, 13; 'its pagan premises', Eisenstadt, *Japanese*, 235; 'from an archaic to an axial …', Bellah, *Imagining*, 10; the 'new religions', see 'New Religions' in *Kodansha Encyclopedia*, article by H.Byron Earhart. 'One reason why Japan entered …', Van Wolferen, *Enigma*, 318–19.

8. Out of the mirror

'Crab-writing', Griffis, *Mikado*, II, 366; 'The first observation a foreigner makes …', Morse, *Day*, I, 221; 'In Fukuzawa's thinking …', Nakamura, 'Yukichi Fukuzawa …'; 'Japanese society does indeed challenge …', Clammer, *Difference*, 3, 132; 'It is in this spirit penetrating …', Singer, *Sword*, 167; 'there is not only one trajectory …', Clammer, *Difference*, 127, 23; 'We seek to reassure ourselves …', Smith, *Japanese*, 139; 'By looking carefully at Japan …', Maraini, *Patterns*, 12; 'Their ways cannot become ours …', Singer, *Sword*, 104; 'But this awakening …', Singer, *Sword*, 67.

Website, bibliography and recommended reading

This book is a brief synthesis of fifteen years of thinking about Japan. It is based on my published and unpublished writings which treat a number of the themes in greater depth. All of the writings as well as films of visits and other materials are on my website, www.alanmacfarlane.com, at the location www.alanmacfarlane.com/ japan/book.html. The writings (and films) chronicle my journey of discovery from first rough impressions and confusions through to this book. There are also a set of films on 'Youtube' under the name 'ayabaya'.

If you know little about Japan and want to start to experience this other world, those marked with (***) are the dozen books which helped me most to understand the world within the mirror.

There are also numerous excellent articles on all aspects of Japanese life in the *Kodansha Encyclopedia of Japan* (Tokyo, Kodansha, 1983), and the two-volume version, *Japan – an Illustrated Encyclopedia* (Tokyo, Kodansha, 1993) is also excellent. Martin Collcutt, Marius Jansen and Isao Kumakura, *Cultural Atlas of Japan* (Oxford, Phaidon Press, 1988) is a good introduction to the rich cultural tradition.

All the following books are published in London, unless otherwise indicated.

Alcock, Sir Rutherford, *The Capital of the Tycoon: Narrative of a Three Years' Residence in Japan* (Longman Green, 1863), 2 vols.

Arnold, Sir Edwin, *Seas and Lands* (Longmans, 1895)

Bacon, Alice Mabel, *Japanese Girls and Women* (Gay and Bird, revised edn, 1902)

Barthes, Roland, *Empire of Signs* (Cape, 1982), trans. Richard Howard

Bayley, David H., 'Police, crime and the community in Japan', in George De Vos (ed.), *Institutions for change in Japanese society* (Berkeley, Univ. of California Press, 1982)

Bellah, Robert N., *Tokugawa Religion* (Glencoe, Illinois, The Free Press, 1957)

Bellah, Robert N., *Imagining Japan* (Berkeley, Univ. of California Press, 2003)

Benedict, Ruth, *The Chrysanthemum and the Sword* (Routledge and Kegan Paul, 1967) ***

Bird, Isabella, *Unbeaten Tracks in Japan* (Virago, [1880] 1984) ***

Blacker, Carmen, *The Catalpa Bow; A Study of Shamanistic Practices in Japan* (Unwin, 2nd edn, 1986)

Chamberlain, Basil Hall, *Japanese Things* (Tokyo, Tuttle, [1904]1971) ***

Clammer, John, *Difference and Modernity* (Kegan Paul International, 1995)

Cortazzi, Hugh, *Dr Willis in Japan 1862–1877* (Athlone, 1985)

Dale, Peter N., *The Myth of Japanese Uniqueness* (Routledge, 1988)

Dore, Ronald, *Flexible Rigidities* (Athlone Press, 1988)

Endo, Shusaku, *Samurai* (Penguin, 1983), trans. Van C. Gessel

Eisenstadt, S. N., *Japanese Civilisation* (Univ. of Chicago Press, 1996)

Enright, D. J., *The World of Dew* (Secker and Warburg, 1955)

Fukuzawa, Yukichi, *The Autobiography of Yukichi Fukuzawa* (New York, Schocken Books, pb. edn, 1972), trans. Eiichi Kiyooka ***

Fukuzawa, Yukichi, *An Outline of a Theory of Civilisation* (Tokyo, Sophia University, [1875] 1973), trans. David A. Dilworth and G. Cameron Hurst

Griffis, William E., *The Mikado's Empire* (Harper, 1903), 2 vols.

Haley, John O., 'Sheathing the sword of justice in Japan: an essay on law without sanctions', *Journal of Japanese Studies*, 8 (2), (1982)

Haley, John O., 'Criminal justice in Japan', *Journal of Japanese Studies*, 18 (2), (1992)

Hall, John W, *Japan; From Prehistory to Modern Times* (Tokyo, Tuttle, 1968)

Hall, John W. (ed.), *The Cambridge History of Japan*, volume 4 (Cambridge Univ. Press, 1991)

Hane, Mikiso, *Peasants, Rebels and Outcastes* (New York, Pantheon Books, 1982)

Hearn, Lafcadio, *Kokoro; Hints and Echoes of Japanese Inner Life* (Tokyo, Tuttle, [1895], 1972)

Hearn, Lafcadio, *Gleanings in Buddha Fields* (Kegan Paul, Trench and Trubner, 1898)

Hearn, Lafcadio, *Japan; An Interpretation* (New York, Macmillan, 1904) ***

Hearn, Lafcadio, *Out of the East* (Jonathan Cape, 1927)

Hendry, Joy, *Understanding Japanese Society* (Croom Helm, 1987)

Jacobs, Norman, *The Origins of Modern Capitalism and Eastern Asia* (Hong Kong Univ. Press, 1958)

Kaempfer, Engelbert, *The History of Japan* (Curzon Press, [1727] 1993) trans. J. G. Sheuchzer, 3 vols.

Koestler, Arthur, *The Lotus and the Robot* (Hutchinson, 1960)

Kondo, Dorinne, *Crafting Selves* (Univ. of Chicago Press, 1990)

Lebra, Takie Suiyama, *Japanese Patterns of Behavior* (Honolulu, Univ. of Hawaii Press, 1976)

Lowell, Percival, *The Soul of the Far East* (Kegan Paul, Trench and Trubner, 1888)

Macfarlane, Charles, *Japan: An Account, Geographical and Historical* (New York, Putnam, 1852)

Maraini, Fosco, *Meeting with Japan* (Hutchinson, 1959), trans. Eric Mosbacher ***

Maraini, Fosco, *Japan; Patterns of Continuity* (Tokyo, Kodansha International, 1971)

Maraini, Fosco, *Tokyo* (Amsterdam, Time Life Books, 1978)

Maruyama, Masao, *Thought and Behaviour in Modern Japanese Politics* (Oxford Univ. Press, expanded edn, 1969), ed. Ivan Morris ***

Maruyama, Masao, 'The structure of *Matsurigoto*: the *basso ostinato* of Japanese political life', in *Themes and Theories in Modern Japanese History*, eds. Sue Henny and Jean-Pierre Lehmann (Athlone Press, 1988)

Maruyama, Masao, 'Proto-type, Old layer and *Basso ostinato*' in *The Collected Works of Maruyama Masao*, volume 12 (Tokyo, 1996), [This passage translated by Kenichi Nakamura]

Matsumoto, Michihiro, *The Unspoken Way: Haragei* (Tokyo, Kodansha, 1988)

Morris, Ivan, *The World of the Shining Prince* (Penguin, 1979)

Morse, Edward S., *Japan Day by Day* (Tokyo, Kobunsha, 1936), 2 vols. ***

Morse, Edward S., *Japanese Homes and Their Surroundings* (New York, Dover [1886], 1961)

Nakamura, Toshiko, 'Yukichi Fukuzawa's ideas on family and the history of civilization' [http://www.alanmacfarlane.com/TEXTS/toshiko_fukuzawa.pdf]

Nakane, Chie, *Japanese Society* (Pelican, 1973)

Nitobe, Inazo, *Bushido; The Soul of Japan* (Tokyo, Tuttle, [1905] 1969)

Ohnuki-Tierney, Emiko, *Illness and Culture in Contemporary Japan* (Cambridge Univ. Press, 1984)

Okakura, Kakuzo, *The Book of Tea* (Tokyo, Kodansha [1906], 1989)

Oliphant Laurence, *Narrative of the Earl of Elgin's Mission to China and Japan* (Blackwood, 1859), 2 vols.

Ozaki, Robert S., *The Japanese; A Cultural Portrait* (Tokyo, Tuttle 1978)

Passin, Herbert, 'Japanese Society' in *International Encyclopedia of the Social Sciences* (Macmillan, 1968)

Ratzell, Friedrich, *The History of Mankind* (Macmillan, 1896), trans A. J. Butler, 3 vols.

Reischauer, Edwin O., *The Japanese Today* (Tokyo, Tuttle, 1988)

Riesman, David, *Conversations in Japan* (Allen Lane, 1967)

Saikaku, Ihara, *The Japanese Family Storehouse* (Cambridge Univ. Press, [1688] 1969), trans. G.W. Sargent

Sansom, G. B., *The Western World and Japan* (Cresset Press, 1950)

Scidmore, Eliza R., *Jinrikisha Days in Japan* (New York, Harper, 1891)

Singer, Kurt, *Mirror, Sword and Jewel* (Tokyo, Kodansha, pb. edn, 1981) ***

Smith, Robert J., *Japanese Society* (Cambridge Univ. Press, 1983) ***

Sugimoto, Yoshio, *An Introduction of Japanese Society* (Cambridge Univ. Press, 2nd edn, 2003) ***

Tames, Richard (ed.), *Encounters with Japan* (Stroud, Alan Sutton, 1991)

Tanizaki, Junichiro, *In Praise of Shadows* (Tokyo, Tuttle [1933], 1974), trans. Thomas J. Harper and Edward G. Seidensticker ***

Thunberg, Charles Peter, *Travels in Europe, Africa and Asia* (London [1793], 3rd edn, 1796), 4 vols.

Tocqueville, Alexis de, *Memoir, Letters, and Remains of Alexis de Tocqueville* (Cambridge, Macmillan, 1961), 2 vols.

Tocqueville, Alexis de, *Journeys to England and Ireland* (New York, Anchor Books, 1968), ed. J. P. Mayer and translated by George Lawrence and J. P. Mayer

Van Meerdervoort, Pompe, *Five Years in Japan, 1857–1863* (Tokyo, Sophia Univ., 1970), trans. Elizabeth P. Wittermans and John Z. Bower

Van Wolferen, Karel, *The Enigma of Japanese Power; People and Politics in a Stateless Nation* (Tokyo, Tokyo, 1993)

Von Siebold, Philipp F., *Manners and Customs of the Japanese in the Nineteenth Century* (Tokyo, Tuttle, [1841] 1973), trans. Terence Barrow

Wigmore, John Henry (ed.), *Law and Justice in Tokugawa Japan* (Univ. of Tokyo Press, 1969)

Yamamura, Kozo (ed.), *The Cambridge History of Japan*, volume III (Cambridge Univ. Press, 1990)

Yapp, Peter (ed.), *The Travellers' Dictionary of Quotation* (Routledge and Kegan Paul, 1983)

Yoshino, Kosaku, *Cultural Nationalism in Contemporary Japan* (Routledge, 1992)

Index

A

abortion 70
adoption 80, 83
advertising 39, 41
Africa, Africans 189, 214
afterlife 177, 185, 191, 192, 199
agriculture 1, 50, 54, 94
Ainu people 1, 132, 169–70, 225
Alcock, Sir Rutherford 40, 56, 110, 149, 230
alcohol 2, 53, 137
amae (mother–son relationship) 86
Amaterasu (goddess) 173, 202
Amino, Yoshihiko 75, 211
ancestor tablets 81
ancestors 200
animals, domesticated 50, 53–4, 57
anime films 24, 176
animism 178, 192, 195–6
anthropologists: understanding social systems
    214–15
anti-consumerism 46
anti-feminism 221
anti-intellectualism 121, 221
anti-*nihonjinron* 12, 14
anti-orientalism 15
Arabs: treatment of Africans 191
architecture 1, 147
Armenians 191
Arnold, Edwin 8
Arnold, Matthew 220
artist-craftsmen 23
arts and crafts 2, 20
Asahi Shimbun newspaper 126–7
Assam 125
Association 103, 106
assymetry 147

Aston, W. G. 175
astrology 182
'Axial Age' concept 192, 194–8, 202, 216

B

Bacon, Alice 38, 86, 94, 102, 230
Bacon, Francis 144
Baconian empiricism 213
bamboo 21, 52, 72, 190
Banto, Yamagata 187
Barthes, Roland 142
    An Empire of Signs 25
baseball 37
bathing 34–5, 72, 165
Beer, Lawrence 133–4
Bellah, Robert 197, 198, 210
    Imagining Japan 195
Benedict, Ruth 30–31, 209
    The Chrysanthemum and the Sword 10
Bird, Isabella 8, 29, 41, 54, 70, 87, 209, 230
Blacker, Carmen 34, 179
Blake, William 223
body, the
    Japanese attitude towards 41–2, 43
    nudity 34, 35, 37–8, 39
    pornography and prostitution 39–43
    Western ambivalence towards 41
    western use of bodies as sexually
        provoking objects 38–9
body language 153, 159
Bolshevist terror methods 123
bon festival 185–6
bonding 91–2
bonsai 21
book-publishing 120, 121
Brahmins 122

Britain
 capital intensive 70
 destruction of Tasmanians 168
 marriage 86
 skill efficiency 70
 see also England
British Council 1, 134
British Empire 130
brothels 40, 41
bubonic plague 67-8
Buddha, the 6, 53, 177, 178, 182, 193
Buddhism 1, 6, 24, 25, 30, 46, 48, 76, 111,
 122, 145, 166, 173, 176-9, 185, 186, 193,
 194-8, 200, 201, 203, 205, 223
burakumin 166-8, 225
bureaucracy 116-19, 139, 221
Burma 124
bushi-do (the 'way of the warrior') 110-111
business world 106
butsudan (Buddhist ancestor cabinets) 173,
 185, 186

C
calligraphy 21, 47, 152, 153
Calvin, John 202
Cambridge 14, 146
Cambridge University 117
cameras 58
capital punishment 135
capitalism 1, 60, 61, 62, 64, 65, 133, 171,
 204, 211, 213, 221, 223
car industry 21, 58
Carroll, Lewis 153
caste system 164
Central Asia 195
ceremonies, cycle of 142
Chamberlain, Basil Hall 25, 55-6, 147, 150,
 181, 182, 230
 'The Invention of a New Religion'
 110-111
 Japanese Things 110
chance 182-3
change 145, 146
Chartres cathedral 34
Chen, Shing-Jen 89-90
cherry blossom 15
Chikamatsu, Monzaemon 105
children
 child prostitution 40

education 88-9
and *kami* 180
treatment of 87-91, 93-4, 158
China
 attitude to war compared with that of
 Japan 125
 bureaucracy 118, 119
 child-rearing 89
 Chinese homes 28
 clan property 65
 clan system 78
 'comfort women' in 42
 compared with Japan 1, 7, 11, 12
 Confucian examination system 122
 Confucian template 195
 and construction of a new world order
 223
 court paraphernalia 118
 culture 21
 Emperor 114
 eras 145
 exports to Japan 58
 famine 67
 great inventions of 207
 influence on Japan 24, 48, 49, 202-3, 205
 marriage 68, 83
 overshadows Japan for centuries 130, 205
 surpassed by Japan industrially and
 militarily 55
 triads 138
 written characters (*kanji*) 203
Chinese art 49
cholera 69
Christianity, Christians 6, 29, 76, 98, 111,
 112, 131, 179, 180, 189, 193, 200, 201, 203
 Calvinist 181
 morality plays 33
chrysanthemums 15, 30
cities 4-5, 21, 28, 45, 128, 141, 216
civil litigation 133
Clammer, John 210, 214, 224
cleanliness 163-6, 169-70
climate 51
clothing 69
 innocence in 39
 materials 72
 overlap in the way young people dress 95
 'reformed' 41
collectivism 79

'comfort women' 42, 43
communism 1, 219, 221, 223
Community 103–6
company collusion 59–60
computer games 21, 24
computers 4, 21, 57
Confucianism 1, 6, 48, 122, 145, 177, 178, 179, 185, 194–5, 197, 198, 199, 201, 203, 223
Confucius 6, 182, 193
constitution 122, 131
consumerism 71, 72, 84
contraception 68
Contract 214
court cases 7
crime 2, 7, 122, 133–8
culture shock 11, 19, 48, 72–3
currency 62–3

D
daimyos (nobles) 34, 108
Dale, Peter: The Myth of Japanese Uniqueness 13–14
Darwin, Charles 145
dating agencies 85
death marches 128
death rituals 176
'defence force' 122, 219
democracy 114–15, 155, 171, 204, 220
Descartes, René 195
Deshima island, off Nagasaki 8
disease 67–8
divination 184
divorce 85, 86, 206
'divorce within marriage' 87
Dore, Ronald 107, 213
dowry 65
dreams 182
Dresden, fire-bombing of 131
drugs 135, 137, 138
Dürer, Albrecht 20
Durkheim, Emile 113
Dutch visitors 8, 55, 169–70, 203
dysentery 68

E
Earls Colne, Essex 147
earthquakes 51–2, 72, 127, 145, 183
East Asia 131, 162

ecology 12, 191, 207, 222
economics 11
economy
    ambivalence towards money and competition 60, 62
    and capitalism 60, 61, 62
    company and factory ethos 59
    company collusion 59–60
    currency 62–3
    decentralised 118
    economic relationships 63–4
    individual economic decisions 61
    manufacturing 61
    payment for goods and services 63
    small businesses 59
    trading empire 61
    veneer of modern efficiency and technical ability 58
Edo 45
    Shogunate 109, 111
    see also Tokyo
education 6, 88–9, 91, 95, 101, 110, 120
egalitarianism 101, 107
Eight Diagrams of classical China 182
Einstein, Albert 216
Eisenstadt, S. N. 194–5, 197–8, 210
Elgin mission 31, 37, 56
Elijah 195
Emperor 1, 53, 78, 100, 108–114, 116, 126, 143, 167, 178
employment
    hard working 54–5, 71
    lifetime security of employment and mutual trust 59
    national income 67, 72, 102–3
    overstaffed institutions 64
    small family firms 59
    women 94
Endo, Shusaku 76
energy use 70
England
    attitude to their culture 204
    and bureaucracy 119
    character of the English 153–4
    compared with Japan 12
    crime rate 134
    inherited wealth and degrading poverty 102
    law 10

mongrel population 206
property system compared with that of
    Japan 65–7
Puritans 25
Tocqueville on 16–17
see also Britain
English Common Law 158
Enright, D. J. 99–100
eras 143, 228
erotic art 40
Escher, M. C. 221
eta 166
ethics 179, 192
ethnocentric universalism 13
etiquette 158–63
Europe
    four 'estates' or ranks 101–2
    Japan compared with 11
Evans, Pritchard, Edward 116
evil 181, 185, 190, 191, 192

F
family 1, 79–82, 105, 212, 215–16
famine 52, 67
fascism 222
Fenollosa, Ernest 21–2, 23
feudalism 102, 108, 109
First Sino-Japanese War (1894–5) 131
flowers 30–31
food
    diet 1, 2, 44
    empty centre 141
    obsession with fish 50
    presentation 44
    proteins 70
    raw food 2, 44
forests 53
Foucault, Michel 150
France
    attitude to their culture 204
    centrally planned 118
    impressionists 22
Fujiwara 62
Fukuzawa, Yukichi 12, 60, 77, 122, 150,
    159–60, 191, 210, 212
    divides the world into four 'kinds'
    130–31
futon (bed-roll) 27
'futures' markets 62

G
gadgetry 2, 21
Galbraith, J. K. 68
gardens 2, 21, 30, 31–2, 45, 205, 217
    imperial 53
    Zen 47
geishas 2, 15, 40, 165
gender relations 94–7
Geneva Convention 130
geography 50, 51, 205, 207
germ warfare 129
Germany
    bureaucracy 118
    Japanese army and fighting methods
        modelled on Germany 123–4
    Nazi 124
    treatment of the Jews 131, 189
    visitors to Japan 8
giri (fulfilment of contractual relations)
    103–4, 105
glass 52, 57
good 185, 190, 191, 192
good-luck charms 182–4
Greece, Ancient 29, 193
Greek philosophy 213, 217
Griffis, W. E. 8, 17–18, 40, 57, 118, 124,
    142–3, 211, 233
'guilt' culture 187
gun crimes 123
gunpowder weapons 57, 58, 123, 203
Gurung people, Nepal 163

H
haiku 100, 120, 150, 153
Hayley, John O. 136
Handel, George Frideric 34
Hara, Hiroko 90
Hayami, Akira 208
Hearn, Lafcadio 8–9, 28, 56, 83, 124–5, 154,
    174–5, 211, 212, 233
Hegel, Georg Wilhelm Friedrich 179
Heibonsha dictionary 138
Hendry, Joy 78, 213
Heraclitus 195
hibachi (heated pit) 27
hierarchy 99–102, 107
hikikomori (shut-in young people) 228
Hinduism, Hindus 164, 176, 181, 189, 201
hinin 166

Hirata, Atsutane 179
Hiroshige, Utagawa 24
Hiroshima 56
Hokkaido 168
Hokkaido University: Law Faculty 1
Hokusai, Katsushika 24
Holism 217
Homer 195
homes, housing 4, 27–8, 52, 58, 69–70, 76, 140
honne (back) 140, 188
Honshu island 108, 168
horoscopy 184
hotoke (spirits) 185, 186
Hsu, Francis 106
Huns 129, 131

I
ie (male-related lineage) 80, 105–6
ikebana 21
Imamiya-Ebisu Shrine, Osaka City 174
imperialism 110, 128, 224
imports 59
India
     caste system 65, 78
     and construction of a new world order 223
     famine 67
     four 'estates' or ranks 101–2
     marriage 68
     peasant holdings 65
     religion 21, 193, 200
     working hours 54
individualism, the individual 74–7, 79, 107, 214
industrial blight 2
industrialisation 54–5, 70, 112
infant mortality rate 69
infanticide 70
inheritance 66, 80
Internet dating 85
inventiveness 55–7
Iran 195
Isaiah 195
Ise Shinto shrine 11, 41, 45, 173, 184
Islam 203, 224, 226
Italy: working hours 54
Iwakura Mission 111
Iwane, General Matsui 128

Izanagi 165

J
Jacobs, Norman 212
Japan
     aesthetics 1, 21, 23, 24, 48, 49
     American occupation 42
     America's post-war influence 204
     character 2, 10
     Chinese influence on 24, 48, 49, 204–5, 207
     'collective-mutual-assistance system' 115
     compared with China 1, 7, 11, 12
     compared with England 12
     compared with Europe 11
     compared with Korea 12
     early sense of national identity and difference 208–9
     economy 1–2, 3, 12, 21, 55, 58–64, 133
     fewer possessions than Americans 67
     gentleness/brutality 123
     high level of ritual 183–5
     Japanese army and fighting methods modelled on Germany 123–4
     'the Japanese way' 226
     Korean influence on 24, 205
     'middle ages' 108–9
     opening up of (from 1870s) 48
     overshadowed by China for centuries 130, 205
     post-war austerity 71–2
     pressure to conform 79
     reunification 68, 109
     Second World War 42, 71, 100, 124, 126, 131, 229
     self-image 12–13
     'small group' society 78
     three great waves of in-migration 208
     a tightly knit society 79
     uniqueness 224
     a water empire 50–51
Japan Mail 39
Japanese art
     becomes famous in the West 22
     bright and shadow sides of 24–5, 48
     and Chinese art 1
     indirectness and allusion 25–6
     influences and is influenced by the West 48

institutionalisation of 22–3
love of subtlety 26
Japanese navy 124
Jaspers, Karl 194, 213
Jeremiah 195
Jews 132, 191
'Jomon' culture area 208
Jomon period 48
Judaism 165, 195, 203
justice system 118

K
kabuki theatre 2, 24, 48, 61, 175
Kaempfer, Engelbert 40
Kamakura Buddhism 198
kami 34, 53, 175, 177, 179–81, 186, 191, 200, 225
Kant, Immanuel 179
karaoke 2, 36–7
karma 181
Kato 179
Kazuo, Osumi 198
Keats, John 21, 48, 223
Keio University 63, 122
King's College, Cambridge 66
   Fellows' Garden 26
kinship 3, 11, 80, 81, 105, 106, 109, 115, 168, 222
kissing 38–9, 158
knights 125
Kobe 37
kohun ('the child role') 100
Kodansha Encyclopedia 105, 202–203
Koestler, Arthur 59, 151, 160–71
Kojien (Japanese dictionary) 140
Kujiki 165
Kokugikan (Hall of Skill), Tokyo 32
Kondo, Dorinne 213
Korea
   Chinese invasion of 125, 130
   colonial 113
   'comfort women' in 41
   compared with Japan 12
   exports to Japan 58
   exuberant colours in art 25
   immigrants 131, 227
   influence on Japan 24, 207
   language 148, 154
Korean War (1592–8) 123, 128

kshatrya 125
Kuril Islands 169
kyo 78
Kyoto 11, 21, 165
   booksellers 120
   ceremonial centre 24, 108
   court 45
   patronage 109
   publishers 120
   religious buildings 200

L
lacquer-work 21, 23, 26, 58
lactose intolerance 54
lamas 178
language 1, 148–55, 172, 204
   Chinese written characters (*kanji*) 205
   and gender 95, 96
   inequality 100
   origins 148–9
   and speech 149, 150–52
   time 142
Lao-tzu 195
law 11, 20, 121, 132–3
Lebra, Takie 107, 210
Lenin, Vladimir 224
Leonardo da Vinci 177
Liberal Democratic Party 115
libraries 121
life cycle 92–3
lifestyle 70
literacy 119, 22, 167, 218
literary tradition 120, 207
living standard 4, 54
logic 133, 8, 178, 179, 199, 218, 227
loneliness 77–8, 84, 222–23
Lost in Translation (film) 2
love 83–4
Lowell, Percival 9, 31–2, 37, 38
Luther, Martin 202

M
Macfarlane, Alan
   accepts Visiting Scholarship to Japan 1
   first impressions of Japan (1990) 4–7
   lectures in anthropology 2
   preconceptions of Japan 1–2
   second visit to Japan (1993) 11
   works in a Nepalese village 175–6

Macfarlane, Charles 94, 120
Macfarlane, Sarah 1
Machiavelli, Niccolò 201
Maitland, F. W. 12
make-up 39
malaria 69
Manchuria 113, 128
Mandarin system 121, 203
manga 2, 21, 24, 161
manufacturing 61, 64, 70
Maraini, Fosco 31, 39, 114, 151, 156, 165,
    212–213, 225
marriage 68, 82–7, 96–7, 104, 106, 107,
    167–8, 208
Martin, Gerry 12
Maruyama, Masao 77, 100, 126, 145–6, 171
Marvel, Andrew 36
Marx, Karl 224
Marxism 215
Matsumoto, Michihiro 156, 193
Matsuyama 129
measles 68
Meerdevort, Pompe van 40
Meiji Constitution 111–12
Meiji government 22, 111
Meiji Restoration 8, 42, 110, 145, 197, 213
Meiji shrine 178
merchants 33, 45, 61
meritocracy 101
Merleau-Ponty, Maurice 149
micro-ecologies 51
middle class 102–3, 109
Middle East 193
Milne, A. A. 167
mingei 22
miniaturisation 26, 27
minimalism 58, 71
Ministry of Education 125–6
Miyazaki, Hayao 174, 179
monasteries, Buddhist 121
Mongols 128, 130, 207
monsoons 52
morality 189–91, 192
More, Sir Thomas: *Utopia* 16
Morris, Ivan 149–50
Morris, William 22
Morse, Edward 20, 21, 32, 38, 45–6, 75,
    87–8, 122–3, 155–6, 210, 211, 233
    Japanese Homes and their Environs 28

mother-son relationship (*amae*) 85–6
Mount Fuji 45
Mozart, Wolfgang Amadeus 34
mulberry 52, 72
Murasaki, Lady: *The Tale of Genji* 96, 149
Muslims 189
mutual surveillance 136
'My Neighbour Totoro' (animated film)
    174

N
Nagas of Assam 128
Nagasaki 45, 55
    Bay 70
    Harbour 170
Nagoya 163
Nakamura, Hajime 157, 196–7
Nakamura, Professor Kenichi 116, 171, 180
    attitude to the past 144
    and charms 182–3
    on children 89
    and communication 154
    invites the author to visit Japan 1
    Japan as 'a one-way mirror' 11
    on Japanese currency 62–3
    on Japanese language 149
    and Japanese post-war attitude 145
    meets the author 4
    on the middle class 102–3
    on religiosity 178
    on the *renga* 153
    and ritual 184
    on visiting the Fellows' Garden, King's
        College 26
    and writing of *Japan Through the Looking
        Glass* 12
Nakamura, Professor Toshiko 116, 180
    on children 89, 91
    and Kenichi's invitation to the author 1
    life cycle 93
    meets the author 4
    on payment for goods and services 63
    and religion 6
    and ritual 184
    and writing of *Japan Through the Looking
        Glass* 12
    on Yukichi Fukuzawa 212
Nakane, Chie 81, 154, 213
name cards 75, 185

Nanking massacres 129
Napoleon Bonaparte 58
Nara 21
Narita airport, near Tokyo 4
nationalist movement, post-war rise of 23
nature 29–30, 35
   bridging of perceived gap between nature
      and culture 47–8
   desire to bring it into the cities 45–6
   man's interaction with 48–9
neo-Confucianism 46, 109, 199
Nepal 3, 94, 163, 178
netsuke 21
New Guinea 217
'new religions 201–203
New Year's Day 178, 180
New York 135
Newton, Sir Isaac 144
Nichiren Buddhism 198
nihonjinron (Japanese cultural nationalism)
   12, 13–14
Nikko shrine 11, 45, 175
ninjo (loving empathy) 105
Nitobe, Inazo 155, 178, 196
Noh drama 33–4, 48, 101, 171, 176
Norinaga, Motoori 177
nuclear weapons 122, 128
nudity 34, 35, 37–8, 39
Nuer people (of Sudan and Ethiopia) 116
numbers 148–9

O
occidentalism 12, 16
Ogyu, Sorai 200
Ohnuki-Tierney, Emiko 160, 213
Okakura, Kakuzo 22, 23
Old Testament prophets 195
omamori (good luck charm) 183–4
omote (surface) 141
on concept 99
orientalism 12, 15
arigami 21
Orwell, George: The Lion and the Unicorn 17
Osaka: merchants in 45, 61
otherness 27, 28, 205
over-conformity 2
oyabun ('the father role') 100
Ozaki, Robert 115, 127, 130
Ozaki, Yukio 114

P
pachinko (pin-ball parlours) 36, 162
painting 21
palmistry 184
parks 45
Passin, Herbert 100, 155
past, attitude to the 145–6
patriotism 110
patronage 110
Pearl Harbour 129
personal names 74–5, 231
personal pronouns 74, 151
physiognomy 183
Pill, the 68
'pillow books' 40
Plato 195
Poe, Edgar Allan 181
police 133, 135–8
political system 114–15
politics 3, 11, 109
   a main function of 115
   and religion 110
pollution 2
population 1, 12, 50, 54, 68–9, 70
porcelain 22, 48
'pork-barrel' system 116
pornography 2, 39–43
Portuguese
   gunpowder weapons 58, 122
   visitors 8, 169–70, 205
postmodernism 12
pottery 21, 48, 58, 100, 207
power
   acceptance of 227
   diffused 116, 140, 218
   distributed, unbureaucratic 119
   Japanese civilisation underpinned by
      political power 115
   military 116
   vertical organisation of 117–18
'power-dwarfing' 100
predestination 181
'Princess Mononoke' (film) 181
prisoner-of-war camps 128, 129, 131
prisoners, treatment of 129–30
prisons 135–6
property 11, 64–7, 104
prostitution 40
Protestant reformation 199–200

Protestant work ethic 97
Protestantism, Protestants 100, 189, 197
Prussian army 123
public hot baths 34–5, 43
punctuality 142
purity 164–5

R
racial marginalisation 168–9
racism 131, 224
rebirth 30, 181
recycling 70, 71
Reischauer, Edwin 98
relativism 12
religion 1
    and cleanliness 164
    'guilt' culture vs. 'shame' culture 187–8
    high level of ritual 183–5, 216
    in India 21, 193, 200
    Japan as the one non-Axial modern
        civilisation 195–6
    lack of developed theology or sacred
        text 175
    lack of malevolent ancestors 181
    lack of a relationship between religion
        and ethics 191–2
    lack of uniformity 118
    multiple paths 178–9, 187, 200
    'new religions 200–201
    and politics 110
    quasi-religious traditions 46
    religiosity 173–5, 178
    and sin 181–2
    see also Buddhism; Christianity; kami;
        Shinto; Taoism
Renaissance: separation of artist and
    craftsman 23
renga (collaborative poem) 153
resource-conserving 70
retirement 92–3
reverse orientalism see occidentalism
rice 1, 53–4, 70, 72
Riesman, David 78–9, 120, 188
ringi process (group decision-making) 100
Rissho Koseikai 201
Rodin, Auguste: 'The Kiss' 39
Royal Navy 125
rural bias 45
Ruskin, John 22, 220

Russia
    bureaucracy 119
    during the Soviet regime 113
    famine 67
    surpassed by Japan industrially and
        militarily 55
Russo-Japanese War (1904–5) 131
ryo-kan (old-style inn) 27
Ryuku archipelago 51, 206

S
Saikaku, Ihara 61, 82, 92
Saito, Professor Osamu 70
sake 2, 53, 184
Sakhalin 129, 206
Sakurai, Professor Eiji 62
salvation 195
samurai warriors 2, 15, 33, 63, 122, 124–5,
    197
Sansom, George 133, 213
Sapir-Whorf hypothesis 155
Sapporo, Hokkaido 4, 45
Scidmore, Eliza 31, 53, 149, 233
seasons 142
Second Sino-Japanese War (1937–45) 126–7
Second World War 71, 131
    behaviour of Japanese military 2, 126,
        229
    'comfort women' in 42
    the Emperor system 101
sensei 99–100
sex
    'comfort women' 42, 43
    Japanese attitude to 41, 43
    pornography 39–43
    prostitution 40
    sexual slavery 42
    Western attitudes to 43
Shakespeare, William: The Tempest 226–7
shamanism 33, 112, 168, 178, 182, 194, 202,
    203, 204
'shame' culture 189, 190
Shinto 5–6, 32, 33, 46, 110, 111–12, 122,
    178, 180, 196–9, 202, 203
    cleanliness 164, 165
    fused with Buddhism 198
    kami (Shinto deities) 34, 53, 175, 178
    rituals 166
    and sake 53

shrines, Shinto 5–6, 32, 41, 165, 174, 175,
    177, 185, 197
Shogunate 108, 109, 110, 116, 201
shoji (shutters) 46
shrines 28, 29, 80, 141, 153, 180
    Buddhist 173
    near striking features 174
    rural 45
    and *sake* 53
    Shinto 5–6, 32, 41, 165, 173, 174, 176,
        184, 196
    tokonoma 36
    two kinds of 145
Siebold, Philipp Franz von 95, 137, 183
silk industry 94
sin 181–2, 194
'sincerity' 170–71
Singer, Kurt 10, 28, 113, 115, 119, 123, 132,
    147, 209, 210, 216, 218–19, 227
    Mirror, Sword and Jewel 227
small groups, commitment to 106–7
smallpox 68
Smith, Robert 150, 187, 212, 223
Smith, Thomas 212
socialisation 88
society, forms of 3
Soka Gakkai 201
soto (public) 141
South America 214
South East Asia 214
space, concept of 141
Spain: working hours 54
Spencer, Herbert 212
status 216
stock market 60
Stoics 183
Sugimoto, Yoshio 115, 136
suicide 2, 225
sumo wrestling 2, 15, 32–3, 163–4, 174
symmetry 148

T
Taine, Hippolyte: *Notes upon England* 17
tamagotchi (computerised pet) 57
tanin (non-blood relationship) 105
Tanizaki, Junichiro 44
    In Praise of Shadows 26
tanka 100
Taoism 146, 201

Tasmanians 168
tatami matting 27, 35, 147
tatemae (front) 140, 188
taxation 64
tea 1, 70, 72, 174
    bowls 48
    ceremony 2, 35–6, 78, 153, 184, 207
    houses 15, 94
technology
    adoption of Western technologies 205
    Japanese inventiveness 55–7
    lack of interest in 57–8
temples 2, 21, 28, 29, 173, 174, 183
Tenno religion 112–13
Tennyson, Alfred, Lord 222
Thai language 154
Thailand: personal names 74
Thunberg, Charles Peter 55, 74–5
Tibet, Chinese invasion of 125
time 142–6
Tocqueville, Alexis de 18, 120, 223
    Democracy in America, L'Ancien Regime
        16–17
toilets 163, 164
tokonoma shrine 36
Tokugawa Shogunate 109, 111, 197
Tokyo 56
    art of 24
    centre of government from seventeenth
        century 24
    crime in 134
    earthquakes in 51–2
    empty centre 141
    fire-bombing of 128
    'homeless' people in 102
    imperial gardens 53
    oshiwara 42
    see also Edo
Tokyo University 22, 151
Tokyo University of Fine Arts and Music 22
Toshiba factory, north of Tokyo 199
Toson, Shimazaki: *The Broken Commandment*
    167
towns, middle-sized 46
toys 56
Trades Union Congresses 35
Tsue, Takao 176
tsunami (tidal wave) 52, 128, 183
Turks: treatment of Armenians 191

typhoid 68
typhoons 146

U
uchi (private) 140–41
ukiyoe (Japanese prints) 22, 24
United States
    baseball 17, 37
    car industry 58
    crime 134, 135
    economy 20
    identification with the group category 79
    inherited wealth and degrading poverty 102
    more co-operative and trusting than the Japanese 79
    more possessions than the Japanese 67
    occupation of Japan 42
    police 135
    post-war influence on Japan 206
    system of manufacture 70
universities 91, 95, 101, 121, 122
University of Cambridge 3
Upanishads 195
ura (deep) 140
urinals 39

V
Valente, Father 77
Van Wolferen, Karel 126–7, 204
    The Enigma of Japanese Power 116
Victoria and Albert Museum, London 207
Vietnam
    Chinese invasion of 125
    personal names 74
Vogel, Ezra 141, 213
volcanoes 52, 127, 145, 183

W
war and peace 122–32, 139
war criminals 126

Watanabe, Professor Hiroshi 200
wealth distribution 101
Weber, Max 212
West, the
    child-rearing 89, 90
    economic rationality 73
    individualism 74
    Japan's difference 204
    macro-inventions 207
    obsession with technology 58
    profligacy and super-abundance 71
westernisation 10, 13, 48, 221
'white man's burden' 127
Wigmore, J. H. 135
Willis, William 124
witchcraft 183, 194
women
    gender relations 94–7
    hard-working 94, 96
    marginalised 225
Wordsworth, William 48, 222
work ethic 97–9

Y
yakuza 2, 137–8, 174
Yanagi, Muneyoshi 22
Yanagita, Kunio 212–213
Yeats, W. B. 48, 222
'yellow man's burden' 131
Yoshikawa, Professor Hiroshi 65
Yoshino, Kosaku 11
    Cultural Nationalism in Contemporary Japan 13
yoshiwara 41, 42

Z
zaibatsu system 60
Zarathustra 195
Zen Buddhism 24, 26, 47, 100, 198
Zen meditation 153
Zoroastra 195